FINDING
YOUR
IRISH ANCESTORS
IN
NEW YORK CITY

Joseph Buggy

Published by
Genealogical Publishing Company
3600 Clipper Mill Rd., #260
Baltimore, Maryland 21211-1953

ISBN 978-0-8063-1988-9

Made in the United States of America

For my parents, Michael and Marian

Contents

Acknowledgments

This book is a product of working as a genealogist in the greatest city in the world. It has mostly been a lone venture but there are some important people to thank. My non-genealogical spouse, Christina, has been a constant source of encouragement and patience. Her proof-reading ability and no-nonsense attitude brought a focus to the early drafts. My editor, Patricia Mansfield Phelan, has been clearing the mist from my writing for the last few years. She has an excellent ability to translate my Hiberno-English into something readable. The staff at the Milstein Genealogy Room, New York Public Library at Bryant Park provided a wonderful arena to research and write this book. It's my second favorite place in the city. Lastly, to all the Irish genealogy researchers and writers in Gotham who have come before me and left a body of work to be enthralled with and amazed by.

Abbreviations

AD	Assembly District
AL	Alabama
AOH	Ancient Order of Hibernians
AZ	Arizona
CA	California
CL	Chronological List
CT	Connecticut
CUNY	City University of New York
DC	District of Columbia
DIFHR	*Directory of Irish Family History Research*
ED	Election District
FHC	Family History Center
FHL	Family History Library
GB	Great Britain
IAG	*Irish American Genealogist* (formerly the *Irish Genealogical Helper*)
IF	*Irish Families*
IFH	*Irish Family History*
IFHFN	*Irish Family History Forum Newsletter*
IGQ	*Irish Genealogical Quarterly*
IHL	*Irish Heritage Links*
IL	Illinois
IN	Indiana
INS	Immigration and Naturalization Service
IR	*Irish Roots*
ISGB	*Irish/Scottish Gaelic Bulletin*
IT	*Irish Tree*
JAIHS	*The Recorder: Journal of the American Irish Historical Society*
LDS	Church of Jesus Christ of Latter-day Saints
MA	Massachusetts
MD	Maryland
MI	Michigan
MO	Missouri
MN	Minnesota
MT	Montana
NC	North Carolina
NH	New Hampshire
NJ	New Jersey
NY	New York
NYC	New York City
NYIH	*New York Irish History*
NYIHR	New York Irish History Roundtable
NYIHRN	*New York Irish History Roundtable Newsletter*
NYPD	New York Police Department
NYU	New York University
OH	Ohio
OR	Oregon
PA	Pennsylvania
SC	South Carolina

SUNY	State University of New York
TIHA	*The Irish at Home and Abroad*
TR	*The New York Genealogical and Biographical Record*
TS	*The Septs*
TWU	Transport Workers Union
US	United States
USCIS	United States Citizenship and Immigration Service
UT	Utah
VA	Virginia
WI	Wisconsin
WPA	Works Progress Administration

1 Introduction

The aim of this book is to present a comprehensive overview for anyone wishing to trace their Irish ancestors within the five boroughs of New York City. It is especially beneficial for those researching ancestors from the beginning of the 19th century to the early 20th. The Irish immigrant ancestor who arrived in New York offers researchers a good chance of finding the place of origin in Ireland, whether he or she settled in the city for generations or moved on soon after arrival. Helping you find that place of origin is one the central objectives of this book. To assist you in your search, detailed information about records, resources, and strategies are provided.

What's Inside?
The history of Irish emigration to the United States, and to New York City in particular, has been covered extensively and has been detailed in a number of excellent publications.[1] This book does not set out to retell that story. Instead, it provides resources and strategies for tracing Irish ancestors in New York City.

Chapters Two and Three introduce you to records in the city. Fundamental sources such as censuses and vital records are covered, along with underutilized records that can be of particular use when tracing Irish ancestors.

Following this, we delve deeper into researching the Irish in New York City. Chapter Four focuses on research strategies you can use if you hit those genealogical brick walls. Immigrants from particular Irish counties often settled in certain parts of the city, and this is discussed in detail in Chapter Five. Twenty-one different record sets and sources are then discussed in Chapter Six. They give the place of origin in Ireland for over 160,000 19th century immigrants and for many hundreds of thousands more in the 20th century.

The Roman Catholic Church is the focus of Chapters Seven through Nine. A historical analysis shows how and why the Church is so important for Irish genealogical research. This is followed by the most detailed listing to date of every Catholic parish that has ever existed in the five boroughs. The all-important start dates for parish registers are included. Next, a chapter on cemeteries lists every known Catholic burial ground that has existed in the city. Public and nondenominational burial grounds have also been included in this chapter to aid researchers.

The concluding chapters of the book present comprehensive lists of periodicals, websites, and other publications that will aid your research and provide a wider understanding of the lives of the Irish in New York City.

Over the last few decades there have been some major developments in the study of Irish genealogy in New York City. B-Ann Moorhouse's 1981 article "Researching the Irish born of New York City"[2] and the discovery of the records of the Emigrant Savings Bank in the mid-1990s spring to mind. These are just two examples of the numerous niche sources that are now available. *Tracing Your New York City Irish Ancestors* brings these sources together for the first time and builds upon it with additional insight.

Where do I Start?
Start your family history journey by writing down what you know about your ancestry. Begin with your parents' genealogical information—dates and places of birth, marriage, death; parents' names; occupation; religion; etc., then work your way back through the earlier generations. Next, gather information, photographs, and documents from relatives. Make sure to speak to those relatives in older generations. There is no point spending weeks trying to discover the year your great-grandfather died if one of your aunts has the answer, or even better, his death certificate.

One important guideline to follow in your research is to treat family stories as clues rather than absolute truth. When tales of ancestors have passed down through numerous generations, they often become distorted. I have come across many examples where the documentation has proved the family story to be untrue, or only partially true. For example, ancestors who were supposedly born in Cork and Galway turned out to have left Ireland from the Cork and Galway ports; they were natives of neighboring counties. In another case, a family assumed that a great-grandfather was buried in Calvary Cemetery in Queens, but in fact he was interred in Holy Cross Cemetery in Brooklyn. In a final example, a family found a 19th Century census form that claimed "Ireland" as an ancestor's birthplace. But further research showed the person had been born in New York City to recent immigrants from Ireland.

As well as being wary about stories from the past, you should also be skeptical about genealogical information you find online. The Internet has revolutionized genealogical research and made it easier. However, the Internet also contains erroneously researched family trees, transcriptions errors, and other incorrect information. Use every online source that you can, but remember, just because something is on the Internet does not make it accurate.

Why Not Go Straight to Irish Records?
Many people starting out on their genealogical search know that their ancestors came from Ireland. An Irish surname or family tradition often indicates this. As a result, there can be a strong urge to bypass New York City records and jump straight into Irish ones. But genealogical records in Ireland can present difficulties. There is a preponderance of names such as Kelly, Ryan, O'Reilly, and O'Brien. You will be surprised how many unrelated Patrick Murphys can live in one parish and while it has been exaggerated, the loss of genealogical records in the Public Records Office fire in 1922—in particular many 19th century censuses—has made genealogical research in Ireland more challenging. Consequently, it is essential to start your Irish genealogical research in the United States.

After you have compiled all the known genealogical information about your New York Irish family, it is time to start researching in the New York City records. Doing so will allow you to fully document the lives of those who emigrated from Ireland and hopefully find their exact place of origin. Then the real fun can begin: researching in Ireland's genealogical records.

Lastly, a word of advice. Your family's journey from Ireland to New York will be incredibly important to you, but a good genealogist is objective with their research. Try to collect as many primary documents as possible. Look for footnotes and citations in the research of others to learn where they got their information from. Evidence is key; the more you have, the stronger your claims can be about your ancestors.

Certain records are indispensable whether you are tracing Irish ancestors or those of another ethnicity or religious affiliation. In the following pages, we will briefly discuss these sources and where to access them. Whether you have in-depth knowledge of your Irish ancestors in New York City or are just beginning your search, you should fully utilize these sources before turning to the resources outlined in the later chapters.

Finding information about Irish immigrants and their family members has a reputation for being difficult. Therefore, try to obtain every record that you can. Very occasionally the records outlined in this chapter will provide the sought-after Irish homestead. In my time researching in New York City vital records, I have come across six birth, marriage and death records that listed a county of birth in Ireland. It goes to show that you should not dismiss vital records even if you already know, for example, a date of death or where the family lived in the 1920 U.S. Federal Census. Unfortunately, those examples were few and far between and the place of origin in Ireland will generally not be found in the records outlined in this chapter. However, by consulting all of the following record sets, you can establish a foundation for your research. This will enable you to consult other records that are more likely to contain the place of origin.

What follows is a brief description of the U.S. federal census, the New York State census, New York City vital records, city directories, and wills and letters of administration. Also included is an overview of the type of information you will find in each record set about Irish immigrants and their descendants. Websites and relevant information about the New York City institutions where you can find these records are also provided at the end of the chapter.

U.S. Federal Census, 1790–1940
The U.S. federal census has been conducted every ten years since 1790, and those records are available to everyone from 1790 to 1880 and 1900 to 1940. The 1890 federal census was destroyed in a fire. The early censuses (1790–1840) list only the names of free heads of household; they give numerical representations for the rest of the people in the household. These can include both family and non-family members. From the 1850 census onward all members of a household are listed, along with their state or country of birth. For those born in Ireland only the country is usually mentioned; it is very rare to see a county or town given.

From 1880 onwards the census asks for each individual's relationship to the head of household. A great deal of information is given on census population schedules from 1900; for example, "month and year of birth" and "number of years married" in 1900; "year of immigration to the United States" in 1900 and 1910; and "if naturalized, year of naturalization" in 1920.

The Irish in the Federal Census
The vast majority of Irish immigrants will be found in the federal censuses from 1860 onward. However, some immigrants who arrived two or three years before a census was taken had less chance of being enumerated, especially if they did not initially stay with already established family or friends. Instead, they might have lived in the rear accommodation of a tenement. These dwellings, which were often just glorified outhouses, were sometimes passed over by census enumerators, or they simply did not know they were there.

The spectacularly repetitive use of first names among the Irish; the commonality of their surnames, and their often estimated ages (usually rounded to years ending in zero or five) mean it can be hard to locate the correct family or immigrant in census records. For example, one could easily image this as a typical Irish family on a census document—James Kelly, age 35, and wife Ann, age 30, with children Michael, age 4, and Catherine age 2. When examining a census record, treat any age over ten as an estimate, with the potential for a wider margin of error the older a person is. Therefore, the earlier an individual appears in a census, the more accurate the age will generally be.

Access
Indexes to all U.S. federal censuses are available for free on Familysearch.org, as are the images for the 1850, 1870, and 1940 censuses. Indexes and images for the 1940 census are also free on the National Archives website, Nara.gov, and, after registration, on a number of commercial genealogy websites, such as Ancestry.com, Censusrecords.com, Archives.com, and Findmypast.com. All census images from 1790 to 1940 are available for free on Archive.org (https://archive.org/details/us_census) but are not indexed. You can search the indexes and images of the 1880 census for free on Ancestry.com. Images and indexes of all federal censuses can be viewed for a fee on the previously mentioned commercial websites.

New York State Census, 1825–1925
The state of New York conducted a census every ten years from 1825 to 1875, skipped the 1880s, and then conducted censuses in 1892, 1905, 1915, and 1925. Unfortunately many of these records have been lost or destroyed. What follows is a table of the state censuses available, dented by 'X', for the five counties that make up New York City:

	1825	1835	1845	1855	1865	1875	1892	1905	1915	1925
New York (Manhattan)				X				X	X	X
Kings (Brooklyn)				X	X	X	X	X	X	X
Queens							X		X	X
Bronx[i]								X	X	X
Richmond (Staten Island)				X	X	X			X	X

The Irish in the New York State Census
Finding the Irish in the New York State censuses has many of the same difficulties as in the U.S. federal census. See the previous section, "The Irish in the U.S. Federal Census", for further information.

Access
Indexes for the 1855, 1875, 1892, 1905, 1915, and 1925 censuses and images for 1855, 1865, 1875, 1892, and 1905 are available for free on Familysearch.org. Ancestry.com and Archives.com have indexes and images for 1892, 1915, and 1925. Ancestry.com offers free access to its collection of New York state census records to all residents of New York state.

Microfilms exist for all counties where records are available. These microfilms are available at the New York City Municipal Archives; the Irma and Paul Milstein Division of United States History, Local History and Genealogy (hereafter called Milstein Genealogy Room) at the New York Public Library's main branch and the Church of Jesus Christ of Latter-day Saints (LDS) Family History centers, via the LDS Family History Library in Salt Lake City, Utah (see https://familysearch.org/search to search the LDS library microfilm catalog). Individual counties in New York State also have the original records and microfilm copies at county libraries, archives, and local government offices.

The New York Genealogical & Biographical Society has digitized the census schedules of Ward 17 for 1855, and members can access them on the society website, Newyorkfamilyhistoryschool.org. Ward 17

---

[i] Prior to 1905 Bronx County was enumerated with New York County.

covered an area in the East Village bounded by Houston St., Avenue A, 14th St., and Fourth Ave. /Bowery.

Vital Records, 1795–Present
New York City began keeping records of deaths in 1795 and births and marriages in the late 1840s. An outline of records available at the Municipal Archives in Manhattan follows. For all certificates listed there are microfilm and computer database indexes available on-site. Vital records can contain a wide range of information beyond names and dates of vital events. Parents' names are asked for on marriage and death records. Further information such as cemetery of burial, occupation and age can also be found on death records. A free index for many years of New York City vital records is available on the websites of the Italian Genealogical Group (www.italiangen.org) and the German Genealogy Group (www.theggg.org).

Birth Certificates and Geographic Birth Index
Manhattan: certificates, July 1847–1848, July 1853–1909 / geographic birth index, 1880–1914
Brooklyn: certificates, 1866–1909 / geographic birth Index, 1898–1910
Queens: certificates, 1847–1897 (with gaps), 1898–1909 / geographic birth index, 1898–1917
Bronx: 1874–1897 (included in Manhattan), 1898–1909 / geographic birth index, 1898–1910
Staten Island: certificates, 1847–1897 (with gaps), 1898–1909 / geographic birth Index, 1898–1907

Marriage Certificates and Licenses
Manhattan: certificates, June 1847–1848, June 1853–1937 / licenses, 1908–1929 / license index, 1908–1951
Brooklyn: certificates, 1847–1895 (various Kings County towns[ii]), 1866–1937 / licenses, 1908–1929 / license index, 1908–1951
Queens: certificates, 1847–1897 (with gaps), 1898–1937 / licenses, 1908–1929 / license Index, 1908–1953
Bronx: certificates, 1874–1897 (included in Manhattan), 1898–1937 / licenses, 1914–1929 / license index, 1908–1951
Staten Island: certificates, 1847–1897 (with gaps), 1898–1937 / licenses, 1908–1929 / license index, 1908–1960

Death Certificates
Manhattan: 1795, 1802–1804, 1808, 1812–1948
Brooklyn: 1847–1895 (various Kings County towns), 1847–1853, 1857–1948
Queens: 1847–1897 (with gaps), 1898–1948
Bronx: 1874–1897 (included in Manhattan), 1898–1948
Staten Island: 1847–1897 (with gaps), 1898–1948

Milstein Genealogy Room Holdings
The following microfilm and print indexes for New York City are available:
Births, 1866-1982
Deaths, 1888-1982
Marriages (arranged by groom's name), 1888-1937
Marriages (arranged by bride's name), 1869-1937

[ii] Kings County consisted of a number of towns in the 18th and 19th century before Brooklyn became a part of New York City in 1898. The towns were Brooklyn, Bushwick, New Lots, New Utrecht, Gravesend, Flatbush, and Flatlands.

Further Information
Records of births after 1909 and deaths after 1948 are kept at the New York City Department of Health. The department does not have public research rooms, and there are restrictions on access to the records. See their website (www.nyc.gov/html/doh/html/vr/vr.shtml) for further information.

Marriage certificates and marriage licenses after 1929 are located at the Office of the City Clerk. The Municipal Archives has microfilm copies of marriage license indexes that cover 1908–1951. It's a good idea to consult these indexes to pinpoint marriages for the years 1938 to 1951 as there is no research facility at the Office of the City Clerk.

According to the City Clerk's website, "a marriage record older than 50 years from today's date is considered a historic record and is available to the general public."[3] But anecdotal evidence points to a lack of clarity as to whether this statement is valid, and so you might find the rule is enforced from the start of the year as opposed to "today's date." The City Clerk's website also states that you can search for a marriage in more than one year; however, in most cases you can search only one year if you go to the office. If searches are needed for subsequent years, responses will be mailed to you, which can take up to four weeks. See the City Clerk's website for information about access to marriage records that are less than 50 years old (www.cityclerk.nyc.gov/html/marriage/records.shtml).

- Ancestry.com has the databases *New York City, Births, 1891–1902; New York City, Marriages, 1600s–1800s;* and *New York City, Deaths, 1892–1902.*

- Archives.com has the databases *New York City Births, 1891–1902; New York City Marriage Index, 1622–1899;* and *New York City Death Records, 1892–1902.*

- Familysearch.org has the databases *New York, Births and Christenings, 1640–1962* and *New York, Deaths and Burials, 1795–1952.*

- Worldvitalrecords.com has the databases *Births Reported in Manhattan, New York, 1901; Births Reported in Manhattan, New York, 1902; Marriages Reported, Manhattan, 1901; Marriages Reported in Manhattan, 1902; Deaths Reported in Manhattan, 1901;* and *Deaths Reported in Manhattan, 1902.*

The Irish in Vital Records
Many Irish immigrants did not report births, marriages, and deaths to New York City authorities. For example, before 1910 only about 75 percent of all births were reported, and this figure was even lower among Catholics.[4] There were a number of reasons for this. The Catholic Church was the focal point in the life of Irish immigrants. As a result, many of them believed that the recording of baptisms and marriages in Church registers fulfilled both their religious and civil obligations.[5] When a physician or midwife was present at a birth it was recorded. However, many Irish women were assisted in childbirth by female relatives or older neighbors, and the birth went unreported.[6] Also, in some instances, as in Brooklyn, civil registration of births was not mandated by law until 1866.[7] While legal requirements might change overnight, the practices and customs of an immigrant population can be much slower to change.

City Directories, 1786–1934
City directories list inhabitants, businesses, or both, usually in alphabetical order by surname or business name. The first New York City directory was published in 1786, the last in 1934. Telephone directories then took their place. There are separate city directories for Manhattan/Bronx, Brooklyn, Queens, and Staten Island.

New York City directories usually give a head of household's name, address, and occupation. When a married male head of household died, his widow was often listed in subsequent years. City directories also contain myriad other information such as maps, city departments and other public bodies, and religious congregations. Much of this information can assist with your genealogical research. For example, a city directory will list all Catholic churches that existed in the year of publication, along with their addresses. If you have an address for your ancestors this can help you pinpoint their nearest church. Relevant baptismal and marriage records could be in the registers of that church. It is worth noting the 1933/34 city directory. It was the last one published before the advent of telephone directories, but unlike all previous years, it listed all adults that lived at an address, including non-head of household spouses and any adult children.

The Irish in City Directories
In general, Irish immigrants will not be found every year in New York City directories, especially not in the first decade after their arrival. The search for employment saw them move regularly, and as a result they might be listed every few years and possibly at a variety of addresses. This was especially true for laborers and domestics, occupations which many Irish had. For these workers, the often exploitative nature of their work and poor conditions and wages meant they had no loyalty to an employer.[8]

So how do you know which is "your Patrick Murphy" in the long list of Patrick Murphys in the directory? After marriage and the birth of a child many couples did try to stay at the same address, or at least in the same neighborhood. Thus it is important to map out potentially relevant entries in the directory to see how close the street addresses are to each other. Finally, you are much more likely to find Irish immigrants and their descendants at the same address year after year if they had reliable employment, especially in the public service or the police department.

Many Irish women will appear in city directories as widows because their husbands died at a relatively younger age. The widow was usually listed within a year or two after her husband's death. This can be a clue when trying to identify an ancestor from a list of similar names.

Up to the mid-1840s the New York City directory did not include laborers, but the Brooklyn directory did.[9] Also, note that the person listed in a city directory was usually the main earner in the household and therefore could be a son instead of a father. The first appearance of a son in a city directory often indicates that he had married recently or had a first child.[10]

Access
The website Fold3.com has all but six years of Manhattan/Bronx and Brooklyn directories from 1786 to 1922 available online, for a fee. The Milstein Genealogy Room has microfilms of New York City directories from 1786 to 1934 for different years and boroughs. Ancestry.com has a collection of New York City directories beginning in 1830 for Manhattan and 1862 for Brooklyn. The Brooklyn Public Library has digitized Brooklyn directories beginning in 1855
(http://www.bklynpubliclibrary.org/brooklyn-collection/digitized-brooklyn-city-directories).
Consult the Brooklyn Public Library and Queens Library for information about access to city directories for each borough. The 1840 Brooklyn directory has been transcribed at
http://distantcousin.com/Directories/NY/1840/Brooklyn. Another subscription website, Worldvitalrecords.com, has directory databases for a small number of early 20th century years. Directories for all available boroughs and years can be ordered on microfilm to your local LDS family history center from the Family History Library in Salt Lake City, Utah.

Naturalization Records
The vast majority of immigrants to the United States became naturalized citizens. The Naturalization Act of 1802 created a three-step process for becoming an American citizen. First, the immigrant filed a

declaration of intention to become a citizen (known as "first papers"). Immigrants could do this at any time, and many did so shortly after arriving in New York. After a period of two to five years the immigrant could then file a petition for naturalization ("second papers").

Before 1906 there was no central repository for New York City naturalizations. A person could start, continue, and finish the naturalization process at any court. Therefore researchers should try to work out which courts were near an immigrant's home or place of work. For naturalizations that occurred after 27 September 1906, the United States Citizenship and Immigration Service (USCIS, formerly the INS) will have a copy of the records.

Keep in mind that not all immigrants became citizens. Some never applied and others never followed up on their declaration of intention. Also, up to 1922 women and children were automatically naturalized if the woman/mother married a citizen or if the husband/father became naturalized. After 1922 they also had to go through the naturalization process. See the "Naturalization Records" section in Chapter 6 for further information about naturalization records.

<u>The Irish in Naturalization Records</u>

The majority of Irish immigrants became U.S. citizens through the proscribed method. However, a few were naturalized in return for voting for Tammany Hall political candidates or in exchange for going to fight in the Civil War. In these ad hoc and illegal examples no paperwork was filed.[11]

Up to 1922, Ireland was a part of the United Kingdom of Great Britain and Ireland. After that date the southern twenty-six counties formed the Irish Free State. All through the 19th and early 20th centuries, people from Ireland renounced allegiance to the British monarch when they became citizens of the United States. Therefore, their nationality is usually listed as "British", "Great Britain", "GB and Ireland", or "English" on naturalization documentation.

Finally, some Irish immigrants chose not to be naturalized. A strong attachment to the home country and the negative anti-Catholicism of the Know-Nothing movement[iii] contributed to this.

<u>Access</u>

See the USCIS website, www.uscis.gov/genealogy, for naturalization records after 27 September 1906. Indexes and records from 1792 up to the 1906 date are available via many sources. *Index to Petitions for Naturalization Filed in New York City, 1792–1989* is available on Ancestry.com. The actual naturalization papers could be held at the local court, the National Archives and Records Administration in Manhattan, or available as digital images on Ancestry.com, Familysearch.org and a range of other commercial and free websites.

Wills and Letters of Administration

A will is a legal document in which a person—the testator—names an executor to manage their estate after they die. It also provides for the transfer of the deceased person's estate to beneficiaries after his or her death. If a person dies, and does not leave a will, and there are no executors appointed or living, then a letter of administration to deal with the estate of the deceased is granted by a county surrogate court. Information that is usually found in a will includes: the name and address of the testator; the names of the beneficiaries; the names of the executors; the names of the witnesses; and the dates that the will was made and probated.

In New York City each county/borough has a surrogate's court where copies of wills and letters of administration can be obtained. Following is an outline of what each surrogate's court has:

New York County (Manhattan): Wills, 1662 – Present / Letters of Administration, 1662 – Present
Kings County (Brooklyn): Wills, 1787 – Present / Letters of Administration, 1817 – Present

---

[iii] This was a political organization, active in the mid-19th century, which was hostile to, and occasionally violent towards, immigrants and Catholics.

Queens County: Wills, 1787 – Present / Letters of Administration, 1787 – Present
Bronx County[iv]: Wills, 1914 – Present / Letters of Administration, 1914 – Present
Richmond County (Staten Island): Wills, 1787 – Present / Letters of Administration, 1787 – Present

The Irish in Wills and Letters of Administration

To make a will or have a letter of administration issued one needs to have assets. Therefore, a researcher might assume that 19th century Irish immigrants, who made up the vast majority of the lower classes, did not have estates that had to be dealt with after their death. However, wills and letters of administration should not be overlooked. A sizable group of Irish immigrants and their descendants accumulated assets within one generation. Even those at the bottom of the socioeconomic ladder sometimes made wills to ensure there would be something for their children if the parents succumbed, as they often did, to the many common terminal diseases or to an accident.

Also, those named as beneficiaries might not only be in New York City. Immigrants who came to the U.S. sent money back to their families in Ireland in the form of the famous remittance. Therefore, a provision could be made in a will to remit money to named family members in Ireland. These named family members, along with any addresses provided, would be valuable information.

Access

Wills and letters of administration are available from the relevant county surrogate's court. See the following "Institutions" section for addresses, websites, and contact details. Indexes and digital images for wills and letters of administration from Kings County (Brooklyn) and Queens County are available on Familysearch.org in the databases *New York, Kings County Estate Files, 1866-1923* and *New York, Queens County Probate Records, 1785-1950* respectively.

Institutions

Following is a list of the main institutions that house records for New York City genealogical research. For the contact details of other institutions you might consult *Genealogical Resources in the New York Metropolitan Area* (2003), edited by Estelle M. Guzik.

Brooklyn Historical Society
128 Pierrepont St., Brooklyn, NY 11201
(718) 222-4111
http://brooklynhistory.org
Includes a library, archive, manuscripts, oral histories, photographs and more.

Brooklyn Public Library (Central Library)
10 Grand Army Plaza, Brooklyn, NY 11238
(718) 230-2100
www.bklynpubliclibrary.org
Includes the Brooklyn Collection, History, Biography and Religion Division, and much more.

Center for Jewish History
15 West 16th St., New York, NY 10011
(212) 294-8301
www.cjh.org
The CJH is a Family History Center where you can view LDS microfilms.

[iv] See Manhattan for pre-1914.

Family History Center (Brooklyn)
343 Court St., Brooklyn, NY 11231
(718) 875-2161
https://familysearch.org/learn/wiki/en/Brooklyn_New_York_Family_History_Center
Access the Family History Center portal and all microfilms from the LDS collection at the Family History Library, Salt Lake City, Utah.

Family History Center (Bronx)
211 E Kingsbridge Rd., Bronx, NY 10458
(718) 561-7824
https://familysearch.org/learn/wiki/en/Bronx_New_York_Family_History_Center
Access the Family History Center portal and all microfilms from the LDS collection at the Family History Library, Salt Lake City, Utah.

Family History Center (Manhattan)
125 Columbus Ave., New York, NY 10023
(212) 799-2414
http://www.nynyfhc.blogspot.com
Access the Family History Center portal and all microfilms from the LDS collection at the Family History Library, Salt Lake City, Utah.

Family History Center (Queens)
40-24 62nd St., Woodside, NY 11377
(718) 478-5337
https://familysearch.org/learn/wiki/en/Queens_New_York_Family_History_Center
Access the Family History Center portal and all microfilms from the LDS collection at the Family History Library, Salt Lake City, Utah.

Family History Center (Staten Island)
913 Rockland Ave., Staten Island, NY 10314
(718) 370-2376
https://familysearch.org/learn/wiki/en/Staten_Island_New_York_Family_History_Center
Access the Family History Center portal and all microfilms from the LDS collection at the Family History Library, Salt Lake City, Utah.

National Archives and Records Administration
1 Bowling Green, New York, NY 10004
1-866-840-1752 or (212) 401-1620
www.archives.gov/northeast/nyc
Naturalization documents, New York State vital record indexes, passenger lists, and more.

New York City Department of Health
Bureau of Vital Records
125 Worth St., Room 133, New York, NY 10013
(212) 788-4500
www.nyc.gov/html/doh/html/vr/vr.shtml
Post-1909 birth certificates and post-1948 death certificates.

New York City Department of Records and Information Services
Municipal Archives
31 Chambers St., Room 103, New York, NY 10007
(212) 788-8580 or (212) 566-5292
www.nyc.gov/html/records
Pre-1910 birth certificates, pre-1938 marriage certificates, pre-1949 death certificates, 1909–1928 marriage licenses, 1880-1917 geographic birth indexes, and more.

New York Genealogical and Biographical Society
36 West 44th St., 7th Floor, New York, NY 10036
(212) 755-8532
www.newyorkfamilyhistory.org
This is the oldest genealogical society in New York City.

New-York Historical Society
170 Central Park West, New York, NY 10024
(212) 873-3400
http://www.nyhistory.org
A huge range of collections including the Patricia D. Klingenstein Library which has maps, newspapers, photographs, printed material and much more.

New York Public Library
Stephen A. Schwarzman Building ("Main Branch")
Fifth Avenue at 42nd St., New York, NY 10018
(917) 275-6975
www.nypl.org
Includes the General Research Division; Irma and Paul Milstein Division of United States History, Local History and Genealogy; Lionel Pincus and Princess Firyal Map Division; DeWitt Wallace Periodical Room; and others.

Office of the City Clerk
Municipal Building, Room 252
Centre and Chambers Streets, New York, NY 10007
(212) 669-8898
www.nyc.gov/portal/site/cityclerkformsonline
Post-1937 marriage certificates and licenses.

Queens Library
Central Library and Archives
89-11 Merrick Blvd., Queens, NY 11432
(718) 990-0770
www.queenslibrary.org
Includes genealogical holdings, maps, newspapers, and more.

Surrogate's Court, Bronx County
851 Grand Concourse, Bronx, NY 10451
(718) 618-2300
www.nycourts.gov/courts/12jd/index.shtml
Post-1913 wills and letters of administration; see Surrogate's Court, New York County for pre-1914.

Surrogate's Court, Kings County (Brooklyn)
2 Johnson St., Brooklyn, NY 11201
(347) 404-9700
www.nycourts.gov/courts/2jd/index.shtml
Post-1786 wills and post-1816 letters of administration.

Surrogate's Court, New York County (Manhattan)
Municipal Archives
31 Chambers St., New York, NY 10007
(646) 386-5000
www.nycourts.gov/courts/1jd/surrogates
Post-1661 wills and letters of administration.

Surrogate's Court, Queens County
88-11 Sutphin Blvd., Jamaica, NY 11435
(718) 298-0400/0500
www.nycourts.gov/courts/11jd/surrogates/index.shtml
Post-1786 wills and letters of administration.

Surrogate's Court, Richmond County (Staten Island)
18 Richmond Terrace, Staten Island, NY 10301
(718) 675-8500
www.nycourts.gov/courts/13jd/surrogates/index.shtml
Post-1786 wills and letters of administration.

United States Citizenship and Immigration Service
111 Massachusetts Ave. N.W., Headquarters Building,
Washington, DC 20529
www.uscis.gov
Post-25 September 1906 naturalization records.

Useful Resources

Bailey, Rosalie F. "Guide to Genealogical and Biographical Sources for New York City: 1783–1855 with Supplement 1855–1898." *New England Historical and Genealogical Register*. Vol. 106. 1952. pp. 244-258; Vol. 107. 1953. pp. 5-26, 82-92, 162-178, 242-251; Vol. 108. 1954. pp. 5-18.

Familysearch Wiki Page—New York City
www.familysearch.org/learn/wiki/en/New_York_City,_New_York

Guzik, Estelle M. *Genealogical Resources in the New York Metropolitan Area*. New York, NY: Jewish Genealogical Society. 2003.

Harry Macy, Jr. "Before the Five-Borough City: The Old Cities, Towns and Villages that Came Together to Form Greater New York." *The New York Genealogical and Biographical Society Newsletter*. Winter 1998.

Murphy DeGrazia, Laura, Ed. *New York Family History Handbook: Research Guide and Gazetteer*. New York, NY: New York Biographical and Genealogical Society. 2013.

Murphy DeGrazia, Laura. *Research in New York City, Long Island and Westchester County*. Arlington, VA: National Genealogical Society. 2013.

New York City, New York Online Historical Directories
https://sites.google.com/site/onlinedirectorysite/Home/usa/ny/newyorkcity

Scott, Kenneth. "Some Materials for Genealogical Research in New York City." *National Genealogical Society Quarterly*. Vol. 50. 1962. p. 150–152.

3 Underutilized Records

The main genealogical resources to consult when tracing ancestors include state and federal census records; birth, marriage, and death records; city directories; and church records, many of which were discussed in Chapter 2. In New York City there are a number of other sources that are ideally suited for tracing Irish ancestors. There are some fundamental historical reasons why these resources have become important. These include (1) the socioeconomic status of new immigrants from Ireland; (2) a prevailing mood of distrust and hostility against the Irish; (3) the development of the Tammany Hall political machine and its patronage system; and (4) the importance to Irish people of secure public sector employment.

In the mid-1800s when Irish immigrants began coming to the U.S. in huge numbers, they started out on the bottom rung of the social and economic ladder. Those from a lower socioeconomic status were more likely to be victims of crime, commit crime, have poorer mental and physical health, and have a greater reliance on charitable, city and state institutions. Statistics from the 1840s to 1860s show that the Irish had the highest rates in all of these categories.

From 1849 to 1858, a total of 4177 people were committed to lunatic asylums in New York City. Of these 3279, or 78.5 percent, were Irish born.[12] In the 1850s the Irish accounted for 60 percent of the almshouse population, 70 percent of the recipients of charity, and more than half of those arrested for drunkenness.[13] A New York Tribune article from August 1870 reported that about 460,000 Irish-born immigrants and their American born children had been arrested in the previous ten years.[14] It was a sad and dangerous time to be Irish in New York City. However, there is a silver lining in this cloud of despair. Crimes, asylum committals, and poorhouse admissions created both records and newspaper articles. The following will explain how these social and economic forces have contributed to a variety of record sets that are important to the Irish genealogist.

Almshouse Collection
Beginning in the decades before the American Revolution, New York City provided assistance to those who were destitute, abandoned or who could not look after themselves. There were almshouses and hospitals at various locations and also a workhouse on Blackwell's Island, now Roosevelt Island. From 1816 to 1848 the main city almshouse was at Bellevue Hospital. It then moved to Blackwell's Island and was known as the "City Home" from 1903 onward.

All of the surviving almshouse records are located at the New York City Municipal Archives. The relevant genealogical records consist of admissions, discharges and death information. Other records in this set, such as almshouse population records, contain statistical and financial information. The Almshouse Collection begins in 1758, but in reality there are very few entries until 1800. Up to about 1830, people born in Ireland are in the minority, mentioned on average in one of every fifteen entries. From 1830 the Irish-born become more frequent in the pages of the ledger books reaching a majority during the Famine years.

For example, from 10–13 September 1848 most of those admitted to the almshouse on Blackwell's Island were born in Ireland. Their ages ranged from the twenties to the sixties and names such as Burke, Dougherty, Costello, and Molloy will be familiar to many.[15] The reasons for their admission show the suffering that was common-place: various diseases, "destitution", and "vagrancy". Even "old age" was listed, primarily for widows who had no family to take them in.

The admission and discharge books include many little notes and comments that can offer insight into the character of a person or provide vital clues about what happened to him or her. For example, John

Brown's entry includes the following information: "[age] 30, b. Ireland, date of admission 2 September 1846, in October eloped from hospital—Bellevue almshouse."[16] A 27 February 1851 entry noted that Sarah Hill, 26, born in Ireland was, "admitted 3 times in 7 months."[17] Then there was also John McCawley, 60, born in Ireland, admitted 27 January 1848: "in April 1848 eloped by scaling the wall after refused to go to Randall's Island."[18] The comment "eloped on a pass" appears on many pages for Irish-born admittals. Conditions must have been bad for inmates to abscond and not want to return. From time to time one finds the comment "drowned", with one particularly tragic: "drowned, jumped in the river, east Channel."

This Almshouse Collection contains countless examples of a group of people who are often hard to trace—that is, women before they married or after they were widowed. Apart from domestic service, not many employment opportunities existed outside the home, and if a woman was abandoned, widowed, or became a single mother she often ended up in the almshouse. Older unmarried women often could not escape the almshouse as domestic work offered little security in their old age. When it was deemed they had outlived their usefulness as a domestic, this was compounded by not having children to take them in.[19]

One example in particular shows the importance of family to Irish women living in the various institutions. Seven Irish women with the names Breslin, Casey, Dyer, Higgins, Somerset, Cashen, and Graham were discharged from the almshouse on 4 March 1857. They were all women in their twenties and thirties and some had been in the almshouse for over a year and a half. Most were mothers, and of all their children the oldest was only two and a half. What was the reason for their being discharged? In the columns beside the women's names is the notation, "Discharged. Refused to have children to Randall's Island" where there was an orphan asylum and poor house in the 19th century.[20] They preferred to be put out on the street than to have their children go to an orphan asylum.

Two types of death records are also in the Almshouse collection: certificates and ledgers. The Irish feature regularly in both. These sources can be particular useful when ancestors can't be found in city vital records in the second half of the 19th century. For example, death certificates for 1853–1877 provide information such as name, age, nativity, cause of death, occupation, condition, how long the person was in New York City, and a "remarks" section that often gives the name of the cemetery where the deceased was buried. The ledgers record such information as name, age, nativity, disease, and name and address of friend. Sadly, about 40 percent of entries have the comment "no friend." You might also find the word "died" beside the names in the discharge and admission records.

When consulting Almshouse records, it is advisable to use the finding aid, available from the staff in the Municipal Archives. The complete set of records is not in chronological order or grouped by type of record. However, certain years are grouped together within admission, discharge, death, and census records. Within these groupings, some records are in alphabetical order and others are arranged chronologically. Many of the almshouse records are available via microfilm from the LDS family history library, search New York, New York (City) - Poorhouses, poor law, etc.. in the "subjects" box of the online catalog. Also, see the "Census of Inmates in Almshouse and Poorhouses" section in Chapter 6 for more information about almshouse records.

Potter's Field

The sad reality for many of those admitted to the almshouse, or for those who couldn't even make it into a city institution, was that life was short and ended with burial in Potter's Field, also known as City Cemetery. Since 1869 pauper's burials have been on Hart Island, off the coast of the Bronx in Long Island Sound. Burials began on the island during the Civil War, but once the city bought the island in 1869 it became the main place of burial for the poor, the destitute, and those with no family to claim them. In 1977 a fire destroyed many of the burial records, but those that survived are available on microfilm at the Municipal Archives.

The Potter's Field records cover the years 1881 to 1985 but there are gaps. Records are arranged by trench number and then date of burial, so having a date of death makes it easier to find someone in these records. Information includes name, age, date, cause, and place of death. There is also administrative information for each burial including grave number, burial permit, and date of permit. From 1889 separate trenches were used for Catholic burials. These segregated plots are also given their own sections in the records, which might make it easier to identify Irish burials. However, this assumes that the authorities knew the deceased was Catholic.

More information about Hart Island and its history can be found on the website, www.hartisland.net. This website also has burial records that cover the period 1980 to December 2011. They are transcriptions from the records of the Department of Corrections and a subscription is needed to carry out a search. Microfilms of potter's field records are available from the LDS family history for the years 1881 to 1931. See *Hart Island (New York) city cemetery records, 1881-1931* on the Familysearch.org catalog for more information.

Public Sector Employment
The Tammany Society was a political organization founded in New York City in the late 18th century. It was intimately associated with the Democratic party of that era. Beginning with the mayoral victory of 1854, the Tammany Society dominated politics in the city until the 1930s. The 1854 victory occurred just a couple of years after the Famine generation of Irish migrants arrived in New York. Between 1846 and 1851 over 600,000 men, women, and children had come to New York to escape starvation and death in Ireland. This was a ready-made ethnic voting bloc, and the well-known ward bosses ensured that the famous saying "Vote early and vote often" was observed. However, this was not just a one-way process. Loyal voting resulted in thousands of Irish immigrants and their descendants securing positions in the various city departments and public sector organizations. For the Irish immigrants these jobs provided a steady income and job security, something they had never experienced in Ireland.

Beginning in 1883, the City of New York published an annual list of all its public sector employees. These included occupations such as police officers, firefighters, teachers and sanitation employees. The civil lists, as they are known, were published in the *City Record*. They record the name of each employee of the City of New York, the home address, annual salary, and date of entry into the civil service. The lists are publicly available up to 1968 but do include some gaps in the early years. It helps to know what city department the person worked in as this is how the records are arranged; the names are not indexed. For the police department the records are further divided by precinct. The civil lists are on microfilm for all years. Currently, the years 1902, 1908, 1923, and 1931 have been inputted to a searchable database. Both record formats can be consulted at the Municipal Archives.

Newspapers
Historically newspapers have been used to give a voice to a particular political, religious, or ethnic viewpoint. In the 19th century many U.S. natives were alarmed by the rapid increase in the number of immigrants coming from Europe, and from Catholic Ireland in particular. Members of the New York City establishment, such as Reverend William C. Brownlee, were most vocal in articulating their virulent anti-Catholic beliefs. As a result, newspapers began to appear that defended Catholicism and were aimed at the increasing number of Irish immigrants.

By 1828 there were twenty newspapers being published in New York City.[21] Many were short-lived affairs but numerous papers were founded later in the 19th century that were published for decades or that are still around today. Of all New York papers the *New York Times* is the most well-known, but many other titles focused on the Irish community.

Most of the early 19th-century Irish American papers lasted only a few years, including the *Exile*, the *Western Star and Harp of Erin*, and the *Shamrock Hibernian Chronicle*. However, their brevity of publication should not be dismissed. For example, the *Shamrock Hibernian Chronicle* contains many passenger lists which give the names of those arriving in New York City and their county or exact place of origin in Ireland (see the "Passenger Lists" section in Chapter 6 for more information). It also includes some "Information Wanted" advertisements that people placed when they were searching for relatives who had emigrated to America and from whom nothing had been heard. The *Truth Teller*, a newspaper that promoted the viewpoint of Catholics in the city, also carried the "Information Wanted" ads (see the "Newspapers" section in Chapter 6 for more information).

The second half of the 1800s saw the emergence of Irish American newspapers that were printed with more frequency. Three such examples were the *Irish News*, *Weekly World*, and *Irish World*, which ran for between five and fifteen years. The standout publication of the era was the *Irish-American*. Its first edition was issued in 1849, and it was published every week for the next sixty-six years. It reported on the Irish American community in New York City as well as providing news from Ireland, and so it contains a significant amount of genealogical information. Two sections of interest—"New York and Vicinity" and "Personal"—often contained information about funerals, weddings, and land sales. Another section, concerning the 69th Infantry Regiment—the famous Fighting 69th, which has Irish-born and first-generation Americans in its ranks—includes lists of volunteers and deaths of veterans.

The following list provides information about Irish American and Catholic newspapers that were published in New York City. All of these newspapers can be found in the American Historical Newspapers microfilms at the New York Public Library Main Branch, Manhattan, Room 100–Periodicals and Microfilm Room. The list gives the name, chronological years of publication, and where else you can access copies in New York City and State. It is rare for an institution to have a complete holding of every copy of a newspaper that was published. Therefore, you should inquire of each institution as to what years they have copies for. For information about where to access holdings of these newspapers outside of New York State, see the *U.S. Newspaper Directory, 1690–Present* on the Library of Congress Chronicling America website, http://chroniclingamerica.loc.gov.

Where to Find Irish American Newspapers

1810–1813 *Shamrock Hibernian Chronicle* (succeeded by the *Shamrock*, 1814–1817)
New-York Historical Society, Manhattan
New York University, Manhattan
Fordham University, Bronx
Queens College, Flushing, Queens
GenealogyBank, www.genealogybank.com (Images) ($)[v]
Stony Brook University, Stony Brook
New York State Library, Albany
Buffalo State College, Buffalo

1812–1813 *Western Star and Harp of Erin*
New-York Historical Society, Manhattan
New York University, Manhattan
Library of Congress – Chronicling America http://chroniclingamerica.loc.gov (images)
GenealogyBank, www.genealogybank.com (images) ($)
Stony Book University, Stony Brook
New York State Library, Albany
Buffalo and Erie County Public Library, Buffalo

[v] $ indicates a fee paying site.

1814–1817   *Shamrock* (successor to the *Shamrock Hibernian Chronicle*, 1810–1817)
New-York Historical Society, Manhattan
New York University, Manhattan
Fordham University, Bronx
Queens College, Flushing, Queens
GenealogyBank, www.genealogybank.com (images) ($)
Stony Brook University, Stony Brook
New York State Library, Albany
Buffalo State College, Buffalo

1817   *Exile*
New-York Historical Society, Manhattan
New York University, Manhattan
Stony Brook University, Stony Brook
GenealogyBank, www.genealogybank.com (images) ($)
New York State Library, Albany
Cornell University, Ithaca
Syracuse University, Syracuse
Buffalo and Erie County Public Library, Buffalo
State University of New York at Buffalo, Buffalo

1825–1855   *Truth Teller*
New York-Historical Society, Manhattan
New York State Library, Albany

1843–184?   *Irish Volunteer*
New-York Historical Society, Manhattan
New York State Library, Albany

1849–1915   *Irish-American*
GenealogyBank, www.genealogybank.com (images) ($)
Iona College, New Rochelle
New York State Library, Albany

1849–1918   *New-York Freeman's Journal and Catholic Register*
New-York Historical Society, Manhattan
New York State Library, Albany
Cornell University, Cornell
Niagara University, Niagara
Syracuse University, Syracuse

1856–1861   *Irish News*
New-York Historical Society, Manhattan
American Irish Historical Society, Manhattan
New York State Library, Albany
New York University, Manhattan

1859–1861   *Phoenix*
New-York State Library, Albany

1866–1874   *Irish People*
             American Irish Historical Society, Manhattan
             New York State Library, Albany

1867–1872   *Irish Citizen*
             New-York Historical Society, Manhattan
             GenealogyBank, www.genealogybank.com (images, 1867–1868 only) ($)
             New York State Library, Albany
             Cornell University, Cornell

1867–1905   *New York News*
             Unknown where copies are available
             The paper was founded in 1855 as a pro–Confederacy publication. In 1867 it changed to
             a pro–Catholic, pro–Tammany Hall newspaper.

1870–1878   *Irish World*
             New York State Library, Albany

1871–188?   *Irish Democrat*
             New York State Library, Albany

1881–1885   *Irish Nation*
             GenealogyBank, www.genealogybank.com (images, 1881–1883 only) ($)
             New York State Library, Albany

1878–1951   *Irish World and American Industrial Liberator* (merged with *Gaelic American* in 1951 to
             create the *Irish World and American Industrial Liberator and Gaelic American*)
             New-York Historical Society, Manhattan
             GenealogyBank, www.genealogybank.com (images, 1890–1905 only) ($)
             Franklin D. Roosevelt Library, Hyde Park
             New York State Library, Albany
             University of Rochester, Rochester

1893–1911   *Irish-American Advocate*
             Iona College, New Rochelle
             New York State Library, Albany

1903–1951   *Gaelic American* (merged with the *Irish World and American Industrial Liberator* in 1951
             to create the *Irish World and American Industrial Liberator and Gaelic American*)
             New-York Historical Society, Manhattan
             Fordham University, Bronx
             New York State Library, Albany

1928–Present *Irish Echo*
             Irish Echo Newspaper Corporation, www.irishecho.com
             American Irish Historical Society, Manhattan
             New York State Library, Albany

1932–?   *Irish-American Advance*
             New York State Library, Albany

1935–Present   *Woodside Herald*
                Woodside Herald, www.woodsideherald.com
                Nassau County Museum Reference Library, East Meadow
                Queens Borough Public Library, Flushing, Queens
                New York State Library, Albany

One of the best examples of how the Internet has made genealogical research considerably easier has been the digitization of newspapers. Once it would have taken countless hours to search all the newspapers in a certain year for a particular event. Now, thanks to optical character recognition software, which is used to scan printed newspaper pages, keywords associated with an event or person can be searched and actual newspaper articles returned immediately.

After the Famine, Brooklyn practically became an Irish county in America. By 1855 one-third of all people in Brooklyn had been born in Ireland, making them the largest immigrant group in Kings County.[22] Therefore the main paper, the *Brooklyn Daily Eagle*, is a genealogical gold mine. Thanks to Tom Tryinski and the Brooklyn Public Library the *Eagle* is available online at www.fultonhistory.com for the years 1841 to 1955 and at http://eagle.brooklynpubliclibrary.org for the years 1841 to 1902. The paper includes many news articles, reports, death notices, and obituaries that have helped break through a brick wall or provided information about the character and personality of an ancestor.

Many more New York City and State newspapers can also be searched on the excellent Fultonhistory.com website. This site can seem difficult to use at first, and you might be confused by the initial welcome to Old Fulton New York Post Cards. But don't give up. It is definitely worth persevering with for the vast range of digitized newspapers. Read the FAQ_Help_Index section to become familiar with the different types of searches that can be carried out and to see the full list of the newspapers on the site.

When searching a newspaper for the names of your ancestors, don't forget to plug the address at which they lived into the search engine. Many news stories refer to something that happened at an address, such as a fire or accident, without giving the names of those involved. It might happen that the event occurred during the years your ancestors lived there. The article could further mention "an Irish family with five children", exactly the type of family you have been looking for.
To get all the relevant hits, be sure to read some articles from the time period of interest to see how street addresses were written in the paper. For example, it could be "127 E 67 St", "127 East 67th St.", "127 E 67th" etc. Understanding how a newspaper reported street address will allow you to get all the relevant hits for a particular address that is pertinent to you research.

Useful Resource
Genealogy Bank Irish American newspapers www.genealogybank.com/gbnk/ethnic/irish_american

A Black Sheep in the Family: Criminal Ancestors
Even though it's said that crime doesn't pay, crime can pay off in spectacular ways when you are researching Irish ancestors. As previously discussed, in August 1870 the *New York Tribune* estimated that in the previous ten years there had been almost half a million arrests of Irish-born immigrants and their children for all sorts of crimes, ranging from petty theft to murder.[23] Many times just being Irish was enough justification for being arrested and charged, whether the person committed the crime or not. This anti-Irish prejudice means that huge numbers of records were left for genealogists to discover.

The reporting of proceedings at local, state, and federal courts has been a favorite of newspapers from the earliest times. Details of physical appearance, biographical information, and a wealth of other details can be found in 19th and early 20th century newspaper reports of court proceedings.

Using microfilmed and digitized newspapers, you can find much of the information needed to access court records for an ancestor who was arrested or tried for a crime. The article usually gives the date, court name, charge, and judges' name. New York City has an outstanding collection of court records. There is a record of every felon convicted in the city from 1684 to 1966. From 1790 onward there are indictment papers and case files for every felon arrest, and from 1800 onward every misdemeanor and violation is recorded in a docket book. Most records in these collections are indexed chronologically and then by the name of the defendant. Court records can be found at the New York City Municipal Archives.

Useful Resources
Arons, Ron. *Wanted! U.S. Criminal Records Sources and Research Methodology*. Oakland, CA: Criminal Research Press. 2009.

Lesser Known New York City Censuses
As discussed in Chapter 2, the U.S. federal and New York State censuses are fundamental record sets for all genealogical researchers. However, since the late 1700s various other censuses have been conducted that concerned New York City.

From 1795 to 1829 various "census of the inhabitants" were conducted. A considerable portion of these censuses has been destroyed, but the existing cluster of censuses conducted in 1816, 1819, and 1821 offer more details than do the 1810 and 1820 federal censuses, including the names of women. These censuses are available on microfilm at the Municipal Archives.

One part of the U.S. federal census that was not previously discussed in this chapter is the census mortality schedules. In the 1850, 1860, 1870 and 1880 censuses, information was also collected about those who had died in all states in the year preceding the date the census was taken. While not specific to New York City, this can be a valuable resource given the higher mortality rates for Irish immigrants (discussed further in Chapters 4 and 5) and their propensity to not register deaths with city authorities (discussed in the "Vital Records" section of Chapter 2). All of these censuses began on 1 June, so information was collected on those who died since the previous 1 June (e.g., 1 June 1859 to 31 May 1860). Questions asked included name, age, whether widowed, place of birth (state, territory, or country), month in which the death occurred, occupation, cause of death, and parents' birthplaces (added in 1870). Ancestry.com has the database *U.S. Census Mortality Schedules, New York, 1850-1880*. See the website, www.mortalityschedules.com, for more information.

In 1890 New York City politicians believed that the federal census of that year undercounted the inhabitants of Manhattan. So they arranged for the police force to carry out a census with officers recording names in ledger books. Known as the 1890 police census, this has become an important record set because the 1890 federal census was destroyed. Just over 88 percent of the ledger books (894 of 1008) have survived. To find a person or family you must know the address as the census is arranged in books, first by electoral and assembly districts and then by address. *Aid to Finding Addresses in the 1890 New York City Police Census* by Howard M. Jenson will show you on which microfilm and in which book to find an address. The police census is available on microfilm at the Municipal Archives, LDS Family History Centers (https://familysearch.org/search/catalog/203070), and the Milstein Genealogy Room. A small proportion of the names, 51,000 from twenty-six ledger books, have been indexed and are available on Ancestry.com.

Useful Resources
Joslyn, Rodger D. "New York City Censuses for 1816, 1819 and 1821." *New York Genealogical and Biographical Society Newsletter*. No. 4. Winter edition. 1992.

Jensen, Howard M. *Aid to Finding Addresses in the 1890 New York City Police Census*. Maryland: Heritage Books. 2003.

Tracing your Irish ancestors in New York City will see you uncover many documents about them and their families. But sooner or later many people hit the genealogical brick wall and they can't trace back any further. This brick wall is regularly encountered by researchers trying to find the place of origin in Ireland. While collecting relevant family documents can get a researcher to the wall, it is often necessary to use different research methodologies to try and break through to the other side. With this in mind, you will find some different approaches in this chapter that should be used.

Spelling Variations–Irish Accents and Illiteracy
A common experience for those tracing their Irish roots is coming across an ancestor's surname spelled differently in various records and documents. Often researchers struggle to find ancestors because of the range of different spellings—for example, Dougherty and Docherty, Galacher and Gallagher (which are just two of at least twenty known variations), McMennamin and MacMenamon, Keefe and O'Keeffe. This quandary leads researchers to wonder if they have the correct family and to ask where their ancestors disappeared to.

For those Irish immigrants who spoke English, the pronunciation and spelling of words and names was influenced by their local accent. The Irish accent could play havoc with how a name was recorded in genealogical records. Just as there are many different accents in the U.S., there are a myriad of accents in Ireland. There are Dublin accents, Cork accents, Kerry accents, west of Ireland accents, and Northern Irish accents, to name but a few. Take the name "O'Neill". In parts of Ireland today this name is pronounced as "Nail". Therefore, an American census enumerator, or city directory compiler, who had never spoken to an Irish person before, would probably record this name as it sounded—Nail.

Coupled with the Irish accent, is the difficulty of how Irish names are pronounced in the Irish language. Gaeilge (Irish) has had a lasting influence on the pronunciations of anglicized spellings of traditional Irish names. For example, in Ireland the name "O'Shaughnessy" is pronounced O'Shock-na-see, as it is Ó Seachnasaigh in Irish, and this pronunciation has influenced how Irish people say the name. Therefore a relevant ancestor might be entered in the U.S. federal census as Timothy O'Shocknessy.

Tied in with the difficulty of understanding Irish accents was the high level of illiteracy among immigrants. At some stage in your research you might come across an "X" where your ancestor should have signed a document, and his or her "signature" will appear in the same handwriting as the person preparing the document. Again, the spelling of the name might be different as the clerk or administrator signing it probably wrote it as it sounded.

When looking at indexes of names on websites or checking online databases, be sure to consider variations of your ancestors' surnames. A good idea is to turn off any "exact match" options on website search engines. A "phonetic" or "soundex" option will give you a broader range of possible matches. If only "exact match" options are available or you just have a long list of names in transcribed records, then you will have to write down different spelling variations of the name you are researching. The best example I have personally come across was a U.S. federal census population schedule where the name "Loughlin" was entered by the enumerator as Rockland! That gives you an idea of how far outside the box you might have to think.

Irish Name Formations
There is a tradition that surnames were introduced to Ireland by Brian Boru, the last high king of Ireland who died at the Battle of Clontarf in 1014. In reality they developed spontaneously. As they developed, *Mac*, meaning "son of", was prefixed to the father's Christian name and *O'*, meaning "grandson of", or its earlier version *Ua*, was prefixed to the grandfather's name.[24] Over time, *Mc* was also used; it is simply an abbreviation of Mac.

It is believed that the oldest fixed surname in Europe is recorded in Ireland. It is found in the Annals of Ireland which note the death of Tigherneach Ua Cleirigh, lord of Aidhne in County Galway, in the year 916.[25]

The *O'*, *Mc*, or *Mac* prefixes can sometimes lead to confusion about country of origin, ancestors whose names don't have prefixes and the difference between *Mc* and *Mac*. As a result, there are four common myths surrounding these prefixes. They are (1) *O'* indicates exclusively Irish origins, while *Mc* and *Mac* are exclusively Scottish; (2) *Mc* indicates Irish origin, and *Mac* indicates Scottish origin; (3) he can't be your ancestor because you spell your name with *Mac* and his name only had *M'* in some Irish records; (4) your ancestors "dropped" the *O'* from their name because they "took the soup"—that is, converted to a Protestant religion from Roman Catholicism during the Famine.

Genealogy was a fundamental part of Gaelic Ireland up to the end of the 16th century. Chieftains could trace their lineages back centuries and used them to prove their right to become the leader of different septs. However, this all began to change in the 16th and 17th centuries, culminating in Oliver Cromwell coming to Ireland and the complete defeat of the Gaelic Irish at the Battle of the Boyne in 1690 and the Battle of Aughrim in 1691. From this point on the *O'* and *Mc/Mac* prefixes were dropped by some and were treated as irrelevant optional extras by English government administrators in Ireland as they recorded names in government document.[26] By the time of the Famine in the mid-19th century, a majority of names in state and church records were not being recorded with the prefix *O'*. It cannot be stressed enough that "dropping the *O'*" and "taking the soup" occurred nowhere nearly as frequently as some people believe. The few documented cases of food for conversion to Protestantism were seized upon and developed into the nationalist myth that huge numbers of Catholics were forced to give up their religion to feed their starving children.[27] But it is simply not true.

The reemergence of prefixes in Irish names began in the last decades of the 1800s with the Gaelic revival in Ireland, led by groups such as *Conradh na Gaeilge*, the Gaelic League. Edward MacLysaght, the chief herald of Ireland from 1943 to 1954, studied the re-emergence of the *O'/Mc/Mac* prefixes.[28] He found the following results for the name *(O') Malley*:

Year	Using Prefix *O'* (%)
c.1855	11
1890	40
1930	91
1958	100

Another example of this trend, more evident in the 20th century, is given by the name *(O') Sullivan*:

Year	Using Prefix *O'* (%)
1866	4
1890	13
1914	20
1944	60

As another wave of Irish immigrants began arriving in America at the end of the 1800s, and into the 1900s, the numbers of those having the *O'/Mc/Mac* prefixes increased. It is entirely possible that some members of a family who came over did not have a prefix before their name while members of the next generation who emigrated did.

Did Your Ancestors Marry of Have Children in Ireland before Emigrating?

A common pattern in Irish migration was for people to come to the U.S. while young and unmarried. This is often reflected in census records showing that both immigrant parents were born in Ireland and all their children born in New York. Luckily for researchers this was not always the case and families with parents already married and children born in Ireland also emigrated. Thanks to parish register information (births, marriages, and sometimes burials) and civil record indexes from Ireland coming online you now have a much better chance of finding the place of origin for ancestors who married in Ireland before emigrating, or better yet, who married and had children before emigrating. There are two main websites for this data: one commercial, Rootsireland.ie, and one that is free, Irishgenealogy.ie. Between them they include over 95 percent of parish registers, as well as many civil birth, marriage, and death records.

A word of warning: if you get matches in these databases for a marriage and three baptisms, then you have very strong proof that you have located the right family and therefore the place of origin. But if you find a matching marriage, or a matching marriage and the baptism of the eldest child, you will have circumstantial evidence, not proof. While the temptation will be strong to claim the family as your own you will still need to do more research. Many names are very common in Ireland, and there could be a number of, for example, Timothy Sullivans and Mary Ryans having a daughter Elizabeth in the 1840s. You need additional evidence before you establish your ancestor's place of origin.

Useful Resources
Irish Family History Foundation, www.rootsireland.ie
Irish Genealogy, www.irishgenealogy.ie

Did Your Ancestors Children Go Back to Ireland?

Mortality rates among Irish adults in the U.S. were much higher when compared to adults who were native born or from other immigrant ethnicities. An 1894 U.S. government report noted that "the excessive death rate among the adults having Irish mothers [in New York City and Brooklyn] as compared with the average death rate of the total whites during the 6-year period [to 31 May 1890] was mainly due to consumption, alcoholism and its consequences, and pneumonia."[29] As a result this left many families headed by one parent, or even worse, left the children orphaned. The orphanages and institutions of the Catholic Church were one option used by families who found themselves in this situation. Another solution was to send children back to Ireland where family members could look after them.

In the 1901 census of Ireland over 6400 people gave their place of birth as America.[30] Almost 67 percent of these were children under 18 years of age, and just over 85 percent were under 30.[vi] This means that the vast majority of these American-born individuals had gone to Ireland at an early stage in their life; they either went alone to family in Ireland or were brought back by an immediate family member or other relative. So if one or both parents of a family you are researching died in the 1870–1900 period, then consult the 1901 and 1911 censuses of Ireland to see if children in that family show up in Ireland, and more crucially, where in Ireland they are living.

Useful Resources
1901 and 1911 censuses of Ireland, http://census.nationalarchives.ie or
http:// genealogy.nationalarchives.ie.

[vi] Figures based on a manual tabulation of those who are listed in the 1901 census of Ireland as born in America and who are under 18 years of age and under 30 years of age.

Was There a Priest in the Family?

In 19th and 20th century Irish society, a child's place in the sibling hierarchy often had a direct effect on his or her future. The eldest-born son usually inherited land or a rental agreement from the local landlord. The eldest daughter was provided with a dowry to marry, but all the other children faced the very real possibility of emigration. However, one son might be educated to become a priest. Having a priest in the family was something to aspire to and was a proud symbol of social status. An old Irish saying refers to a family's pride at having "a bull in the yard and a son in the priesthood."

This tradition continued with Irish immigrants. When a young immigrant family came to New York City, or two young immigrants married, then the rapidly expanding Catholic Church could prove tempting when it came to seeing their sons having a better life than themselves. Having a priest in one's ancestry is most advantageous for the Irish genealogist as extensive information can be found about a priest in seminary records and parish histories.

There are numerous publications about the history of the Catholic Church in New York City. Some of these go into minute detail about parishes and the priests who served them. For example, in the Church of St. Agnes in Manhattan, a Rev. Henry A. Bann, born at Parkstown, County Meath on 15 August 1837, became the parish priest in 1890.[31] In the Church of St. Teresa in Manhattan, Rev. James Boyce, a native of Ardagh, Ireland, and a graduate of Fordham, was the first parish priest.[32] Rev. Edward Corcoran, born in County Westmeath on 4 September 1836, became parish priest of St. Joseph's parish in Brooklyn in 1867.[33]

A search of seminary records can be most useful. From 1864 to 1896, most priests from New York City attended seminary at St. Joseph's in Troy, NY. After 1896 most New York City seminarians went to St. Joseph's in Dunwoodie, NY. There have been other short-lived seminaries as well. Remember too that men who came to the U.S. as young children and were later ordained, could have attended a seminary in Ireland, in another European country such as Italy or France, or in other American states.

Seminaries

Upper Nyack Seminary, Upper Nyack, NY, 1834
The first New York seminary, opening in 1834 with five priests, was destroyed in a fire in 1837.[34]

St. Vincent de Paul Seminary, Lafargeville, NY, 1838
This seminary was deemed to be too remote and it was moved to St. John's College when that seminary opened in 1841.[35]

St. Joseph's Seminary/St. John's College, Fordham, NY, 1840
The seminary began as St. Joseph's Seminary in 1840. When the adjoining St. John's College opened in 1841 there was no clear distinction between the two and so graduates became known as "seminarians of St. John's College".[36] A new seminary building was built on the site in 1845; it ceased functioning in 1860.[37] St. John's College became Fordham University in 1907.

St. Joseph's Theological Seminary of the Province of New York, Troy, NY, 1864–1896
The Troy facility closed in 1896 and the students moved to St. Joseph's Seminary, Dunwoodie, NY.

St. Joseph's Seminary, Dunwoodie, NY, 1896–Present
201 Seminary Avenue
Yonkers, New York 10704
(914) 968-6200
www.dunwoodie.edu
sjs@dunwoodie.edu

Cathedral Preparatory Seminary, Queens, NY, 1914–Present
This minor seminary was originally located in Brooklyn at 555 Washington Ave. The current campus in Queens opened in 1963, and the Brooklyn campus closed in 1985. It is a high school and two-year college seminary for those interested in becoming priests.
56-25 92nd St.
Elmhurst, NY 11373
(718) 592-6800
www.cathedralprepseminary.com

Useful Resources
Culkin, Harry M. *Priests and Parishes of the Diocese of Brooklyn, 1820–1990*. Brooklyn, NY: W. Charles. 1991.

Sharp, John K. *Priests and Parishes of the Diocese of Brooklyn, 1820–1944*. New York: Press of Loughlin Bros. 1944.

It's Not All About the Immigrant
Tracing your ancestry back to an immigrant ancestor can involve a lot of work. Therefore, it can be quite the achievement to uncover who the immigrant ancestor was, especially if he or she came to the U.S. because of the Famine. In such a case, it is a good idea to try and find every available record for this person in the hope that the place of origin in Ireland will be revealed. However, don't become so focused on that immigrant that you forget about the spouse and children. Sometimes it is records of these people that hold the key to unlocking the vital information, as relevant documents asked about parents, or referred to the parents' background.

The lives of an immigrant's children should be investigated to the fullest. If there were eight children in the family, do eight times the research. An obituary of the oldest child might say, for example, that he or she was born in New York just after the parents emigrated from County Laois. The will of the youngest child might leave money, for instance, to an aging aunt in Belmullet, County Mayo, due to a promise made to the parents.

Your Ancestors' FAN Club
Let's say you have conducted research in every resource you can think of but you have found no evidence of a place of origin in Ireland or even a county of origin. It is then time to start tracing the wider circle of people whom your ancestor knew. Irish people are extremely clannish and this has been a dominant feature of their migration to the United States. After receiving the remittance payment to travel to America, many immigrants followed, and at first lived with, their siblings, relatives from older generations, cousins, old-country neighbors, and even just people from the same county. Researching the lives of these people and finding out where they are from in Ireland could be the clue to unlocking where your ancestors are from.

A famous example of this clannishness led to U.S. president Barack Obama visiting Moneygall in County Offaly in 2011. This small village was the home of his maternal ancestor Fulmoth Kearney (variations of this name found in relevant documents include Falmoth and Falmouth). Francis Kearney, an uncle of Fulmoth's, died about 1848 and made land available in Iowa to Fulmoth's father, Joseph Kearney. The condition was that Joseph had to be willing to come to the US.[38] So, Joseph and his family, including son Fulmoth, emigrating in 1850 and the rest is history.

You will have to employ the "FAN club" methodology to conduct research into the lives of the wider circle of people that knew your ancestor. This methodology was brought to prominence by expert genealogist Elizabeth Shown Mills. FAN stands for *F*riends, *A*ssociates, and *N*eighbors. It is also known as collateral research, or cluster research. FAN's might not be related to your family but as many people from the same Irish parish or village settled in the same part of New York City, the FAN's should be investigated.

A good idea when using this methodology is to analyze the surnames that appear on the four census pages before and after your ancestor's listing. It is especially worth examining the names of those who lived in the same building on the earliest census record you can find for your ancestors. If not relatives, the people your ancestors lived with during their first few years of their time in America could well have been from the same place in Ireland.

Note the names of individuals from Ireland, and look for similarities or patterns in the information such as age, occupation, year of immigration and year of naturalization. If any of the names are even slightly unusual consult Edward MacLysaght's *The Surnames of Ireland*, which gives over 4000 names and the Irish counties they are usually associated with.

From 1880 onwards, each census enumerator was given a specific enumeration district. This was a "basic geographic area of a size that could be covered by a single census taker (enumerator) within one census period."[39] In New York City, these enumerator districts were based on city election districts (ED), themselves a sub-division of the city assembly districts (AD). Each ED was the size of a few city blocks and could be covered by one census enumerator. Therefore, if a street forms the boundary between two ED's the north side of a street will be in one ED and the south side of the street will be in another ED. Likewise with the east and west side of an avenue.

So, when looking at your ancestor's neighbors in a census you might be getting only the names of those who lived on one side of the street, if that street was a boundary between two ED's. The side of the street your ancestors lived on could be in one ED, while someone who knew them from the same place in Ireland could be living across the street, but in a different ED.

When checking four pages of the census either side of your ancestor, note the street addresses to make sure both sides of the street are included. Odd numbered buildings will be on one side of a street or avenue and even numbered buildings will be on the other side. If not, find which AD/ED the other side of the street is in and search that one too. You can use the excellent One Step website, http://stevemorse.org, developed by Steve Morse, to work out which AD/ED addresses are located in. It is more difficult to use this approach before 1880 as street names were not recorded on state or federal censuses previous to that year.

Federal censuses before 1880 and New York State censuses before 1892 do not ask about a person's relationship to the head of household. If you do not know the original surname of a married female ancestor, pay close attention to any boarders or lodgers living with her family in censuses before these years. They are not listed as a relative (where the mother is head of household) or in-law (where the father is head of household), but I have seen examples where it was later found out that these boarders or lodgers are related to the wife/mother of a family or have the same surname as the wife/mother from before her marriage. Even after these years relatives can be only listed as a "border" or "lodger" so always take note of their surname.

New York City naturalization records from the 19th century rarely have a place of origin listed. However, chain migration can be evident on these records, so you should apply the FAN club methodology to the names listed as character witnesses. These names could share a surname, indicating a close family relationship; have a different name, but still be related; or be a non-family member. If you find that the witness on your ancestors declaration of intention is not related to them, then there must have been some reason they were asked to do this. They might have been someone your ancestor met through his employment, but they could also have come to the U.S. from your ancestor's home place before yours did.

Useful Resources
MacLysaght, Edward. *The Surnames of Ireland*. Dublin: Irish Academic Press. 1985.

Steve Morse One Step Website–New York State census, http://stevemorse.org/nyc/nyc.php

Steve Morse One Step Website–U.S. federal census, http://stevemorse.org/census/unified.html

5 Where the Irish Lived in New York City

Where did the Irish live in New York City? The simple and unhelpful answer is "almost everywhere." While this answer will obviously be of no aid to your genealogical research, a detailed analysis shows that the Irish were concentrated in different parts of the city during different time periods. It can even be shown that immigrants from different counties congregated in specific parts of the city and on specific streets. Therefore, knowing where they lived in the city can potentially help you find out where your ancestor was born in Ireland.

Understanding the migration patterns of the Irish in the city[vii] can also help you build a more accurate picture of your ancestors' movements. This is particularly important if your ancestors had a low socioeconomic status as this group moved more frequently than did those who were better off. In New York City the Famine immigrants gravitated to Lower Manhattan. Here the oldest housing stock could be found and therefore cheaper rents, along with the most labor-intensive jobs.[40]

Eighty percent of Irish families in New York City moved at least once, but for the majority the move was only a short distance.[41] Individuals and families who were new to the city changed residence much more frequently than did those who had been there for decades. While two-year leases were the norm, weekly and monthly leases were common too.[42] The traditional moving day was the first of May[43] and on this busy day the whole city was on the move.
Three of the main reasons why the Irish moved were a death of a parent, new employment, and the development of transportation in the city. In the majority of cases when a parent died, it was usually the father. Mortality rates for Irish-born men who came to New York were shockingly high, with one estimate of the average lifespan being just ten years.[44]

Movement from Manhattan to Brooklyn was common. In fact, 38 percent of Irish families had moved out of Manhattan by 1859, with the majority going to Brooklyn.[45] The opening of new Catholic churches provides clues as to where the Irish lived and where they moved to in the city. The church was keenly aware of the need for houses of worship for its flock, and tracking the years of formation of new parishes illustrates the migratory patterns of the Irish, especially as they began to move in greater numbers to Queens and the Bronx.

In the pre-Famine period the Irish primarily congregated into the First and Sixth wards, and to a lesser degree in the Fourth and Fifth wards in Lower Manhattan.[viii] In the 1790s this settlement began near the East Side docks on Harman (now East Broadway) and Bancker (now Madison) streets. Steadily, the settlement patterns began to spread inland on the island. This concentration thickened in the fourth and sixth wards with the arrival of hundreds of thousands of Famine immigrants in the mid-19th century. In Brooklyn the Irish also first settled on the waterfront—in the First, Second, Fifth and Sixth wards—with the area just west of the Navy Yard attracting them from the beginning of the 1800s.

[vii] References in this publication to New York City and "the city" include the five boroughs—Manhattan, Brooklyn, Queens, Bronx and Staten Island. The five borough New York City came into being in 1898. Before this Manhattan/New York County also included parts of the Bronx, Brooklyn was a separate city, and Queens and Richmond (Staten Island) were counties. Today, locals in the New York City metropolitan area who use the term "the city" are referring to Manhattan only.
[viii] Wards were political divisions that were introduced in New York City in 1686. An alderman was elected to the city council from each ward. They were abolished in 1938.

Over the decades, these old communities changed, bringing the Irish to new areas of the city in the late 1800s and early 1900s. Hell's Kitchen[ix] and Inwood in Manhattan, Bay Ridge and Flatbush in Brooklyn, and Woodside and Sunnyside in Queens saw the largest growth of Irish immigrants and their descendants. Today, concentrations of Irish born-immigrants can be found in Woodlawn in the Bronx and Woodside in Queens, with Breezy Point in Queens having the highest concentrations of those with Irish ancestry.[46]

In this chapter we present an overview of areas of New York City where the Irish lived. For some areas we can give a lot of information, even down to the streets where people from certain counties resided. For others there is only a general acknowledgment that they were Irish areas. For each borough, you will find these districts broadly arranged by the era in which the Irish began living there. The information is presented largely in chronological order, beginning with the Irish in various wards after the Famine. Coming into the 20th century, the focus on wards changes to specific neighborhoods.

Manhattan
In 1855 the Sixth Ward had about 14,000 residents, of which two-thirds were Irish-born. The Irish county with the highest level of representation was Kerry, followed by Sligo and Cork.[47] The lower half of Mulberry St. attracted immigrants from Cork and Sligo[48], with further concentrations of Sligo natives to be found on Orange St.[49]

The Sixth Ward contained the notorious Five Points, then made up of the intersection of Orange, Cross, and Anthony streets (today the old Five Points is where Baxter and Worth streets meet at Columbus Park). This was a neighborhood that was infamous in the 19th century for poverty, crime, and disease. The Five Points had the most dilapidated and therefore the cheapest tenements in the city, and the low rent attracted Famine immigrants.

A high concentration of immigrants from Kerry, and from the Lansdowne estate around Kenmare in particular, was living in the Five Points by 1860. Indeed, one in seven of all Irish living there was from Kerry, with 75 percent of them from the Lansdowne estate.[50] Kerry natives also clustered on Baxter St. (then known as Orange St.)[51] and Anthony St[52]. In the *American Historical Review*, Tyler Anbinder notes that these Kerry folk were not attracted to the previously established Kerry enclaves of the city, such as the Fourth Ward.[53] Along with Kerry, Sligo and Cork, people from Tipperary and Longford were also evident in the area to the north of city hall and east of the Bowery.[54]

The Sixth Ward shared its southern boundary with the northern boundary of the Fourth ward. In the 1880s and 1890s the New York Kerrymen's Association thrived in the Fourth Ward. This area was once so full of people from the county that it was known as the "Kerry Ward."[55] The Kerry settlement was concentrated around the Church of St. James on James Street.

After the Famine the Seventh Ward become known as the "Cork Ward" due to the number of residents from that county.[56] Monroe St. in particular saw the heaviest concentration, so much so that it became known as "'Cork Row."[57] The records of the Emigrant Savings Bank (see Chapter 6) show that other heavy clusters of Cork immigrants were found in Cherry and Roosevelt streets.[58] Other Munster[x] immigrants, primarily from Limerick, were to be found in the eastern section of the Eighteenth Ward (between Second Ave. and the East River). [59]

[ix] Hell's Kitchen is the area of midtown on the west side of Manhattan. It is also referred to as Chelsea.
[x] The southern–most Irish province containing the counties of Clare, Limerick, Kerry, Cork, Tipperary and Waterford.

Immigrants from Ulster[xi] counties were also heavily represented in various parts of the city. In the 1860s the area between tenth and fourteenth streets near the East River was known as "Mackrelville" due to the numerous poor Irish that lived there and the stereotype of Catholics eating fish on Fridays.[60] This was the northern section of the Eleventh Ward and had a concentration of people from Cavan. Other pockets of Cavan natives could also be found from Eight St. up to Twentieth St., also on the east side[61]

The Thirteenth Ward was home to immigrants from County Tyrone, especially in the western half of the ward toward the East River.[62] Natives of County Antrim were drawn to the Jackson Square area. It is bordered by Greenwich Ave., Eight Ave., and Horatio St. and was in the very northern part of the Ninth Ward.[63] Immigrants from Donegal were found in significant numbers along Mulberry St. in the Tenth Ward[64] and on the west side of the Thirteenth Ward, below Fourteenth St. People from Derry could also be found here.[65]

Some Leinster[xii] counties also saw concentrations based on county of origin. The northern part of the Sixteenth Ward with street numbers in the 20s and the southern part of the adjoining Twentieth Ward (in the 20s and 30s) were home to many Westmeath and Longford immigrants.

Starting in the 1820s and 1830s, the Irish lived in and above Greenwich Village with this area located in the Ninth ward.[66] For the first two decades of the 20th century the west side of Greenwich Village along the East River was dominated by immigrants from County Clare, with the area being nicknamed "County Clare Street."[67] Even before this time, Clare natives were evident on Washington and Greenwich streets.[68] Small pockets of Irish also lived in Harlem at the beginning of the 20th century.[69] These enclaves were found around 113th to 115th streets, between Lexington and Third avenues, and slightly to the south at 100th to 102nd streets, between First and Lexington avenues.

By 1920 the majority of Irish were no longer living in the old Lower Manhattan wards. One of their last residential pockets in Lower Manhattan was located under the Williamsburg Bridge on the Lower East Side.[70] The Irish were concentrated in the area boarded by the East River, Rivington St., Goerk St. (now a public housing complex), and Corlears St. (also a housing complex). After WWI the largest gathering was found in Hell's Kitchen.[71] The Irish were the dominant ethnic group in this area, bordered by the East River, Fortieth St., Seventh Ave., and Seventieth St. Between 1920 and 1940 the Irish population in Washington Heights and Inwood, in northern Manhattan, increased by a factor of almost four.[72] The development of the 207th St. train yards saw many Irish move to Inwood, as they worked for the transportation department and for the companies that existed before the formation of the Metropolitan Transit Authority in the 1960s. Eventually the ethnic makeup of the area began to change, and the Irish began to move away beginning in the 1960s.

Select Manhattan Wards and Their Perimeters

Fourth Ward	East River, Catherine St., Chatham Square, Chatham St., Chatham Row, Spruce St., Gold St. (now Frankfort St.), and Frank St. (now Dover St.)
Fifth Ward	East River, Canal St., Broadway, and Reade St.
Sixth Ward	Broadway, Canal St., Center St., Walker St., Bowery, Chatham Square, Chatham St., and Chatham Row (now Park Row and entrance to Brooklyn Bridge)
Seventh Ward	East River, Catherine St., Division St., and Grand St.
Ninth Ward	Hudson River, Fourteenth St., Sixth Ave., and West Houston St.
Tenth Ward	Spring St., Bowery, Division St., and Clinton St.

[xi] The northern–most Irish province containing the counties of Antrim, Armagh, Cavan, Derry, Donegal, Down, Fermanagh, Monaghan and Tyrone.
[xii] The northern–most Irish province containing the counties of Wexford, Kilkenny, Carlow, Wicklow, Kildare, Laois, Dublin, Offaly, Louth, Meath, Longford and Westmeath.

Eleventh Ward	Rivington St., East River, Fourteenth St., and Avenue B/Clinton St.
Thirteenth Ward	East River, Grand St., Clinton St., and Rivington St.
Sixteenth Ward	Hudson River, West Fourteenth St., Sixth Ave. and, West Twentieth-sixth St.
Eighteenth Ward	East River, East Fourteenth St., Sixth Avenue and East Twentieth-sixth St.
Twentieth Ward	Hudson River, West Twentieth-sixth St., Sixth Ave. and West Fortieth St.

New York State Census: 1855 and 1875

In the following tables, statistics from the 1855 and 1875 New York State censuses show the number of Irish-born immigrants living in the Manhattan wards and the percentage of Irish that made up each ward. To provide additional perspective, the density of Irish born immigrants in each ward has been added.

1855

Ward Ranking	Density[73] (No. of Irish per Square Mile)		Percentage[74]		Number[75]	
1.	Fourth	80,353	First	46.0	Seventeenth	14,815
2.	Second	67,718	Fourth	45.6	Eighteenth	14,666
3.	Fourteenth	56,006	Sixth	42.6	Twentieth	12,853
4.	Seventeenth	32,922	Sixteenth	39.0	Seventh	11,777
5.	Seventh	36,803	Eighteenth	37.1	Sixteenth	11,572
6.	Thirteenth	29,205	Fourteenth	36.2	Sixth	10,845
7.	Eleventh	27,326	Second	35.8	Fourth	10,446
8.	Eighth	26,703	Nineteenth	35.4	Eleventh	9291

1875

Ward Ranking	Density (No. of Irish per Square Mile)		Percentage		Number	
1.	Fourth	51,392	First	35.1	Nineteenth	25,153
2.	Fourteenth	44,387	Fourth	32.1	Eighteenth	16,993
3.	Seventh	38,750	Second	30.8	Twenty-first	16,270
4.	Sixth	33,150	Eighteenth	27.8	Twenty-second	16,057
5.	Twenty-first	25,429	Twenty-first	27.7	Twentieth	15,977
6.	Eighteenth	25,362	Fifth	27.5	Seventh	12,400
7.	Thirteenth	24,747	Seventh	27.2	Twelfth	11,492
8.	Twentieth	23,155	Fourteenth	26.8	Sixteenth	10,434

Brooklyn

The immigration of the Famine Irish saw a huge increase in the numbers of Irish-born people living in Brooklyn. By 1860 just over a quarter of a million people resided there, and 57,000 of those—just over one in five—were born in Ireland.[76] As in Manhattan, many of the immigrants were attracted to living near the waterfront and the Navy Yard so the men and husbands could be near jobs on the docks. As a result these areas became heavily Irish.

Even before the Famine, Irish immigrants had been attracted to this part of Brooklyn. In 1800, a ship builder-turned-developer, John Jackson began advertising this area of the Second and Fifth Wards as Vinegar Hill. He hoped to attract Irish immigrants who had fresh memories of the failed 1798 rebellion, in which the most famous battle was fought on Vinegar Hill in County Wexford.[77]By the middle of the 19th century about half of the residents of this part of Brooklyn were Irish, with numerous men working as dockworkers in the Navy Yard.[78] Many of the female Irish were employed as domestic servants in the nearby Brooklyn Heights brownstones.[79] Over that fifty year period this growing concentration saw the name of the area change from Vinegar Hill to "Irish Town."[80]

In the 1880s the area just to the south of the Navy Yard, Fort Greene in the Eleventh Ward, had a strong concentration of Donegal immigrants.[81] The Irish began to leave Williamsburg for nearby Greenpoint in the second half of the 19th century, as immigrants from Eastern Europeans began to move into Williamsburg. Many new immigrants from County Antrim, from the Cushendall area in particular, came to Greenpoint to work for the McAllister boat towing company, which grew considerably from 1880 onward.[82] One of the parishes in Greenpoint, St. Cecilia, included a large concentration of people from Galway and Mayo.[83] In later decades, from the 1930s through the 1950s, many Irish speakers from Donegal immigrated to St. Theresa parish and the sections of Flatbush to its south.[84] Veronica Place, in this same area, was the most densely population Irish street in Flatbush.[85]

Select Brooklyn Wards and Their Perimeters

First Ward	East River, Atlantic Ave., Clinton St., and Old Fulton St.
Second Ward	East River, Bridge St., Sands St., and Old Fulton St.
Third Ward	Clinton St., Old Fulton Ave./Camden Plaza West, Court St., and Atlantic Ave.
Fourth Ward	Old Fulton Ave./Camden Plaza West, Fulton St., Bridge St., and High St.
Fifth Ward	East River, Navy Yard and Navy St., Johnson St., and Bridge St.
Sixth Ward	East River, Atlantic Ave., Court St., Coles St., and Hamilton Ave.
Seventh Ward	Bedford Ave., Atlantic Ave., Washington Ave., and Flushing Ave.
Tenth Ward	Bergen St., Court St., Fourth Place, 5th St., Second Ave., 1st St., and Fourth Ave.
Eleventh Ward	Flushing Ave., Portland Ave., Washington Ave., and Atlantic Ave.
Twelfth Ward	East River, Hamilton Ave., Coles St., and Smith St.
Fourteenth Ward	East River, North Fourteenth St., Union St., North Second St., 9th St., and Grand St.
Seventeenth Ward	East River, Meeker Ave., Richardson St., Leonard St., Pelt Ave., Van Cott Ave., and North Fourteenth St.

New York State Census: 1855 and 1875

In the following lists, statistics from the 1855 and 1875 New York State censuses show the number of Irish-born immigrants living in the Brooklyn wards and the percentage of Irish that made up each ward.

1855

Ward Ranking	Percentage[86]		Numbers[87]	
1.	Seventh	51.7	Tenth	6690
2.	Twelfth	47.7	Seventh	6471
3.	Second	35.4	Sixth	6463
4.	First	35.2	Fifth	5629
5.	Flatbush	35.1	Eleventh	4985
6.	Sixth	35.0	Fourteenth	4314
7.	Fourteenth	34.8	Twelfth	3332
8.	Fifth	34.4	Second	2967

1875

Ward Ranking	Percentage		Numbers	
1.	Twelfth	30.5	Sixth	9500
2.	Second	30.5	Tenth	6106
3.	Fifth	29.7	Twelfth	5349
4.	Flatbush	28.3	Fifth	5229
5.	Sixth	27.9	Seventh	4525
6.	Ninth	27.5	Eleventh	4020
7.	Tenth	24.6	Ninth	3757
8.	Fourteenth	22.1	Seventeenth	3754

Queens

In the late 1890s the Greater New York Irish Athletic Association (later known as the Irish American Athletic Club) bought land on the western side of Long Island City.[88] The purchase became known as Celtic Park, and Irish immigrants and their descendants used its facilities for playing sports. With Calvary Cemetery nearby, the Irish became very familiar with the area. As a result they began to move to Woodside and Sunnyside, mainly from Hell's Kitchen, beginning in the late 1920s and early 1930s.[89] In the mid-20th century, Woodside was one of the most Irish areas in New York City. Today many other ethnic groups also live in Woodside, but Irish immigrants who arrived in the 1950s and later, can still be found there.

In the late 1910s and early 1920s, many Irish began moving to the Rockaways, mainly to the areas of Seaside and Hammels.[90]Indeed, by the 1940s, Seaside had gained the nickname "Irishtown." Today Breezy Point, on the eastern tip of the Rockaways, is one of the top three areas in the United States with the most Irish ancestry and is known as the "Irish Riviera."

Bronx

While the early history of Irish life in New York City is dominated by Manhattan and Brooklyn, small pockets of the Bronx had Irish habitation before the Famine. There the Irish labored on large employment projects, such as the building of the Harlem Railroad, the Hudson River Railroad, and the Croton Aqueduct in the 1840s. This saw the Irish live close to where they had to work on these projects.[91]

By the 1930s the Irish were firmly established in the Bronx. A concentration of Kerry natives and descendants could be found at the O'Leary Flats housing complex in Parkchester/Stratton Park.[92] The complex was located in the East Bronx, in the area of White Plains Rd. and Wood Ave. When it opened, many Kerry families moved from the south Bronx to this complex. Riverdale and Norwood also saw concentrations of Irish immigrants and their descendants in the 20th century. Today, Woodlawn is home to the highest concentration of Irish-born people in New York City.

Staten Island

Of the five boroughs, the history of the Irish on Staten Island has been written about the least. Nevertheless the Irish inhabited the island and worked there too. While they might not have carved out distinctive Irish areas, the clues left behind in the form of older place names give an indication of where the Irish lived, and possibly from what county some of these inhabitants were from.

After the Famine, many Irish families settled on the lands of the former Egbert farm in central Staten Island. Today this area is known as "Egbertville", but during the 19th century it was variously nicknamed "Tipperary Corners", "New Dublin" and "Young Ireland."[93]

Again after the Famine, the area known as "Vinegar Hill", which was in the St. George area in the vicinity of Monroe and Montgomery avenues, became known as "Cork Hill". The Cork Hill boys and the Rocky Hollow boys used to march against each other and engage in fights.[94]

6 Sources for the Place of Origin in Ireland

As has been mentioned, finding the place of origin in Ireland is the ultimate aim of anyone tracing their Irish ancestors. However, this can be difficult because only "Ireland" appears on most documents giving the birthplace of Irish immigrants. Are there any records from 19th and 20th century New York City that definitely give a place of origin in Ireland? Well, you might be surprised to learn there are many sources. In this chapter records are discussed that provide this vital information for Irish immigrants. About 160,000 people are accounted for in the listed 19th century sources, in addition to the 20th century sources that give the Irish place of origin for hundreds of thousands more.

A full chronological bibliography is available at the end of the chapter. This will outline where you can access online records and gives complete information for published resources. You can use www.worldcat.org to find libraries that have copies of relevant books. It is advisable to check all versions of a set of records that interests you as some online databases might not have all records, when compared to a published version, and vice versa.

Emigrant Industrial Savings Bank

The Emigrant Industrial Savings Bank was founded by the Irish Emigrant Society and opened its doors in 1850. It was originally located on Chambers St., beside the current Municipal Archives, a location ideally suited to attracting a large number of Irish depositors who lived in Lower Manhattan. In all over 170,000 accounts were opened between 1850 and 1883 with the vast majority in the names of Irish men and women.[95]

The genealogical brilliance of these records lies in a subset called the Test Books, in which there are surviving records for the first 66,756 accounts, covering the years 1850–1863.[96] If you bank online, you will be familiar with having to enter passwords and codes to gain access to your bank account. The Emigrant Savings Bank had a similar system. When individuals opened an account, they provided their name, occupation, address, where they were born, when they came to the U.S., on which ship they came, and information about any children, parents, and siblings. When sending a remittance payment home, to prevent impersonation of an account holder, or if a lodgment book was lost, the Test Book was produced, and the account owner was quizzed on the biographical information he or she had provided.

The following 1852 entry for Daniel and Catherine Hanlon vividly illustrates the sheer volume of information that can be found in this set of records.[97] The Hanlons had account number 2571, and Daniel worked as a public porter, with the family living at 110 Cherry St. The rest of the information the Hanlons supplied follows:

About Daniel: Nat[ive][xiii] of Parkmore Co. Kilkenny, Irl. Arr[ive]d NY. May 3 [18]49 per ship McDonald fr[om] L[iver]pool. P[aren]ts dead Fa[ther] Kieran mo[ther] Bridget Keefe. 3 bro[ther]s in NY. John Thomas + James – 1 Patrick in Pittsburgh + Kieran in US – 1 sis[ter] Cath[erine] in Irl – Is m[arrie]d to Cath[erine] Carr, 2 ch[ildren] Kieran + Julia

About his wife Catherine: She is nat[ive] of Cuff Grange – Lornatree [?] Co. Kilkenny, Irl. Arr[ive]d with hus[band] – p[aren]ts dead. Fa[ther] Denis mo[ther] Julia Izzard [?] 1 bro[ther] Tho[ma]s in Hartford 4 sis[ters] Bridget in Hartford Julia in Mass[achusetts]. Mary Ann + Ellen in Irl.

[xiii] Letters and numbers in parenthesis are included to complete words and year. Question marks in parenthesis indicate being unsure about transcription.

Can you image having Daniel and Catherine Hanlon in your family tree and coming across all this information? Other subsets of genealogical note in the surviving Emigrant Savings Bank records are Index Books, Deposit-Account Ledgers, Real Estate Books, and Transfer, Signature and Test Books.

The original records are at the New York Public Library. These records have been digitized and are available on Ancestry.com in the database *New York Emigrant Savings Bank, 1850-1883*. Microfilm copies are also available at the New York Public Library and from the LDS Family History Library. Kevin J. Rich has also transcribed the first 12,482 accounts and published them in three volumes

Tyler Anbinder, a historian at George Washington University, has worked extensively with the accounts of the Emigrant Industrial Savings Bank. Anbinder, working with other historians, is currently transcribing the biographical data, including county of origin, for the first 18,000 accounts of the Emigrant Industrial Savings Bank and will make them available as a downloadable dataset on http://dvn.iq.harvard.edu/dvn/dv/anbinder. He has already published the biographical data for nine hundred account holders on the same website.[98]

Useful Resources
For a complete explanation of the entire set of records see:
Salvato, Richard. *A User's Guide to the Emigrant Savings Bank Records*. New York: New York Public Library Manuscripts and Archives Division. 1997. Available online at:
http://legacy.www.nypl.org/research/chss/spe/rbk/faids/emigrant.pdf.

New York Public Library and Scholarly Resources. *Emigrant Savings Bank Records, 1841-1945*. Wilmington, DE: Scholarly Resources. 2000.

Census of Inmates in Almshouses and Poorhouses
In Chapter 3, we discussed that the Almshouse Collection is an underutilized source. In the 19th and early 20th centuries a separate set of almshouse records was complied for the New York State Board of Charities and can be found on Ancestry.com. A 19th century law required all almshouses and poorhouses in the state to record information about residents on standardized forms. These forms asked about the birthplace of residents and thousands of Irish places of origin are listed.

New York, Census of Inmates in Almshouses and Poorhouses, 1830–1920, contains biographical information for almost 250,000 residents. Forms are filled out to varying degrees, but depending on the year, they may include: name, age, date of admission and discharge, marital status, birthplace, last residence, length of time in the U.S. and in the state, port of entry, naturalization details, occupation, religion, names and addresses of relatives or friends, and information about the parents of residents.

An analysis of this record set shows that the county or place of origin is provided for over 16,000 residents of New York City institutions. The record set begins in 1830 but the first examples of Irish places of origin are found beginning circa 1850. Of course, hundreds of thousands of Irish immigrants came to New York City between 1830 and 1850. A considerable number of these would have entered almshouses and poorhouses. No matter the year, you are encouraged to search this database because of the wealth of information that may assist your search.

Headstone Transcriptions
There has always been a strong volunteer ethos in genealogy. Today researchers can easily access previously difficult or hard-to-find records due to the dedicated work of a volunteer transcriber. The next two publications fall into that category.

A dedicated genealogist named Rosemary Muscarella Ardolina transcribed about eight thousand headstones from Calvary Cemetery, Queens that list a place of origin in Ireland. This is a truly outstanding achievement as Calvary is the biggest cemetery in the United States. Two books, *Old Calvary Cemetery: New Yorkers Carved in Stone* and *Second Calvary Cemetery: New Yorkers Carved in Stone*, are the fruits of Ardolina's countless hours of toil.

Joseph M. Silinonte is a name that should be familiar to anyone doing Irish genealogical research in New York City. In the 1990s Silinonte published two books that list the place of origin for thousands of Irish men and women who lived in 19th century New York City. The first publication, *Tombstones of the Irish Born* gives headstone transcriptions from Holy Cross Cemetery in Brooklyn. The first burial at this cemetery occurred in 1849, and since then countless numbers of primarily Brooklyn Irish have been buried there. In all, Silinonte lists over 5000 names, and every county in Ireland is referenced. Silinonte's second book on marriage records is discussed in the "Marriage Records, Diocese of Brooklyn" section of this chatper.

Our Lady of Mount Carmel Cemetery in Astoria, Queens, was often called the "Irish Famine cemetery" due to the many burials of Famine immigrants from the 1840s to 1890s. Many headstones in this small cemetery noted the deceased's birth place in Ireland. Transcriptions were published in a supplement to *Description of Private and Family Cemeteries in the Borough of Queens*. For more information about this cemetery, see Chapter 9. Some of these transcriptions are also available at http://www.pefagan.com/gen/astoria/mtcarm/mtcframi.htm.

Newspapers

Again, thanks to the dedicated work of genealogists, publications of "Information Wanted" ads are available. As mentioned in Chapter 3, these notices were placed in newspapers by family members or friends looking for Irish immigrants who had not been seen or heard from for a long time. The contact person was often a third party who was more established in the city, more likely to be found in censuses and city directories, and often from the same part of Ireland. All these ads give the place of origin in Ireland for the individual being sought.

Probably the most well know Information Wanted ads are from the "Missing Friends" column in the *Boston Pilot*. Despite being a Boston paper, the *Pilot* has thousands of entries concerning the Irish in New York City. In total, the Information Wanted database, at http://infowanted.bc.edu, has 40,329 entries. More than 3800 of the immigrants being sought arrived at the port in New York City. The targets of the advertisements had last been heard from in the states along the East Coast and beyond. Over six hundred people who placed the ads gave contact addresses in New York City. The database is based on the eight volume work of Ruth-Ann Harris and Donald M. Jacobs and contains transcribed information. Ancestry.com and Americanancestors.org have this database with each entry linked to an original image from the newspaper. See the chronological bibliography at the end of the chapter for full details of all sources.

This post-Famine entry, from 1852, shows how relevant this source is to New York City research:

Of John Kelly, from County Galway, parish Balinakil [Balinakill], townland Gurthunea. When last heard from he was in New York, 66 Cherry Street—supposed to be in Virginia. Any information respecting him will be thankfully received by his wife, Bridget Murphy, No. 2 Elizabeth Street, Brooklyn, NY.[99]

For ads in New York City newspapers, there are two excellent publications by Laura Murphy DeGrazia and Diane Fitzpatrick Haberstroh. *Voices of the Irish Immigrant* is a compilation of these notices from the *Truth Teller* newspaper, covering the years 1825 to 1844. Likewise, *Irish Relatives and Friends* presents notices from the *Irish-American* that were printed in the years 1850 to 1871. Both publications list over 4700 information wanted ads.

This 1863 example, from *Irish Relatives and Friends*, gives names from three generations of the O'Hara family from Ardnaree, Sligo. It shows how rewarding a relevant ad can be:

Of Patrick Henry, a native of the parish of Kilmore Moy, townland of Ardnaree, County Sligo, Ireland, a cooper by trade, and having been brought up in the city of Belfast. When last heard from he was in Baltimore, MD. Also, of his uncles, Patrick and Michael O'Hara, from Ardnaree, County Sligo, sons of Arthur O'Hara. They are twenty years in America. When last heard from, in 1857, they were in Carbondale, Luzerne County, Penn. Any information of them will be thankfully received by Patrick Henry, at No. 71 10th Avenue, near West 15th Street, New York. [100]

In Chapter 3, the genealogical value of the *Brooklyn Daily Eagle* was discussed. This was not an Irish American newspaper, but it did contain large amounts of information about Irish immigrants and their descendants in Brooklyn. Another New York City newspaper of value to those with Irish born ancestors is the *New York Herald*, published from 1835 to 1924.[xiv] This newspaper will be of particular use to those with ancestors who lived in Manhattan.

By about 1850, the average New York City Irish family had learned to utilize the newspaper as a way to relay information to family members in the U.S. and Ireland, especially via more detailed marriage and death notices.[101] Due to the work of genealogist James P. Maher, a staggering 285,000 marriage and death notices have been indexed in his four volume work, *Index to Marriages and Deaths in the New York Herald*, covering the years 1835 to 1876. Over 15,000 of these notices give an Irish place of origin. The index allows you to easily search for a name of interest to your research and, if found, get the date of the edition it was mentioned in.

Full details for each of his four volumes are listed in the bibliography at the end of this chapter. Some editions of this newspaper have been digitized. The years 1840 to 1865 are available via a ProQuest Historical Databases institution subscription at participating libraries. See, for example, the New York Public Library (www.nypl.org/collections/articles-databases/proquest-historical-database).
Ancestry.com has a database, *New York Herald (New York, New York)*, that has digitized editions for the years 1869 to 1872. The same years are also available on Ancestry's affiliate newspaper website, Newspapers.com. Microfilm editions of the newspaper are available at institutions such as the New York Public Library and New York State Library.

The *New York Times* was by no means an "Irish" newspaper in the 19th century. Although, it carried few death notices for the Irish-born, 250 that give the place of origin in Ireland can be found in the 1850–1870 period. These obituaries are for middle-class Irish immigrants in the city who became small-business men and artisans. Their names can be found in *The Irish Middle Class of New York City, 1850-1870*, located at Bobst Library at New York University. This work is the master's thesis of Marion R. Casey, currently a professor of Irish Studies at NYU.

Travel Writing
Some of the most interesting historical accounts from the 18th and 19th centuries are travel memoirs in which the author describes the places they visited and people they met. One such journey was undertaken by the Fenian leader Jeremiah O'Donovan Rossa in the late 1840s. Beginning in Pittsburgh, Pennsylvania, he traveled to Philadelphia and then on to New York City. From there he toured upstate New York, visiting Albany and Troy before heading west to Syracuse and Buffalo. The next stage of his

---

[xiv] This newspaper should not be confused with the *New–York Herald*, published from 1802 to 1817.

trip took him to Cleveland, Ohio, and then back to Pittsburgh, before traveling on to Cincinnati, Ohio, and Louisville, Kentucky. He then returned to Pittsburgh via Cincinnati.

What makes this almost four-hundred page account most interesting to the genealogist is that the author notes where in Ireland every Irish person that he meets on his journey is from. Of one immigrant in Manhattan, he writes: "Mr. Michael Duffy from the townland of Mulloghave, county Monaghan, No. 108 Bank Street, and only four years from his native land'.[102] O'Donovan Rossa conversed with many people in New York City and this example also shows how the information can be cross referenced with other record sets, such as city directories and passenger lists, to be most useful. You can read this book on Archive.org at http://archive.org/details/abriefaccountau00odogoog.

Marriage Records, Diocese of Brooklyn
Joseph Silinonte's second book (see the "Headstone Transcriptions" section in this chatper for a discussion of his first book) is an excellent example of how casting a genealogist's eye over archived or unpublished documents can be hugely beneficial. When Silinonte was invited to view records of marriage dispensations granted in the Roman Catholic Diocese of Brooklyn, he found that many of them listed the names of the parents of the marrying parties; for Irish-born brides and grooms the county of origin in Ireland was given. A dispensation is the relaxation of a rule that would usually inhibit a member of a particular faith from marrying someone.

In 1996 Silinonte published Volume 1 of *Bishop Loughlin's Dispensations,* which covers the years 1859–1866. Almost seven thousand men and women are listed with their county of origin provided. Sadly, Silinonte passed away before he could publish subsequent volumes. There must be thousands more marriage dispensations in the archives of the Diocese of Brooklyn for the years after 1866. Therefore, if you have ancestors who married in a parish in Brooklyn, it is worth writing to the diocesan archives to see if any existing dispensation can be located. You can find contact information for the diocese in Chapter 8.

Church of the Transfiguration Marriage Register
Another rare example of Catholic Church records holding priceless information are the sacramental registers of the Church of the Transfiguration at 29 Mott Street in Manhattan. This church is located in the old Sixth Ward, which was dominated by the Irish after the Famine. The building was purchased from the Episcopalian Church by the Roman Catholic Church in 1853. For six years (1853–1859) the church secretary recorded the county and civil parish of almost every Irish person who was married there.[103] The civil parish of origin for over one thousand people from Ireland is noted. See Manhattan, no. 4 in Chapter 8 for full contact details.

Passenger Lists
Before 1820 the U.S. government did not require that the numbers and particulars of immigrants be recorded. As a result there are no standardized passenger lists or ship manifests for these years. In some ports, however, such as Philadelphia, the names of passengers were sometimes recorded, along with the cargo that landed there.

The first legislation concerning the collation of immigrants was the Steerage Act enacted by Congress on 2 March 1819. The act established standards to be followed by ships carrying passengers to the U.S. and required that the ages, sex, occupation and nativity of each passenger be recorded. From 1820 onward, ships had to provide a list of passengers to customs officers when they arrived at U.S. ports, and hence it became known as "the customs list", more popularly known as a passenger list, or ship manifest. However, the overwhelming majority of these lists provided only the country of origin for the immigrants. Therefore, "Ireland" is all you will find on most customs lists. Despite this, there are publications that give the place of origin in Ireland for many people who came to the United States.

This information comes from various 19th century documents in Britain and Ireland and the Irish genealogist Brian Mitchell has compiled a number of publications. *Irish Passenger Lists, 1803–1806* contains names and places of origin extracted from the Hardwicke papers. Government officials of the day were concerned about a skills shortage and wanted to keep certain people in Ireland. Earl Hardwicke was the Lord Lieutenant of Ireland at the time and had final say on who could emigrate. Copies of approved lists of emigrants were duplicated and sent to his office, resulting in these lists being archived in his official papers. In all, passengers from 109 ships are recorded with the ports of Dublin, Derry, and Belfast providing the vast majority of ships. Over 60 percent of these ships arrived in New York City. The names can also be found in a series of articles published between 1906 and 1912 in the *Register*, the journal of the New England Historical and Genealogical Society. Mary Heaphy, a contributor to the Irish Genealogy Project Archives (www.igp-web.com), has been adding these names to a growing database since 2010.

Mitchell's second publication, *Irish Emigration Lists, 1833–1839,* is another compilation from Irish sources of the names and places of origin of emigrants who sailed to New York City. It focuses on the early work of the Ordnance Survey of Ireland. This survey produced a huge volume of information for the first two counties that were surveyed, Antrim and Derry. As a result there are large lists of immigrants to New York from these two counties. A free index of names from this source is available at www.rootsweb.ancestry.com/~ote/ships/index.htm#irishimm1833.

Some of the earliest New York Irish newspapers carried articles about Irish immigrants disembarking at New York City and, crucially, where they are from. *The Shamrock Hibernian Chronicle* was the main newspaper for the 1810–1820 period and in two publications, *Passenger Lists from Ireland* and *Passengers from Ireland: Lists of Passengers Arriving at American Ports Between 1811 and 1817* you will find names and places found in its articles. There is considerable overlap between the two publication and they lists over 200 ships, with the vast majority providing the names of passengers. Almost 80 percent of the ships arrived in New York City, and most of the manifests give a county or town of origin in Ireland.

The Olive Tree genealogy website (www.olivetreegenealogy.com/ships/irishtousa.shtml) has many transcriptions of passenger lists and indexes of names for the previously discussed passenger list sources, covering the years 1803 to 1839.

Despite the recording of "Ireland" on customs lists, there are exceptions and we should be thankful that some ship captains were overzealous when it came to collecting information about their passengers. For some captains, recording them as being from Ireland was not good enough, and so they collected information about counties and even towns of origin.

Before and during the Famine, in the 1840s and 1850s, the passenger lists of some ships were compiled by people who obtained detailed information on the place of origin or birth for each passenger. In the accompanying table you will find a compilation of such ships. Most of the ships listed below carried between 100 and 200 passengers. It would take countless hours of research to examine all passenger lists from 1820–1891 to see if a place of origin in Ireland is given. While every effort has been made to locate such ships, there are bound to be some missing from the table. Therefore, it is always worthwhile to try and find the passenger ship on which your Irish ancestor came to New York City. Remember, some ships stopped at ports in Ireland on their way from Liverpool, and other British cities, to New York.

The exact question asked on the ship manifest about place of origin or birth is given under the "Passenger List Asks" heading. This has been included as different questions can elicit different answers from immigrants. Caution should be used when a coastal county is given as the answer, particularly one that had a port (e.g., Galway; Moville, Derry; Cobh/Queenstown, Cork; Belfast, Antrim; etc.).

Respondents who spent their last night in Ireland in the town of the port may have given the port name as the answer, depending on how they interpreted the question. For example, being asked their "place of birth" will more than likely see the passenger give the correct answer. But being asked "last place of settlement" might see the passenger volunteer the name of the town they stayed in on their last night—namely the port—as opposed to where they had been living.

Ships to New York City that Give Place of Origin on Customs List

Ship	Sailed From	Arrival Date	Passenger List Asks
Princess Victoria	Liverpool	9 June 1840	Place of birth/Last place of settlement – Name of place within county listed.
Elard	Liverpool	27 April 1842	Where born/Last residence – Name of place within county listed for some entries. Nearly all passengers were from Co. Cork.
Excel	Liverpool	22 June 1843	Place of birth.
Sarah Milledge	Galway	13 May 1848	Last place of settlement – All passengers say Galway.
Adam Carr	Glasgow	26 June 1848	Cannot determine question as top of first page is missing – Vast majority of passengers are Scottish. Those that say they are Irish list Londonderry and Belfast as where they are from.
James Andrews	Galway	28 July 1848	Country of birth/Last place of settlement.
Peter Hattrick	Liverpool	28 July 1848	Last place of settlement.
St. George	Liverpool	21 August 1848	Last place of settlement.
David Cannon	Liverpool	20 Sept 1848	Place of last residence.
Sheridan	Liverpool	15 Dec 1848	Last place of settlement.
James H. Shepherd	Liverpool	29 Jan 1849	The country to which they severally belong – Villages, towns and counties are listed.
Sea	Liverpool	4 June 1849	Country of birth/Last legal residence – Customs list gives name of place within county.
Alexria	Limerick	6 July 1849	Last legal residence – All passengers say Limerick.
Jenny Lind	Belfast	28 Aug 1849	First page asks "the country to which they severally belonged." Pages 2–5 ask "country of birth"/"last legal residence." These pages are possibly from two different customs lists. All passengers on pages 2–5 say Belfast.
Aberdeen	Liverpool	13 March 1850	Last legal residence.
William D. Lewall	Liverpool	5 Sept 1850	The top of the first page of the customs list, including the names of the first twenty-six passengers, is missing but they are indexed under the ship name Sewall on Ancestry.com. The missing part of the page asks for last legal residence.

Assisted emigration to North America happened throughout the 19th century and assisted emigrants make up a small but substantial subset of passenger lists. These emigrants had their passage paid by their landlord, the local Poor Law Union Board of Guardians (a type of public benefit authority that oversaw the running of workhouses), or some other public or private organization. The wide scale poverty and death of the Famine lead to a desperate clamor from Irish people to emigrate. Therefore, assisted emigration was utilized on some estates and in some counties. The work of Eilish Ellis, primarily in her publication *Emigrants from Ireland, 1847–1852: State-Aided Emigration Schemes from Crown Estates in Ireland* has brought to light lists of tenants from various Irish landlord-owned estates that had their passage paid to New York. Importantly these lists give the following information for almost every emigrant: name and age, personal details, date of arrival in New York, name of ship, name of the estate from where they came, and the exact location of the estate in Ireland. The estates were Ballykilcline, County Roscommon; Irvilloughter and Boughill, County Galway; Kingwilliamstown, County Cork; Castlemaine, County Kerry; and Kilconcouse, County Offaly. In total, Ellis provides the names of almost 830 emigrants. The list of emigrants from the Castlemaine estate is available on a Rootsweb page, www.rootsweb.ancestry.com/~irlker/castlemigr.html. Some of these names are available in the Ancestry.com database, *Emigrants from Ireland, 1847–1852.*

The previously mentioned Brian Mitchell has a third publication that gives the place of origin for Irish immigrants to New York City; *Irish Passenger Lists, 1847–1871: Lists of Passengers Sailing from Londonderry to America on Ships of the J. & J. Cooke Line and the McCorkell Line.* While most of the passengers were from the northern counties, not all were; many people often travelled great distances from other parts of Ireland to catch the ship to America. Many of the McCorkell boats listed in this publication went to the port of New York.

The 1891 Immigration Act, which was an updated version of the 1882 Immigration Act, mandated that immigrants arriving in the U.S. provide their name, nationality, last residence, and where they were planning to go in the States. The passenger lists were not created upon entry in the United States but before the ship left port in Europe. Since the shipping company was responsible for returning people who could not gain entry into the U.S. and since they would also have to pay a fine, it was in the company's interest to ensure that all passengers were free of disease, not convicted of a felony and not likely to become a public charge (that is, become reliant on public institutions). By 1893 passenger list forms were standardized and included questions about an immigrant's marital status, last place of residence, destination city, and names and addresses of relatives in the U.S.

While you should definitely look at the passenger list for any ancestor who immigrated to the U.S. after the 1891 Act came into being, keep in mind that until the turn of the century some lists still did not provide a place of origin beyond "Ireland." But, the further after 1891 that your ancestor immigrated, the more information you will find.
The 1891 Immigration Act also saw the federal government assume power over immigration from the individual states. As part of this process the government provided the funding to establish the immigration inspection station on Ellis Island, which opened on 1 January 1892. Ellis Island saw countless Irish immigrants come to, and through, New York City before it closed in November 1954. See the chronological bibliography at the end of this chapter for full details about where to access passenger lists.

Unindexed images for a large amount of seemingly random New York City passenger lists from 1820 to 1957 are available for free on Archive.org. Navigation of these records is not easy and their webpage, https://archive.org/details/vesselpassengercrewnewyork, is a good place to start. It is recommend to use the "all items (most recently added first)" link to access a listing of all scanned passenger lists.

Irish Immigrant Girls Organization
The Mission of Our Lady of the Rosary for the Protection of Irish Immigrant Girls was founded to be a first place of refuge for young single women from Ireland who came to New York. It opened its doors in 1883 and closed in 1926. In 2006 four ledgers containing the names of 60,000 of these women were found by Rev. Peter Meehan at the Church of Our Lady of the Rosary, located at 7 State St. in Lower Manhattan. A county of origin is listed in the ledgers for each woman. In 2012 the Irish Mission at

Watson House Project exhibit was opened to showcase the work of the organization, as well as its records. As this book went to press there were plans to digitize the ledgers and to open a family research center at the church. Contact the Church of Our Lady of the Rosary at (212) 269-6865 for more information. See Manhattan no. 54 in Chapter 8 for all contact details.

Naturalization Records

New York City naturalization records dated before 27 September 1906 usually contain only the name and address of the alien and of a character witness. They almost never include the place of origin in Ireland. The 1906 Naturalization Act changed all this. It decreed that standardized forms for the declaration of intention, petition for naturalization, and certificate of naturalization were to be used. The standardized forms now requested plenty of information of genealogical value including the applicant's name, age, personal description, occupation, place and date of birth, present and last foreign addresses, port of embarkation and entry, date of arrival in U.S., and name of vessel on which they arrived. Just like before 27 September 1906, the alien still applied at the court of their choice. After the legislation was enacted, copies of these forms were to be sent to the newly created Immigration and Naturalization Service (INS) in Washington, D.C.

You can apply for a naturalization record dated after 27 September 1906—but no later than fifty years ago—from the United States Citizenship and Immigration Service (USCIS). USCIS replaced the INS after 9/11. It's a two-step process. You do not need to know the court, or even where the application was made. First, you must apply to have an index search carried out for the USCIS file number for your ancestor. Then you must submit a Record Copy Request based on the file number. Of course, if you already have the file number you do not need to do the first step. See the "Institutions" section of Chapter 2 for the website and address of the USCIS.

Records available through the USCIS Genealogy Program include:
- Naturalization Certificate Files (C-files): 27 September 1906 to 1 April 1956
- Alien Registration Forms: 1 August 1940 to 31 March 1944
- Visa files from: 1 July 1924 to 31 March 1944
- Registry Files: 2March 1929 to 31 March 1944
- Alien Files (A-files) numbered below 8 million (A8000000) and documents therein dated prior to 1 May 1951

Alternatively, if you know the court where the application was made, you can get a copy of the original application documents. There are a number of online indexes and digitized record sets that can help with this process.

- Familysearch.org has *New York, Eastern District Naturalization Petitions, 1865–1957*[xv]; *New York, Southern District Index to Petitions for Naturalization, 1824–1941*[xvi]; *New York, Southern District Naturalization Index, 1917–1950*; and *New York, Southern District, U.S District Court Naturalization Records, 1824–1946*.
- Italiangen.org (Italian Genealogical Group) and theggg.org (German Genealogy Group) have the Eastern District Naturalization Index database, 1865–1957; Southern District Naturalization Index database, 1824–1959; Bronx Borough Supreme Court Naturalization Index database, 1914–1952; Queens Borough Supreme Court Naturalization Index database, 1906–1957; and United States Circuit Court for the Southern District of New York Naturalization Index database, 1906–1911

[xv] The Eastern District includes Brooklyn (Kings County), Queens and Staten Island (Richmond County).
[xvi] The Southern District includes Manhattan (New York County) and the Bronx.

- Ancestry.com has *Index to Declaration of Intent for Naturalization: New York County, 1907–1924; New York County Supreme Court Naturalization Petition Index, 1907-24; New York, Index to Petitions for Naturalization filed in New York City, 1792-1989;* and *New York, Naturalization Records, 1882-1944.* Ancestry.com has a number of other naturalization record sets that are not New York City–specific but most likely contain records of naturalization applications that were made in the city.
- Fold3.com has a number of indexes, including: *Naturalization Index: NY Eastern, Oct. 1906–Nov. 1925; Naturalization Index: NY Eastern, Nov. 1925–Dec. 1957; Naturalization Index: NY Southern Intentions, 1917–1950;* and *Naturalization Index: NY Southern Petitions, 1824–1921.* The website also has digitized records, including: *Naturalizations: NY Eastern, 1865–1937* and *Naturalizations: NY Southern, 1897–1944.*

Chronological Bibliography of Sources

1803–1806   Fothergill, Gerald. "Emigrants to America." *New England Historical and Genealogical Register.* Vol. 60. No. 1 (January 1906)–Vol. 66. No. 3 (October 1912). Available online at www.americanancestors.org/databases.

Igp-web.com. General Ireland and Foreign Records–Emigration. *General Ireland Emigration Records, compiled by Mary Heaphy* [database online]. www.igp-web.com/IGPArchives/ire/countrywide/emigration.htm: 2010.

Mitchell, Brian. *Irish Passenger Lists, 1803–1806: Lists of Passengers Sailing from Ireland to America: Extracted from the Hardwicke Papers.* Baltimore, MD: Genealogical Publishing. 1995.

1811–1817   Hackett, Dominick J., and Charles M. Early. *Passenger Lists from Ireland.* Baltimore: Genealogical Publishing. 1973.

Schlegel, Donald M. *Passengers from Ireland: Lists of Passengers Arriving at American Ports between 1811 and 1817.* Baltimore, MD: Genealogical Publishing. 1980.

1825–1844   DeGrazia, Laura Murphy and Haberstroh, Diane Fitzpatrick. *Voices of the Irish Immigrant: Information Wanted Ads in the Truth Teller, New York City, 1825–1844.* New York, NY: New York Genealogical and Biographical Society. 2005.

1831–1921   Americanancestors.org. *Searching for Missing Friends: Irish Immigrant Advertisements* [database online]. Boston, MA: Americanancestors.org. 2010.

Ancestry.com. *Searching for Missing Friends: Irish Immigrant Advertisements Placed in "The Boston Pilot 1831–1920"* [database online]. Provo, UT: Ancestry.com Operations. 2013.

Harris, Ruth-Ann, and Jacobs, Donald M., Eds. *The Search for Missing Friends: Irish Immigrant Advertisements Placed in the Boston Pilot,* Volumes 1–8. Boston: New England Historical Genealogical Society. 1989–1993. This covers the years 1831–1920.

Infowanted.bc.edu. Boston College Information Wanted. *A Database of Advertisements for Irish Immigrants Published in the Boston Pilot* [database online]. Boston, MA: http://infowanted.bc.edu: 2005.

1833–1839	Ancestry.com. *Irish Emigration Lists, 1833–1839* [database online]. Provo, UT: Ancestry.com Operations. 2006.
	Mitchell, Brian. *Irish Emigration Lists, 1833–1839: Lists of Emigrants Extracted from the Ordnance Survey Memoirs for Counties Londonderry and Antrim.* Baltimore, MD: Genealogical Publishing. 1989.
1835–1876	Ancestry.com. *Index to Marriages and Deaths in the New York Herald 1856-1863 Vol. 2* [database online]. Provo, UT: Ancestry.com Operations. 2006.
	Ancestry.com. *Index to Marriages and Deaths in the New York Herald, Vol. I: 1835-1855* [database online]. Provo, UT: Ancestry.com Operations. 2006.
	Maher, James P. *Index to Marriages and Deaths in the New York Herald, Volume IV: 1871–1876.* Baltimore, MD: Genealogical Publishing. 2006.
	Maher, James P. *Index to Marriages and Deaths in the New York Herald, Volume III: 1864–1870.* Baltimore, MD: Genealogical Publishing. 2000. Republished 2006.
	Maher, James P. *Index to Marriages and Deaths in the New York Herald, Volume II: 1856–1863.* Baltimore, MD: Genealogical Publishing. 1991. Republished 2006.
	Maher, James P. *Index to Marriages and Deaths in the New York Herald, Volume I: 1835–1855.* Baltimore, MD: Genealogical Publishing. 1987.
1841–1926	Queens Borough Public Library. *Description of Private and Family Cemeteries in the Borough of Queens.* Supplementary Volume. Queens, NY: Queens Borough Public Library, 1975. This publication contains headstone transcriptions from Cemetery of the Church of Our Lady of Mount Carmel Parish, Astoria, Queens. Some transcriptions are also available at http://www.pefagan.com/gen/astoria/mtcarm/mtcframi.htm. See Chapter 9, Catholic Cemeteries for more information about this cemetery.
1847-1852	Ancestry.com. Emigrants from Ireland, 1847–1852 [database online]. Provo, UT: Ancestry.com Operations. 2007.
	Ellis, Eilish. *Emigrants from Ireland, 1847–1852: State-Aided Emigration Schemes from Crown Estates in Ireland.* Baltimore: Genealogical Publishing. 1977.
	Ellis, Eilish. "Emigrants from Ireland, 1847–1852: State-Aided Emigration Schemes from Crown Estates in Ireland." *Analecta Hibernica.* No. 22. 1960. pp. 328, 331–394. The list of emigrants from one estate in the publication is available at: www.rootsweb.ancestry.com/~irlker/castlemigr.html.
1847–1871	Mitchell, Brian. *Irish Passenger Lists, 1847–1871: Lists of Passengers Sailing from Londonderry to America on Ships of the J. & J. Cooke Line and the McCorkell Line.* Baltimore: Genealogical Publishing. 1988.

1849–1900   Ardolina, Rosemary Muscarella. *Old Calvary Cemetery: New Yorkers Carved in Stone.* Bowie, MD: Heritage Books. 1996.

Ardolina, Rosemary Muscarella. *Second Calvary Cemetery: New Yorkers Carved in Stone.* Floral Park, NY: Delia Publications. 2000.

1849–1992   Silinonte, Joseph M. *Tombstones of the Irish Born: Cemetery of the Holy Cross, Flatbush, Brooklyn.* Concord, Ontario: Becker Associates. 1992.

c.1850-1920 Ancestry.com. *New York, Census of Inmates in Almshouses and Poorhouses, 1830-1920* [database online]. Provo, UT: Ancestry.com Operations. 2011.
The record set begins in 1830 but place of origin information is found beginning about 1850.

1850–1870   Casey, Marion R. *The Irish Middle Class in New York City 1850–1870.* New York: New York University, master's thesis. 1986.

1850–1871   Ancestry.com. *Irish Relatives and Friends* [database online]. Provo, UT: Ancestry.com Operations. 2006.

DeGrazia, Laura Murphy, and Haberstroh, Diane Fitzpatrick. *Irish Relatives and Friends: From Information Wanted Ads in the Irish–American, 1850–1871.* Baltimore, MD: Genealogical Publishing. 2001.

1850–1883   Ancestry.com. *New York Emigrant Savings Bank, 1850–1883* [database on–line]. Provo, UT: Ancestry.com Operations. 2005.

Harvard.edu. *Replication Data for: Emigrant Bank Sample Used for Journal of American History Article, December 2012* [database on–line]. Cambridge, MA: http://dvn.iq.harvard.edu/dvn/dv/anbinder. 2012.

Rick, Kevin J. *Irish Immigrants of the Emigrant Industrial Savings Bank. Volume I, 1850–1853.* New York, NY: Broadway–Manhattan Co. 2001.

Rich, Kevin J. *Irish Immigrants of the Emigrant Industrial Savings Bank : Test Book Number One. Volume II, Accounts 2501–7500.* Massapequa, NY: Kevin J. Rich. 2005.

Rich, Kevin J. *Irish Immigrants of the Emigrant Industrial Savings Bank : Test Book Number One. Volume III, Accounts 7501–12482.* Massapequa, NY: Kevin J. Rich. 2010.

1853–1859   Church of the Transfiguration. *Marriage Register.* 29 Mott St., New York, NY.

1854–1855   Jeremiah O'Donovan. *A Brief Account of the Author's Interview with His Countrymen and of the Parts of the Emerald Isle, Whence They Emigrated : Together With a Direct Reference to Their Present Location in the Land of Their Adoption, During his Travels Through Various States of the Union in 1854 and 1855.* Pittsburgh, PA: Self-published. 1864.
Available online at: http://archive.org/details/abriefaccountau00odogoog

1859–1866   Silinonte, Joseph M. *Bishop Loughlin's Dispensations, Diocese of Brooklyn: Genealogical Information from the Marriage Dispensation Records of the Roman Catholic Diocese of Brooklyn, Kings, Queens and Suffolk Counties, New York*. New York, NY: Self-published. 1996.

1883–1926   Church of Our Lady of the Rosary Parish. *Ledger Books of the Mission of Our Lady of the Rosary for the Protection of Irish Immigrant Girls*. 7 State Street, NY, New York.

1892–1957   Ancestry.com. *New York Passenger Lists, 1820–1957* [database online]. Provo, UT: Ancestry.com Operations. 2010.
              This record set includes the passenger lists from the table of ships that sailed to New York in the 1840s and 1850s and that were discussed in this chapter as having an Irish place of origin.

              Castlegarden.org *America's First Immigration Center, 1820–1913* [database online]. New York, NY: Castlegarden.org. 2009.

              Ellisisland.org. *Ellis Island/Port of New York Records, 1892–1924* [database online] New York, NY: The State of Liberty–Ellis Island Foundation. 2001.

              Familysearch.org. *New York Passenger Arrival Lists (Ellis Island), 1892–1924* [database online]. Provo, UT: Familysearch.org. 2010.

              Familysearch.org. *New York Passenger Arrival Lists (Ellis Island), 1925–1942* [database online]. Provo, UT: Familysearch.org. 2012.

              Familysearch.org. *New York Passenger and Crew Lists, 1825–1996* [database online]. Provo, UT: Familysearch.org. 2013.

1906–1956   United States Citizenship and Immigration Services. *Naturalization Certificate Files (C-files) from 27 September 1906 to 1 April 1956*. 111 Massachusetts Ave., Headquarters Building, Washington, DC.

7 The Roman Catholic Church

Finding Roman Catholic baptismal and marriage records can sometimes be a difficult process. There is no central repository for Catholic sacramental registers in New York City, and instead all registers are kept at the parish level. Currently, there are 396 parishes in New York City, and numerous former parishes no longer exist or have merged.

The Bronx, Manhattan (New York County), and Staten Island (Richmond County) are in the Archdiocese of New York, while Brooklyn (Kings County) and Queens are in the Diocese of Brooklyn. The Diocese of New York was created in 1808 and elevated to the status of an archdiocese in 1850. The Diocese of Brooklyn was created from the Archdiocese of New York in 1853. At the end of 2013, Manhattan had 95 parishes, the Bronx had 67, Staten Island had 35, Brooklyn had 102, and Queens had 96. Just as in the past, it is inevitable that in the future some parishes will close, others will amalgamate, and more will be formed anew due to demographic changes and financial difficulties.

The first Catholic church in New York City, St. Peter's, was founded in 1785 on the corner of Barclay and Church streets in Lower Manhattan.[104] Later, new parishes were created out of existing parishes, and as the population of Catholics grew in different parts of the city. For the movements of Catholics, two examples can be given. The building of the New York and Harlem Railroad began in the 1830s. This was built from downtown, up the East Side to Yorkville, and then on to Harlem, and saw Catholics who had worked on the railway move to upper Manhattan. Another was due to the social mobility achieved in the closing decades of the 20th century. Again this saw many Irish Catholics move further uptown from the old Fourth, Fifth, and Sixth wards they had dominated in the years after the Famine.

With the founding and amalgamation of so many parishes over the centuries, it is sometimes difficult for researchers to know which parish to contact for sacramental records. For example, a newly married couple might show up living on Dikemann St. in the Red Hook section of Brooklyn in the 1850 federal census, one of the many areas where the post-Famine Irish settled in. Today this street is located in the Visitation of the Blessed Virgin Mary parish. But should you contact this church for the marriage record you would find that no marriages were performed there in years before 1850. Why not? Well, the parish was only founded in 1854. Instead the nearest church at that time was St. Paul's and the couple may have married there. That parish was founded in 1838 and located on the corner of Court and Congress streets.

Traditionally, most Catholic Irish marriages were held in the bride's church. Therefore if you find the groom's family living in the parish where the wedding took place, this is a strong indication that the bride's family lived in the same parish.[105]
Some of the earlier 19th century Catholic churches were German-speaking and some of the later 19th century Churches were Italian-speaking. Therefore, if one of these was the nearest church for an Irish family, they would more than likely have gone to another church that was English speaking. However, these non-English language parishes should not be discounted, because some Irish immigrants married immigrants from other countries and so there are Irish names in the registers of traditionally German, Italian, and Polish parishes.

Despite the importance of the Catholic Church in the lives of Irish immigrants, there are a number of reasons why their baptisms, marriages, and deaths may not appear in registers for the parishes that existed, especially in the first half of the 19th century. First, Catholic emancipation had only been achieved in Ireland with the Roman Catholic Relief Act of 1829. Before this, the Catholic Church in Ireland was a shell of its mid-20th century hegemony. Thus, the majority of Irish people had no interaction with a formal, widely established institutional church, and they brought this lack of religious experience with them to New York City. This also contributed to their lack of understanding of basic Catholic teaching, with a New York City priest commenting that "half of our Irish population here is Catholic merely because Catholicity was the religion of the land of their birth."[106]

Second, there were not a lot of Catholic parishes and clergy in the city. Up to 1840 there were only eight Catholic churches in Manhattan even though the Catholic population was estimated to be eighty to ninety thousand.[107] Third, at those Catholic churches that did exist, the custom of pew renting excluded many Irish immigrants from attending services. According to this custom, adopted from the Episcopal Church, the pews of the Church were rented to parishioners for a fee for a term of up to one year. As a result, many Catholic Irish immigrants "lived on the fringe of parish life,"[108] and so there is very little evidence of them in parish registers. Fourth, unlike baptism and marriage, the death of a Catholic is not considered one of the seven sacraments. There was no obligation to record deaths in a parish register in the same way that baptism and marriages were recorded.

It is important to have an address for your ancestor in order to locate the relevant parish—and hopefully the baptismal and marriage information. Addresses can be found in city directories, in all U.S. federal censuses from 1870 onward, and on documents such as petitions for naturalization. The search for employment led many Irish immigrants and their families to move frequently, so you must try and establish an address as close as possible to the year of the event you wish to obtain information for.

Provide as much detail as possible when calling or writing to a particular parish for a record. Limit the parameters of your search request. For instance, it is not a good idea to request all Murphy baptisms in a thirty-year period. When writing to a parish, make sure to include a donation of, say, $15 to $20, and a stamped, self-addressed envelope. Some parishes have suggested or mandatory charges for searches. Don't be afraid to negotiate on the price, especially if you are requesting multiple register records.

Reaction to your request and response times will vary from positive and quick to negative and slow. While the previous ten years you have spent researching your Irish ancestors is important to you, be prepared to hear a minority of parish secretaries say, "we don't like those kinds of requests." Nevertheless, you will get some sort of a response. Some parishes are excellent, have computerized records and will respond to your query within days. Other parishes are understaffed and get many requests, so you will be waiting months. In this case, a polite follow up phone call might be helpful.

Over the last thirty years many parishes will have celebrated the 100th or even 150th anniversary since their founding. As part of this celebration a booklet is often produced that includes a history of the parish, the names of priests who served there, stories about the parishioners, events of the parish, and so on. These booklets can provide further clues to assist you with your genealogical research, as well as details of the social history of your ancestors.

Many parishes now have websites, which range from basic to in-depth. Some websites give detailed information on the history of the parish, while others don't even mention when the parish was founded.

While the vast majority of Irish immigrants who came from the southern twenty-six counties of Ireland were Catholic, don't discount the possibility of them not being Catholic at all, converting to a different religion, marrying someone of a different faith, or being buried in a non-Catholic graveyard. These factors should be considered especially for ancestors who arrived in the late 18th century and first decades of the 19th. As mentioned, the Catholic Church was not at its institutional and ideological strong point until the latter half of the 19th century. Therefore, before this time, Irish immigrants might have had no real interaction with the New York City Catholic Church, especially if they lived a distance from one of the few early Catholic churches. Episcopal, Dutch Reformed, and other denominations were much more established in the city in this period. It is therefore possible that those who immigrated by themselves, worked with, or interacted with non-Catholics, married a non-Catholic, or needed an emergency saying of the last rites might be found in the Church registers of another religious denomination.

Parish Registers: Microfilm, Print, and Online
The registers of some parishes have been microfilmed and transcribed by organizations such as the LDS church and are available via microfilm, online transcriptions and/or in print. However, the vast majority of parish registers in New York City are not available to view at LDS Family History Centers. In 2008 the Vatican ordered all Catholic dioceses not to give their sacramental registers to the Mormon Church for scanning or microfilming.

Manhattan
Church of St. Clare
Family History Library film 1289417: Baptisms, 1903–1914
FHL film 1289418: Baptisms, 1914–1923
FHL film 1289419: Baptisms, 1923–1940 / Marriages, 1904–1915
FHL film 1289420: Marriages, 1915–1940 / Confirmations, 1905–1939

Church of Sts. Cyril and Methodius
FHL film 1289296: Financial and status reports, 1914–1968 / Baptisms, 1910–1966
FHL film 1289297: Baptisms, 1966–1980 / First communions, 1923–1942, 1951–1980 / Confirmations, 1923–1942, 1952–1954, 1968–1979 / Marriages, 1913–1980 / Death reports, 1910, 1971–1975
FHL film 1289414: Deaths, 1942–1980

Church of St. Peter
Sherman, Constance Denise. "Baptismal records of St. Peter's Church, New York City, 1787–1800." *National Genealogical Society Quarterly*, Vol. 68. No. 1. March 1980. p. 21–30; Vol. 68. No. 2. June 1980. p. 129–136; Vol. 68. No. 3. September 1980. p. 203–212.
This is also available at the LDS Family History Library: Book 973 B2ng v. 68 (1980).

Church of St. Raphael
FHL film 1289414: Baptisms, 1886–1916
FHL film 1289415: Baptisms, 1916–1975 / Marriages, 1886–1890
FHL film 1289416: Marriages, 1890–1974

Brooklyn
Our Lady of Sorrows Parish
Baptisms, 1890–1942 / Marriages, 1890–1942
Available at http://theggg.org/churchdb.stm
Mostly parishioners of German ethnicity, but Irish names are found in the entries.

St. Leonard of Port Maurice Parish
Baptisms, 1872–1978 / Conformations, 1872–1978 / Marriages, 1872–1978
Available at http://theggg.org/churchdb.stm
Mostly parishioners of German ethnicity, but Irish names are found in the entries.

St Paul Parish
Baptisms, 1839–1857 / Marriages, 1839–1857
Reilly, James. *St. Paul's Roman Catholic Church, Court Street, Brooklyn, New York. Baptism Register July 22, 1839–July 12, 1857; Marriage Register August 7, 1839–August 18, 1857.* Salt Lake City, UT: Redmond. 1996.

Baptisms, 1857–1900 / Marriages, 1857–1900
Reilly, James. *St. Paul's Roman Catholic Church, Brooklyn, New York: Baptism and Marriage Registers, 1857–1900.* Salt Lake City, UT: Redmond Press. 1996.

Raghallaigh, Eibhilín. *St. Paul's Roman Catholic Church, Brooklyn, New York: The Irish Parish. Baptism and Marriage Registers, 6 September 1857–30 December 1900*. Floral Park, NY: Delia Publications. 2001.

Ancestry.com. *Brooklyn, New York Catholic Church Baptism Records, 1837–1900* [database online]. Provo, UT: Ancestry.com Operations. 2008.

Parish Publications

All churches listed are in Manhattan unless otherwise stated. All of these publications are available at the New York Public Library Milstein Genealogy Room. Consult www.worldcat.org to find the nearest library that has a copy of a publication you are interested in. Failing that, you might have to contact the relevant parish to find information about where the publication is available. All contact details for each parish can be found in Chapter 8.

All Saints	All Saints Parish. *All Saints Parish—100th Anniversary*. New York: parish publication. 1981.
Immaculate Conception (Staten Island)	Immaculate Conception Parish. *History of the Parish of Immaculate Conception on the occasion of the 75th anniversary, 1887–1962*. New York: parish publication. 1962.
Mary Help of Christians	Honig, Deborah. "The Church of Mary, Help of Christians, New York City: The National Parish as a Solution to the Italian Problem." New York, NY: Columbia University, master's thesis. 1966.
Our Lady of Mercy (Bronx)	Schuyler, Joseph B. *Northern Parish: A Sociological and Pastoral study*. Chicago: Loyola University Press. 1960.
Sacred Heart	Brown, Henry J. *One Step Above Hell's Kitchen: Sacred Heart Parish in Clinton*. New York, NY: Sacred Heart Church. 1977. The full name of this parish is Sacred Heart of Jesus.
St. Agnes	St. Agnes Parish. *The Golden Jubilee of St. Agnes Parish, New York City, 1873–1923*. New York, NY: parish publication. 1923.
St. Alphonsus	Murphy, Francis X. *The Centennial History of Saint Alphonsus Parish*. New York, NY: parish publication. 1947.
St. Ann	Brown, Henry J. *St. Ann's on East Twelfth Street, New York City 1852–1952*. New York, NY: Roman Catholic Church of St. Ann. 1952.
St. Brigid	O'Flaherty, Patrick. "The History of St. Brigid's Parish in the City of New York Under the Administration of Patrick F. McSweeney." New York, NY: Fordham University, master's thesis. 1952.
	Author unknown. *Souvenir of the Consecration Year of St. Brigid Church, 1849–1889*. New York, NY: publisher unknown. 1889.
St. Fidelis (Queens)	Hass, James E. *St. Fidelis Parish in College Point, New York. The First 75 Years, 1856–1931: A History*. Baltimore, MD: Gateway Press. 2006.

St. James	St. James Church. *Centennial Anniversary, Church of St. James, 1827–1927*. New York, NY: publisher unknown. 1927.
St. Joseph	Shelley, Thomas J. *Greenwich Village Catholics: St. Joseph's Church and the Evolution of an Urban Faith Community, 1829-2002*. Washington, D.C: Catholic University of America Press. 2003.
St. Ignatius (Brooklyn)	Trabold, Robert. "Building an Immigrant Community: St. Ignatius Parish, 1971–1981." Suffolk, NY: Long Island University, master's thesis. 1982.
St. Ignatius Loyola	Dooley, Patrick J. *Fifty Years in Yorkville, or Annals of the Parish of St. Ignatius Loyola and St. Lawrence O'Toole*. New York, NY: Parish House. 1917.
St. Michael	Brown, Henry J. *The Parish of St. Michael, 1857–1957: A Century of Grace on the West Side*. New York, NY: Church of St. Michael. 1957.
St. Monica	Kelly, George A. *The Story of St. Monica's Parish, New York City, 1879–1954*. New York, NY: Monica Press. 1954.
St. Patrick (Old)	Carthy, Mary Peter. *Old St Patrick's, New York's First Cathedral*. New York, NY: U.S. Catholic Historical Society. 1947.
St. Paul (Brooklyn)	Noll, Evelyn F. "The History of St. Paul's Church in Brooklyn." St. John's, Canada: St. John's University, master's thesis. 1944.
St. Peter	Hartfield, Anne. "Profile of a Pluralistic Parish: St. Peter's Roman Catholic Church, 1785-1815." *Journal of American Ethnic History*. Vol. 12. No. 3. 1993. pp. 30–59.
	Ryan, Leo R. *Old St Peter's: The Mother Church of Catholic New York (1785–1985)*. New York: U. S. Catholic Historical Society. 1935.
St. Peter Claver (Brooklyn)	Davis, Victoria M. "St. Peter Claver Parish, Brooklyn: African American Mission, Way-Station or Home?" Burnaby, Canada: Simon Frasier University, master's thesis. 1994.
St. Philip Neri (Bronx)	St. Philip Neri Parish. *Golden Jubilee of St. Philip Neri Parish, Sunday, October 3 1948*. Bronx, NY: parish publication. 1948.
St. Teresa of Avila (Brooklyn)	Cass, John. *The History of St. Theresa's Parish, 1874–1924*. Brooklyn, NY: privately published. 1924. The name of the parish today has a different spelling than in the title of this publication.
St. Thomas Aquinas (Brooklyn)	St. Thomas Aquinas Parish. *100th Anniversary, St. Thomas Aquinas Parish, Flatlands, Brooklyn, 1885–1985*. New York, NY: parish publication. 1985.

Parish Fairs

In the second half of the 19th century, Catholic immigrants from Ireland and beyond were coming to New York City in huge numbers and the Church was struggling to keep up with the need for infrastructure. As a result, the Church was constantly collecting money for the building of the next parish church, school, or institution. Along with parish collections and donations, parish fairs were very successful at raising funds. They were yearly events where a large range of goods and services were on sale, competitions were held, and prizes given for various activities. The largest fairs took place in the 1870s and 1880s, culminating in the St. Patrick's Cathedral fair, where many parishes were represented.[109]

For the genealogist, an interesting aspect of the parish fairs was that they were organized and run by women. For the year 1878 an extensive list, *Journal of the Fair for the New St. Patrick's Cathedral, has* survived. It contains the names of male and female prize winners and of the women who organized the fair at St. Patrick's Cathedral.[110] Many prizes were given out for each parish, and the name and address of each winner (both male and female) is listed. Along with this are the names of the organizers and from which parish they were from. Various formats for women's names are used, such as Miss A. Kelly, Mrs. James O'Rourke, Mrs. B O'Rourke, and Catherine Dunne, etc. The fact that all the names are divided by parish helps to distinguish between the more common names. This interesting publication can be found at the New York Public Library Milstein Genealogy Room.

8 Roman Catholic Parishes of New York City

In this chapter you will find a list, arranged by borough, of every Roman Catholic parish that has existed in New York City since the founding of the first parish, St. Peter's, in 1785. The official name of the parish was obtained from the websites of the Archdiocese of New York (www.archny.org) and the Diocese of Brooklyn (http://dioceseofbrooklyn.org). All parish names are also arranged alphabetically in the index at the end of the book.

For each parish, the list provides the year of foundation and notes about initial formation, boundary, and ethnicity, where available. This information came from *The Catholic Church in the United States of America* (hereafter Catholic Church)[111], *New York City Inventory of the Church Archives—Roman Catholic Church* (hereafter WPA) [112], *Chronological List of Brooklyn Parishes, 1822-2008* (hereafter CL Brooklyn)[113] and *Chronological List of Queens Parishes 1843-2009* (hereafter CL Queens)[114]. If the ethnicity of 19th and early 20th century parishes is not stated, it can be assumed to be English-speaking and was more than likely founded for a predominantly Irish congregation.

For some parishes there are conflicting dates of establishment in the sources. In canonical terms a parish was regarded as founded when the first permanent resident priest was appointed.[115] However, masses, baptisms, and marriages regularly occurred before this date. Some parish websites give the date the church building was built as the date of the founding of the parish. But in many cases, the parish was created before that date, with masses said at another location, such as the house of a Catholic. When the parish began to operate (you will sometimes see this noted as "erected") is used as the date of foundation so as to avoid confusion, where possible, and to best serve the interests of genealogists. This was often before a resident priest was appointed or permanent church was built.

The start date of baptismal and marriage registers for all parishes is included in this list. Death register information, which is only available for some parishes, is also given. This information came from WPA, CL Brooklyn, and CL Queens. It is recommended you take the start dates of the parish registers as an accurate but not infallible guide, particularly for those that do not correspond with the starting date of the parish. Do not discount a parish of potential interest due to the date of the registers beginning two or three years after the parish was founded. It is still advisable to contact that parish, if just to eliminate it from your research inquiries.
In some cases, parish registers will predate the foundation year of the parish. This is due to the congregations hearing mass and receiving sacraments in private dwellings, halls, and other churches. It can also be due to the parish starting out as a mission of another parish before it officially began to operate as a separate parish.

Church location, contact details, and website information, where available, have been provided for all current parishes. Some Catholic churches in New York City have changed address since their foundation due to population shifts, congregation sizes outgrowing the church building capacity, fires, and the purchasing of new lots to build larger churches and adjoining schools. Keep this in mind when using an ancestor's address to ascertain a possible parish. However, in only a small number of cases did a church move a substantial distance from its original location. Usually, the address only changed by a few blocks, at most.

Some of the parishes that previously existed are now closed. In the lists, closed parishes are marked with a single asterisk (*) before their name. Since the beginning of the 20th century, many city parishes have merged with neighboring parishes. They are indicated by a double asterisk (**). To obtain records for these parishes you will have to write to the relevant diocesan authorities or other parishes, if indicated.

Both the Archdiocese of New York and Diocese of Brooklyn have offices to which you can write to for information about their parishes, including the location of registers from closed parishes. For the Archdiocese of New York (Manhattan, Bronx and Staten Island) send a self-addressed stamped envelope to:

Vicar General's Office
1011 First Avenue
New York, NY 10022

For the Diocese of Brooklyn (Brooklyn and Queens) send a self-addressed stamped envelope to one of the following:

Chancery Office
Roman Catholic Diocese of Brooklyn
75 Greene Ave.—PO Box C
Brooklyn, NY 11202
(718) 399-5900

Office of Diocesan Archives
310 Prospect Park West
Brooklyn, NY 11215
(718) 965-7300

Useful Resources
Culkin, Harry M. *Parochial Boundary Map of Roman Catholic Diocese of Brooklyn*. New York: Self-published. 1983.
This publication shows the boundaries of every parish in Brooklyn as it looked in the early 1980s. It is available at the Map Division (room 117), New York Public Library Main Branch, 5th Avenue at 42nd Street. However, it is stored at an offsite facility so you will not be able to request and view it on the same day.

Manhattan
Archdiocese of New York: 94 active parishes

1. Church of St. Peter, 1795   Baptisms, 1787 / Marriages, 1802
16 Barclay St., New York, NY 10007   (212) 233-8355 m097@archny.org
www.stpetersrcnyc.org
St. Peter's was the only Catholic Church serving New York City, Brooklyn and northern New Jersey for
many years. It was estimated that there were only about four hundred Catholics in the city when the
parish was formed. See Chapter 7, Parish Publications for more information. St. Peter's also has a
mission chapel:

> St. Joseph's Chapel
> 385 South End Ave., New York, NY 10280   (212) 466-0131 m084@archny.org
> http://www.sjchapel.org

2. Church of St. Patrick, 1809   Baptisms and Marriages, 1820
263 Mulberry St., New York, NY 10012   (212) 226-8075 m094@archny.org
www.oldsaintpatricks.com
This is known as the "Old Cathedral." The church did not open until 1815. See Chapter 7, Parish
Publications for more information.

3. Church of St. Mary, 1826   Baptisms and Marriages, 1848
28 Attorney St., New York, NY 10002   (212) 674-3266 m089@archny.org
The first church was at Sherriff St. but was destroyed in a fire in 1831. The second church was on Grand
St., with the third church opening in 1833. From 1833 to 1835 German Catholics used the basement to
worship between the building of the first and second church at St. Nicholas parish (no. 6). St. Mary's
present church was built in 1871.

4. Church of the Transfiguration, 1827   Baptisms and Marriages, 1825
29 Mott St., New York, NY 10013   (212) 962-5157 m110@archny.org
www.transfigurationnyc.org
The parish was known as Christ Church from 1827 to 1837. The first church was on Ann St., then
Chambers St., with the present church purchased in 1853. See Chapter 6 for more information about
Church of the Transfiguration parish registers.

5. Church of St. Joseph, 1829   Baptisms and Marriages, 1833
371 Sixth Ave., New York, NY 10014   (212) 741-1274/7 m081@archny.org
The original chapel was on Grove St. until the present church opened in 1883. The original parish
boundaries were from Canal St. to 20th St. See Chapter 7, Parish Publications for more information.

*6. Church of St. Nicholas, 1833 German   Baptisms and Marriages, 1833
This church is closed and was demolished in 1960. The original Church was at Delancey and Pitt streets
before a new church was built on East 2nd St. In between, the parishioners worshipped in the basement
of St. Mary's church (no. 3) for a short while.

7. Church of St. Paul, 1834   Baptisms, 1834 / Marriages, 1835
113 East 117th St., New York, NY 10035   (212) 534-4422 m095@archny.org
www.stpaulchurchive.org

8. Church of St. James, 1834
23 Oliver St., New York, NY 10038
www.stjamesandstjoseph.org

Baptisms and Marriages, 1836
(212) 233-0161 m075@archny.org

The first church was on James St. See Chapter 7, Parish Publications for more information.

9. Church of St. John the Baptist, 1840 German
210 West 31st St., New York, NY 10001

Baptisms, Marriages, and Deaths 1840
(212) 564-9070 m077@archny.org

The original church was on West 30th St. near 7th Ave.

10. Church of St. John the Evangelist, 1840
348 East 55th St., New York, NY 10022

Baptisms and Marriages, 1840
(212) 753-8418 m078@archny.org

The original church was on East 50th St.

11. Church of St. Vincent de Paul, 1841 French
116 West 24th St., New York, NY 10011

Baptisms, 1840 / Marriages, 1840 / Deaths, 1904
(212) 243-4727 m109@archny.org

The original church was on West 23rd St.

12. Church of the Nativity, 1842
44 2nd Ave., New York, NY 10003

Baptisms and Marriages, 1842 / Deaths, 1918
(212) 674-8590 m022@archny.org

13. Church of St. Andrew, 1842
20 Cardinal Hayes Place, New York, NY 10007

Baptisms and Marriages, 1842
(212) 962-3972 m049@archny.org

The parish also has marriage and death registers for the "City Prison Chapel", beginning 1908 and 1911, respectively

14. Church of the Most Holy Redeemer, 1844 German
173 East 3rd St., New York, NY 10009

Baptisms, Marriages, and Deaths, 1877
(212) 673-4224 m020@archny.org

15. Church of St. Francis of Assisi, 1844 German
135 West 31st St., New York, NY 10001

Baptisms and Marriages, 1844
(212) 736-8500 m068@archny.org

16. Church of St. Columba, 1845
343 West 25th St., New York, NY 10001

Baptisms and Marriages, 1845 / Deaths, 1928
(212) 807-8876 m061@archny.org

Parishioners previously went to St. Joseph's (no. 5) on West Washington Place. The parish originally covered the areas between the East and North (Hudson) rivers and 14th and 42nd streets.

*17. Church of St. Alphonsus, 1847 German   Baptisms, 1847 / Marriages, 1848 / Deaths, 1847
This parish closed in 1980, with records transferred to St. Anthony of Padua parish (no. 31). The original church was on Thompson St., then the parish moved to West Broadway in 1870. Founded from St. Joseph's parish (no. 5). See Chapter 7, Parish Publications for more information.

18. Church of St. Francis Xavier, 1847
55 West 15th St., New York, NY 10011
www.sfxavier.org

Baptisms and Marriages, 1851
(212) 627-2100 m070@archny.org

Also known as Church of the Holy Name of Jesus. The parish has its origins in a church dedicated to the Holy Name of Jesus that burned down on 28 January 1848 on Elizabeth St., near Walker St. Founded out of St. Joseph's parish (no. 5).

**19. Church of St. Stephen 1848 (now called Church of Our Lady of the Scapular and St. Stephen, see no. 130)

Baptisms, 1849 / Marriages, 1850 / St. Stephen Bellevue Hospital Emergency Baptisms, 1850–1908

The original Church of St. Stephen was on East 28th St. and Madison Ave. St. Stephen's parish was created from St. John the Evangelist parish (no. 10). St. Stephen's parish merged with Our Lady of the Scapular (no. 68) in 1989. This new parish then merged with Church of Sacred Hearts of Jesus and Mary (no. 106) in 2008.

*20. Church of St. Brigid, 1848   Baptisms and Marriages, 1849 / Deaths, 1848

http://saintbrigidsaintemeric.org

This parish closed in 2004 and all records are at the Church of St. Emeric (no. 132). The archdiocese received a substantial donation in 2008 to repair and reopen the church building. The church was rededicated in January 2013 and is still at Ave. B and 8th St. On the parish website its name is Church of St. Brigid–St. Emeric, but the website of the archdiocese does not have a listing for St. Brigid, only for the Church of St. Emeric. Therefore, this is not considered a merged parish. See Chapter 7, Parish Publications for more information.

21. Church of St. Ignatius Loyola, 1851   Baptisms, Marriages, and Deaths, 1851
980 Park Ave., New York, NY 10028   (212) 288-3588 m074@archny.org
www.saintignatiusloyola.org

The original church was on 4th Ave. and 84th St. See Chapter 7, Parish Publications for more information.

22. Church of the Holy Cross, 1852   Baptisms and Marriages, 1852 / Deaths, 1932
329 West 42nd St., New York, NY 10036   (212) 246-4732 m009@archny.org
http://holycrossnyc.com

Original parish territory was from the west side of 5th Ave. to the Hudson River and from the north side of 31st St. to Yonkers.

*23. Church of St. Ann, 1852   Baptisms and Marriages, 1852

The original church was at East 8th St. and then moved to 110 East 12th St. The year it closed is unknown. See Chapter 7, Parish Publications for more information.

24. Church of the Annunciation, 1853   Baptisms, Marriages, and Deaths, 1853
88 Convent Ave., New York, NY 10027   (212) 234-1919 m002@archny.org

The parish originally covered the area north of 100th St. and west of 8th Ave.

25. Church of the Immaculate Conception, 1855   Baptisms and Marriages, 1855
414 East 14th St., New York, NY 10009   (212) 254-0200 m016@archny.org

See Chapter 7, Parish Publications for more information.

26. Church of St. Michael, 1857   Baptisms, Marriages, and Deaths, 1857
424 West 34th St., New York, NY 10001   (212) 563-2575 m091@archny.org
www.stmichaelnyc.com

The parish originally covered the area from 28th to 38th streets and from 6th Ave. to the Hudson River. Original church was on West 31st St. and 9th Ave. The current church opened in 1907. See Chapter 7, Parish Publications for more information.

*27. Church of the Assumption, 1858 German   Baptisms and Marriages, 1858
Closed in an unknown year but was open in the early 1940s. The church was at 427 West 40th St.

*28. Church of St. Boniface, 1858 German   Baptisms, 1858 / Marriages, 1859 / Deaths, 1921
The parish closed in 1950 and the records are now housed at the Church of the Holy Family (no. 114).
The original Church was on 2nd Ave. and 47th St. The boundary was the southeast corner of 3rd Ave.
and 49th St. to the East river; the East River, from the south side of 49th St to the south side of 45th St;
the south side of 45th St. on the East River to the northwest corner of 2nd Ave. and 45th St.; then north
on 2nd Ave to the south side of 47th St.; then west on 47th St to 3rd Ave.; and north on the east side of
3rd Ave. to the south east corner of 49th St.

29. Church of St. Paul the Apostle, 1858   Baptisms, 1858 / Marriages, 1860
415 West 59th St., New York, NY 10019   (212) 265-3209 m096@archny.org
www.stpaultheapostle.org
The original church was on West 60th St.

*30. Church of St. Gabriel, 1858   Baptisms and Marriages, 1859 / Deaths, 1859
The parish closed in 1938. The original church was on East 37th St. Before the parish was founded, most
parishioners attended St. John the Evangelist (no. 10).

31. Church of St. Anthony of Padua, 1859   Baptisms, 1859 / Marriages, 1866 / Deaths, 1925
154 Sullivan St., New York, NY 10012   (212) 777-2755 m052@archny.org
The church closed in 1860 but reopened in 1865. The original church was on Canal St. It was founded
from St. Joseph's parish (no. 5).

32. Church of St. Joseph of the Holy Family, 1859   Baptisms and Marriages, 1859 / Deaths, 1923
405 West 125th St., New York, NY 10027   (212) 662-9125 m083@archny.org
Services were held at Sacred Heart Convent (this is now Manhattanville College), Manhattanville until
the church was built in 1860. Manhattanville is now a part of west Harlem.

33. Church of St. Teresa, 1863   Baptisms and Marriages, 1863 / Deaths, 1914
141 Henry St., New York, NY 10002   (212) 233-0233 m104@archny.org
The parish was formed from St. Mary's parish (no. 3).

34. Church of the Holy Innocents, 1866   Baptisms and Marriages, 1866
128 West 37th St., New York, NY 10018   (212) 279-5861 m012@archny.org
www.innocents.com
The parish was formed from parts of St. Stephen's (no. 19), Holy Cross (no. 22), St. Columba (no. 16), St.
Michael's (no. 26) and St. Patrick's Old Cathedral (no. 2) parishes.

35. Church of the Holy Name of Jesus, 1867   Baptisms and Marriages, 1867
207 West 96th St., New York, NY 10025   (212) 749-0276 m013@archny.org
When Holy Name of Jesus parish was founded the area was known as Bloomingdale and was comprised
of cottages and shanties. The parish was formed from St. Paul the Apostle parish (no. 29). The original
church was on the north side of 97th St between Amsterdam Ave. and Broadway.

36. Church of Our Lady of Sorrows, 1867 German   Baptisms, Marriages, and Deaths, 1867
213 Stanton St., New York, NY 10002   (212) 673-0900/01 m038@archny.org
The ethnicity of this parish had changed to Italian by the early 20th Century. It was formed out of St.
Mary's parish (no. 3).

37. Church of St. Vincent Ferrer, 1867   Baptisms and Marriages, 1867 / Deaths, 1924
869 Lexington Ave., New York, NY 10065   (212) 744-2080 m108@archny.org
www.csvf.org

*38. Church of St. Rose, 1868   Baptisms, 1868-1935 / Marriages, 1868-1935
The church was located at 42 Cannon St. and the parish closed in the 1960s. It was formed out of St. Mary's parish (no. 3). When the church was built, it was known as St. Rose of Lima but later became St. Rose when the St. Rose of Lima parish (no. 85) was founded in 1901. Baptism and marriage records for after 1935 are located at St. Mary's church (no. 3).

**39. Church of St. Bernard, 1868 (now called Church of Our Lady of Guadalupe at St. Bernard, see no. 131)
Baptisms, 1868 / Marriages, 1868
St. Bernard's was created out of St. Joseph (no. 5) and St. Columba (no. 16) parishes and its original place of worship was on 13th St. between 9th and 10th avenues. It merged with Our Lady of Guadalupe in 2003 (no. 86).

40. Church of the Epiphany, 1868   Baptisms and Marriages, 1868
239 East 21st St., New York, NY 10010   (212) 475-1966 m005@archny.org
www.theepiphanychurch.org
The parish was formed due to the overcrowding in St. Ann (no. 23), St. Stephen (no. 19) and St. Francis Xavier (no. 18). The original boundary was from 18th to 24th streets and from the east side of Broadway to the East River. An Italian congregation was formed in the parish in 1901.

41. Church of St. Elizabeth, 1869   Baptisms and Marriages, 1869
268 Wadsworth Ave., New York, NY 10033   (212) 568-8803 m064@archny.org
The parish was originally formed for the Catholics in the neighborhood of Fort Washington (Manhattan) and Spuyten Duyvil (Bronx). Their first formal church was at St. John's (Bronx no. 10) in Knightsbridge, where they worshipped until the church in St. Elizabeth's parish was opened about 1871.

*42. Church of Our Lady of Perpetual Help, 1871 Bohemian (German)   Baptisms and Marriages, 1874
This parish closed in 1998. The first congregation formed in the basement of St. Nicholas's (no. 6). The first church was built on East 4th St. and was dedicated to St. Cyril and Methodius in 1875. The parish moved uptown as Bohemian immigrants were doing so and their Church opened in 1887. It was located at 321 East 61st St.

43. Church of St. Agnes, 1873   Baptisms and Marriages, 1873
141 East 43rd St., New York, NY 10017   (212) 682-5722 m045@archny.org
The original parish territory was between Madison and Third avenues, 34th and 42nd streets, with a strip extending to the East River between 42nd and 47th streets. The Church of St. Agnes was formed from the parishes of St. Stephen (no. 19), St. Gabriel (no. 30) and St. Patrick's Old Cathedral (no. 2). See Chapter 7, Parish Publications for more information.

44. Church of St. Cecilia, 1873   Baptisms and Marriages, 1873
125 East 105th St., New York, NY 10029   (212) 534-1350 m058@archny.org
This parish was created out of the southern portion of St. Paul's parish (no. 7).

45. Church of St. Joseph, 1873 German   Baptisms and Marriages, 1859 / Deaths, 1916
404 East 87th St., New York, NY 10128   (212) 289-6030 m082@archny.org
http://stjosephsyorkville.org
The first services were held at the Asylum Chapel of the Redemptorist Fathers on 3rd Ave. until the
current church was built in 1874. Baptisms before 1873 come from the Church of St. Joseph orphan
asylum, which was located at East 89th St. and Ave. A.

46. Church of St. Stanislaus, 1873 Polish   Baptisms, 1887 / Marriages, 1881 / Deaths, 1887
101 East 7th St., New York, NY 10009   (212) 475-4576 m101@archny.org
www.stanislauschurch.com
This parish was formed out of St. Mary's (no. 3). The first church was in Henry St., the second on the
corner of Stanton and Forsyth streets. The current church building opened in 1901.

*47. Church of St. Mary Magdalene, 1873 German   Baptisms and Marriages, 1873
The parish closed in 1945. It was originally located at 529 East 17th and then on Ave. D, between 12th
and 13th streets.

48. Church of the Sacred Heart of Jesus, 1876   Baptisms and Marriages, 1876
457 West 51st St., New York, NY 10019   (212) 265-5020 m043@archny.org
www.shjnyc.com
Sacred Heart parish of Jesus was formed out of St. Paul the Apostle (no. 29) and Holy Cross (no. 22)
parishes. The originally boundary was 54th St. to 4th St. and from 7th Ave. to the Hudson River. See
Chapter 7, Parish Publications for more information.

49. Church of All Saints, 1879   Baptisms, 1880 / Marriages, 1880 / Deaths, 1919
47 East 129th St., New York, NY 10035   (212) 534-3535 m093@archny.org
The congregation originally worshiped at Harlem Hall at 3rd Ave. and 130th St., then Lincoln Hall at 4th
Ave. and 129th St., then back to Harlem Hall. The present church was built in 1893. See Chapter 7, Parish
Publications for more information.

50. St. Patrick's Cathedral, 1879   Baptisms and Marriages, 1879
460 Madison Ave. (at 51st St.), New York, NY 10022   (212) 753-2261 m001@archny.org
www.saintpatrickscathedral.org

51. Church of St. Monica, 1879   Baptisms and Marriages, 1880
413 East 79th St., New York, NY 10021   (212) 288-6250/1 info@churchofstmonica.org
www.churchofstmonica.org
See Chapter 7, Parish Publications for more information.

*52. Church of St. Leo, 1880   Baptisms, Marriages, and Deaths, 1880–1908
St. Leo's, which closed as a parish church in 1908, was located at East 28th St. between Madison and 5th
avenues. It was founded within the boundaries of St. Stephen's parish (no. 19). St. Leo's had a mortuary
chapel at 9 East 28th St., which provided spiritual care, regardless of faith, for those who died in hotels
etc., or were from outside of the city. Since 1909 the parish has been a part of to St. Stephen's (no. 19).
The Sisters of Marie Reparatrice were given this Church in 1910 when they were exiled from France, and
the rectory was turned into a convent. The Church building was demolished in the 1980s.

53. Church of St. Jean Baptiste, 1882 French   Baptisms, Marriages, and Deaths, 1882
184 East 76th St., New York, NY 10021   (212) 288-5082 m076@archny.org
www.stjeanbaptisteny.org
The congregation first worshiped at an older church on East 77th St. until the present church opened in 1884.

54. Church of Our Lady of the Rosary, 1883   Baptisms and Marriages, 1883
7-8 State St., New York, NY 10004   (212) 269-6865 m036@archny.org
www.setonshrine.com
This parish is associated with the Mission for the Protection of Immigrants Girls. See the "Irish Immigrant Girls Organization" section in Chapter 6 for more information.

55. Church of St. Benedict the Moor, 1883 African American   Baptisms and Marriages, 1883
c/o Sacred Heart of Jesus, 457 West 51st St., New York, NY 10019   (212) 265-5020 m053@archny.org
The parish was originally located at 210 Bleeker St., then moved to 320 West 83rd St. It now has mission status.

56. Church of the Holy Rosary, 1884   Baptisms, 1884–1925 / Marriages, 1884–1924
444 East 119th St., New York, NY 10035   (212) 534-0740 glciii@aol.com
www.nyholyrosary.org
Mass was said at the old Church of St. Cecilia (no. 44) before the present church was built toward the end of 1884. Baptismal and marriage registers from 1914 to at least 1942 are in Italian. Registers from 1884 to 1924/5 are in English.

57. Church of Our Lady of Mount Carmel, 1884   Baptisms, 1884 / Marriages, 1883
448 East 116th St., New York, NY 10029   (212) 534-0681 m031@archny.org
The congregation originally worshiped at a temporary chapel on East 111th St.

58. Church of Our Lady of Vilnius, 1885 Lithuanian   Baptisms, 1906 / Marriages, 1906 / Deaths, 1909
32 Dominick St., New York, NY 10013   (212) 255-2648 m040@archny.org
The original congregation met in the basement of Our Lady of Sorrows parish (no. 36). The first priest left in 1886, and parishioners attended other parishes until a Lithuanian priest came to the city in 1905. The congregation began meeting again in the basement of St. Teresa's (no. 33) church. Their first parish church was erected at 568 Broome St. in 1911.

*59. Church of Our Lady (Queen) of Angels, 1886 German   Baptisms and Marriages, 1886
This parish closed in 2007. It was originally located on 199th St. and 2nd Ave., and later on East 112th St.

60. Church of Our Lady of Good Counsel, 1886   Baptisms and Marriages, 1886
230 East 90th St., New York, NY 10028   (212) 289-1742 m026@archny.org
www.olgcny.com

**61. Church of St. Raphael, 1886 (now called Church of Sts. Cyril and Methodius and St. Raphael, see no. 129)
Baptisms and Marriages, 1886
Merged with Sts. Cyril and Methodius (no. 105) in 1974. St. Raphael's first used an old Church at 553 West 50th St., which has also been used by St. Clemens parish (no. 99).

62. Church of St. Catherine of Genoa, 1887   Baptisms, Marriages, and Deaths, 1887
506 West 153rd St., New York, NY 10031   (212) 862-6130 m056@archny.org
The original parish boundary was 145th to 161st streets and from St. Nicholas Place to the Hudson River.

63. Church of the Blessed Sacrament, 1887
152 West 71st St., New York, NY 10023
www.blessedsacramentnyc.com

Baptisms and Marriages, 1887
(212) 877-3111 m010@archny.org

64. Church of St. Veronica, 1887
149 Christopher St., New York, NY 10014

Baptisms and Marriages, 1887 / Deaths, 1888
(212) 924-5628 m107@archny.org

Founded out of St. Joseph's parish (no. 5). First services were held on Washington St. before the current church was built in 1891.

65. Church of St. Charles Borromeo, 1887
211 West 141st St., New York, NY 10030
www.churchofstcharlesborromeoharlem.com

Baptisms and Marriages, 1887 / Deaths, 1933
(212) 281-2100 m059@archny.org

The original place of worship was on 8th Ave. near 141st St; later the church was on 7th Ave. and 141st St.

*66. Church of St. Joachim, 1888 Italian

Baptisms, 1888 / Marriages, 1890 / Deaths, 1888

This parish closed in 1967 and was subsumed into St. Joseph's parish (no. 5). It opened a mission church in 1908 at 18 Catherine Slip.

67. Church of the Guardian Angel, 1888
193 Tenth Ave., New York, NY 10011
www.guardianangelchurch-nyc.org

Baptisms, Marriages, and Deaths, 1888
(212) 929-5966 m007@archny.org

**68. Church of Our Lady of the Scapular, 1889 (now called Church of Our Lady of the Scapular and St. Stephen, see no. 130)
Baptisms, Marriages, and Deaths, 1889
This church was located at 338 East 28th St. St. Stephen's parish (no. 19) merged with Our Lady of the Scapular in 1989. This new parish was merged with Church of Sacred Hearts of Jesus and Mary (no. 106) in 2008.

*69. Church of St. Thomas Apostle, 1889

Baptisms and Marriages, 1889

This parish closed in 2003. The church, built in 1904, was at 260 West 118th St. Before that, an earlier church was at a different location.

*70. Church of St. Joseph, 1890 Maronite (Syrian)

Baptisms and Marriages, 1890

This parish closed in an unknown year. The church was in existence in 1942 at 57 Washington St. but was probably demolished for the Brooklyn Battery Tunnel, which opened in 1950. Parishioners first worshipped at a house at 127 Washington St., which later converted to a chapel and then moved to 81 Washington St. This closed in 1906 and the congregation took refuge in St. Peter's (no. 1), leaving Maronite Catholics with no ethnic based parish. A church was erected in Brooklyn in 1906 (Our Lady of Lebanon Cathedral parish–Brooklyn, no. 99) and this briefly served as the only Maronite parish in New York City. The church at 46 Washington St. was quickly re-established in the same year to serve Manhattan Maronites and it then moved to 57 Washington St.

71. Church of St. Elizabeth of Hungary, 1891 Hungarian/Slovak
211 East 83rd St., New York, NY 10028
www.stelizabethofhungarynyc.org

Baptisms and Marriages, 1891
(212) 734-5747 m065@archny.org

This church traditionally served the Hungarian/Slovak population of New York and Brooklyn.

72. Church of the Most Precious Blood, 1891 Italian   Baptisms and Marriages, 1891 / Deaths, 1932
109 Mulberry St., New York, NY 10013   (212) 226-6427 m021@archny.org

73. Church of Our Lady of Loreto, 1891 Italian   Baptisms and Marriages, 1891 / Deaths, 1920
309 Elizabeth St., New York, NY 10012   (212) 431-9840 m028@archny.org
The original territory was east and west of the Bowery and north of Broome St. This parish was created out of Old St. Patrick Cathedral parish (no. 2).

74. Church of Our Lady of Pompeii, 1892 Italian   Baptisms, Marriages, Deaths, 1892
25 Carmine St., New York, NY 10014   (212) 989-6805 m034@archny.org

75. Church of the Ascension, 1895 German   Baptisms and Marriages, 1895
221 West 107th St., New York, NY 10025   (212) 222-0666 m003@archny.org
www.nyc-ascensionchurch.org
This parish was created from a section of Holy Name of Jesus parish (no. 35) that was north of 101st St.

76. Church of St. John Nepomucene, 1895 Slovak   Baptisms and Marriages, 1895 / Deaths, 1905
411 East 66th St., New York, NY 10021   (212) 734-4613 m079@archny.org
www.stjohnnepomucene.org
The parish was founded out of St. Elizabeth parish (no. 41). The original church was at East 4th St. but was abandoned when a church was built on East 57th St. in 1911.

77. Church of St. Catherine of Siena, 1896   Baptisms and Marriages, 1896
411 East 68th St., New York, NY 10021   (212) 988-8300 m057@archny.org
http://stcatherinenyc.org
The original boundary of the parish was 2nd Ave. to the East River and from 60th St. to the south side of 72nd St. The parish was created out of St. Vincent Ferrer parish (no. 37).

78. Church of St. Francis de Sales, 1896   Baptisms and Marriages, 1896
135 East 96th St., New York, NY 10128   (212) 289-0425 sfds.church@yahoo.com
www.sfdsnyc.org
The original place of worship was on 100th St. on the East Side of Manhattan.

*79. Church of St. Ambrose, 1897   Baptisms, 1898 / Marriages, 1898
This parish closed in 1938. The Church was located at 339 West 54th St. The parish limits were from the west side of 10th Ave. to the North (Hudson) River, from the north side of West 53rd St. to the south side of West 57th St.; and from the west side of 11th Ave. to the North (Hudson) River, from the north side of West 46th St. to West 53rd St.

80. Church of the Holy Trinity, 1898   Baptisms, 1899 / Marriages, 1899 / Deaths, 1934
213 West 82nd St., New York, NY 10024   (212) 787-0634 m015@archny.org
www.htcny.org
The original boundary was from West 79th to 86th streets and from Central Park West to the Hudson River.

81. Church of Mary Help of Christians, 1898 Italian   Baptisms, 1899 / Marriages, 1899 / Deaths, 1935
440 East 12th St., New York, NY 10009   (212) 254-0058 m018@archny.org
The congregation first worshiped in the basement of St. Brigid's Church (no. 20). The original boundary was the East River, East 8th St., East 14th St., and the Bowery. The parish opened their own church in 1908 and the records from 1899 to 1908 are for when the Salesian Missionary Fathers served Italian immigrants in St. Brigid's parish. See Chapter 7, Parish Publications for more information.

82. Church of St. Lucy, 1899 Italian and non-Italian   Baptisms and Marriages, 1899 / Deaths, 1934
344 East 104th St., New York, NY 10029   (212) 534-1470 info@saintlucychurch.com
http://saintlucychurch.com
The original boundaries were from 97th St. to 110th St. and from 2nd Ave. to the East River.

83. Church of St. Aloysius, 1899   Baptisms and Marriages, 1899
219 West 132nd St., New York, NY 10027   (212) 234-2848 m047@archny.org
www.staloysiusharlem.com

84. Church of Our Lady of Lourdes, 1901   Baptisms, Marriages, and Deaths, 1901
472 West 142nd St., New York, NY 10031   (212) 862-4380 m029@archny.org

85. Church of St. Rose of Lima, 1901   Baptisms and Marriages, 1901
510 West 165th St., New York, NY 10032   (212) 568-0091 m099@archny.org

**86. Church of Our Lady of Guadalupe, 1902 (now called Church of Our Lady of Guadalupe at St. Bernard, see no. 131)
Baptisms, 1902 / Marriages, 1902
This church was originally at 229 East 14th St. St. Bernard's parish (no. 39) merged with Our Lady of Guadalupe in 2003.

87. Church of St. Malachy, 1902   Baptisms and Marriages, 1901
239 West 49th St., New York, NY 10019   (212) 489-1340 m087@archny.org
http://actorschapel.org
This parish was founded out of Sacred Heart of Jesus parish (no. 48).

*88. Church of St. Matthew, 1902   Baptisms and Marriages, 1902
Half of the early worshippers in this parish were Italian. This parish closed in 1959. The congregation originally worshiped at 166 West 65th St. The first mass was said in 1903 at the new church on West 67th St. between Amsterdam and West End avenues. The original boundary of the parish was from the north side of 63rd St. to the south side of 69th St. and from Amsterdam Ave. to the Hudson River.

89. Church of St. Stephen of Hungary, 1902 Hungarian   Baptisms and Marriages, 1902 / Deaths, 1907
414 East 82nd St., New York, NY 10028   (212) 861-8500 m103@archny.org
www.saintstephenofhungary.org

90. Church of St. John the Martyr, 1903   Baptisms, 1902 / Marriages, 1903
259 East 71st St., New York, NY 10021   (212) 744-4880 m080@archny.org

*91. Church of St. Clare, 1903 Italian   Baptisms, 1903 / Marriages, 1904 / Deaths, 1903
This parish closed in the 1930s after being demolished for the Lincoln Tunnel which opened in 1937. It was located at 436 West 36th St.

*92. Church of St. George, 1905 Ruthenian Greek   Baptisms, Marriages, and Deaths, 1905
24 East 7th St.
This parish closed in 1977. The original place of worship was a church on East 20th St.; later the church was at 24 East 7th St. In later years many Ukrainians worshipped here.

93. Church of St. Gregory the Great, 1906
144 West 90th St., New York, NY 10024
Baptisms, Marriages, and Deaths, 1908
(212) 724-9766 m073@archny.org
The original territory was from 82nd St. to 96th St. and from Central Park West to the Hudson River. Services were held in a church on West 89th St. until it was destroyed by fire on 22 May 1913. The current building was erected in October 1913.

94. Church of St. Mark the Evangelist, 1906
65 West 138th St., New York, NY 10037
Baptisms and Marriages, 1908
(212) 281-4931 m088@archny.org
The original boundaries were from 134th St. west to 7th Ave. and northeast to the Harlem River.

95. Church of Corpus Christi, 1906
529 West 121st St., New York, NY 10027
www.corpus-christi-nyc.org
Baptisms and Marriages, 1906
(212) 666-9350 m004@archny.org
The parish was formed as an outgrowth of the Newman Club at Columbia University, as well as other Catholic clubs at Barnard and Teachers colleges. The original boundaries were 114th St. to Manhattan Ave. and from Morning and Amsterdam avenues to the Hudson River.

*96. Church of Our Lady of Grace, 1907 Italo-Greek Albanese
Baptisms and Marriages, 1907
This parish closed in 1946. The first church was at 14 Stanton St. A later church was at 18 Stanton St.

97. Church of the Resurrection, 1907
276 West 151st St., New York, NY 10039
Baptisms and Marriages, 1907
(212) 690-7555 m042@archny.org

98. Church of the Incarnation, 1908
1290 St. Nicholas Ave., New York, NY 10033
Baptisms and Marriages, 1908
(212) 927-7474 m017@archny.org

*99. Church of St. Clemens, 1909 Polish
Baptisms and Marriages, 1909 / Deaths, 1921
This parish closed in the 1960s. The church was at 408 West 40th St. Services were first held on 10th Ave. near West 51st St., then on West 50th St. near 11th Ave. before the church on West 40th St. was bought.

100. Church of Notre Dame, 1910
405 West 114th St., New York, NY 10025
www.ndparish.org
Baptisms, Marriages, and Deaths, 1914
(212) 866-1500 m023@archny.org

101. Church of Our Lady of Esperanza, 1910 Hispanic
624 West 156th St., New York, NY 10032
Baptisms and Marriages, 1910
(212) 283-4340 m025@archny.org

102. Church of the Good Shepherd, 1911
608 Isham St., New York, NY 10034
www.goodshepherdnyc.org
Baptisms, Marriages, and Deaths, 1913
(212) 567-1300 m006@archny.org
This parish was formed from St. Elizabeth (no. 41) and St. John (Bronx no. 10).

103. Church of St. Ann, Italian 1911
312 East 110th St., New York, NY 10029
Baptisms, 1904 / Marriages, 1905 / Deaths, 1934
(212) 722-1295 extension 2 m051@archny.org
The parish was formed out of Our Lady of Mount Carmel parish (no. 57). The original church was on East 112th St. Records before 1911 are from when the church was a mission from the parish of Our Lady of Mount Carmel.

*104. Church of St. Mary, 1912 Byzantine-Ruthenian   Baptisms and Marriages, 1912
The date when this parish closed in unknown. It was formed from St. George parish (no. 92) and was located at 246 East 15th St. and then at 227 East 13th St.

**105. Church of Sts. Cyril and Methodius, 1913 Croatian (now called Church of Sts. Cyril and Methodius and St. Raphael, see no. 129)
Baptisms, Marriages, and Deaths, 1913
The parish merged with the Church of St. Raphael (no. 61) in 1974. The original church stood at 552 West 50th St.

106. Church of Sacred Hearts of Jesus and Mary, 1914 Italian   Baptisms and Marriages, 1916
325 East 33rd St., New York, NY 10016   212-213-6027 m044@archny.org
www.churchofststephen.com

*107. Church of St. Sebastian, 1915   Baptisms and Marriages, 1915 / Deaths, 1923
This parish closed in 1971. The church was located on East 26th St.

108. Church of St. Cyril, 1916   Baptisms, Marriages, and Deaths, 1916
62 St. Mark's Place, New York, NY 10003   (212) 674-3442 m063@archny.org

*109. Church of St. Albert, 1917 Belgian   Baptisms and Marriages, 1917
The parish closed in an unknown year. The church was located at 427 West 47th St.

110. Church of Our Lady of Peace, 1918   Baptisms and Marriages, 1918
237 East 62nd St., New York, NY 10021   (212) 838-3189 m033@archny.org
www.ourladyofpeacenyc.org

*111. Church of St. George, 1920   Baptisms, 1890 / Marriages, 1890 / Deaths, 1899
This parish, which closed in 1982, was located at 103 Washington St. Records prior to 1920 are those of services of Catholics of the Melchite rite who attended the Church of St. Peter (no. 1) before the founding of their own parish.

112. Church of St. Joseph, 1924   Baptisms, 1907 / Marriages, 1925 / Deaths, 1925
Five Monroe St., New York, NY 10002   (212) 267-8376 m072@archny.org
www.stjamesandstjoseph.org
This parish was formed out of St. Joachim's parish (no. 66). It is also known as San Giuseppe.

*113. Church of Most Holy Crucifix, 1925   Baptisms and Marriages, 1925
The parish closed in 2005. The church was located at 378 Broome St.

114. Church of the Holy Family, 1927   Baptisms and Marriages, 1927 / Deaths, 1937
315 East 47th St., New York, NY 10017   (212) 753-3401 m011@archny.org

*115. Church of Our Lady of the Miraculous Medal, 1926 Hispanic
Baptisms, 1926 / Marriages, 1927 / Deaths, 1926
This parish closed in the 1980s. The church was located at 114th St. and 7th Ave.

116. Church of Our Lady Queen of Martyrs, 1927   Baptisms, Marriages, and Deaths, 1927
91 Arden St., New York, NY 10040   (212) 567-2637 m035@archny.org

117. Church of the Holy Agony, 1930
1834 Third Ave., New York, NY 10029

Baptisms and Marriages, 1930
(212) 289-5589 m008@archny.org

*118. Church of St. Theresa of Avilla, 1932
This parish closed in 1935. The church was located at 4381 Broadway.

Baptisms, 1932-1935 / Marriages, 1932-1935

*119. Church of St. Hedwig, 1934
Closed in an unknown year, it was located at 62 East 106th St.

Baptisms and Marriages, 1934

120. Church of St. Michael's Chapel, 1936 Russian
266 Mulberry St., New York, NY 10012
http://stmichaelruscath.org/

Baptisms and Marriages, 1936
(212) 226-2644 m112@archny.org

*121. Church of Exaltation of Holy Cross, 1938 Hungarian
Closed in an unknown year, it was located at 323 East 82nd St.

Birth, Marriages, Deaths, 1938

*122. Church of Our Lady Star of the Sea, 1942
This church was used by Catholics at the army base on Governors Island. It was open in the late 1960s
but closed in an unknown year.

Baptisms and Marriages, 1942

123. Church of Our Lady of Victory, 1944
60 William St., New York, NY 10005
http://ourladyofvictorychurch.org
The original church was at 23 William St. The present Church was built in 1947.

Baptisms and Marriages, 1944 / Deaths, unknown
(212) 422-5535 m039@archny.org

124. Church of St. Jude, 1949
431 West 204th St., New York, NY 10034

Baptisms and Marriages, 1949 / Deaths, unknown
(212) 569-3000 m085@archny.org

125. Church of St. Thomas More, 1950
65 East 89th St. (East of Madison Ave.), New York, NY 10128
http://thomasmorechurch.org

Baptisms and Marriages, 1950 / Deaths, unknown
(212) 876-7718 m106@archny.org

126. Church of Our Saviour, 1955
59 Park Ave., New York, NY 10016
www.oursaviournyc.org

Baptisms and Marriages, 1955 / Deaths, unknown
(212) 679-8166 m041@archny.org

*127. Church of Faith, Hope and Charity, 1958   Baptisms and Marriages, 1958-1986 / Deaths, Unknown
This parish closed in 1986. The church was located at Park Ave. and 59th St. from 1958 to 1978 and then
at Park Ave. and 58th St.

128. Church of St. Frances Xavier Cabrini, 1973
564 Main St., Roosevelt Island, NY 10044

Baptisms and Marriages, 1973 / Deaths, Unknown
(212) 832-6778 m115@archny.org

129. Church of Sts. Cyril and Methodius and St. Raphael, 1974
502 West 41st St., New York, NY 10036
St. Raphael's (no. 61) parish merged with Sts. Cyril and Methodius (no. 105) in 1974.

(212) 563-3395 crkva.nyc@verizon.net

130. Church of Our Lady of the Scapular and St. Stephen, 1989/2008
142 East 29th St., New York, NY 10016   (212) 683-1675 m102@archny.org
www.churchofststephen.com
St. Stephen's (no. 19) parish merged with Our Lady of the Scapular (no. 68) in 1989. This new parish merged with Church of Sacred Hearts of Jesus and Mary (no. 106) in 2008.

131. Church of Our Lady of Guadalupe at St. Bernard, 2003
328 West 14th St., New York, NY 10014   (212) 243-0265 m054@archny.org
St. Bernard's (no. 39) parish merged with Our Lady of Guadalupe (no. 86) in 2003.

132. Church of St. Emeric, 2006   Baptisms and Marriages, 2006 / Deaths, Unknown
185 Ave. D, New York, NY 10009   (212) 228-4494 m066@archny.org
http://saintbrigidsaintemeric.org
When St. Brigid's (no. 20) parish closed in 2004 this parish was founded. In January 2013 the old church building from St Brigid's parish was rededicated. On the parish website its name is Church of St. Brigid–St. Emeric, but the website of the archdiocese does not have a listing for St. Brigid, only for the Church of St. Emeric.

Brooklyn
Diocese of Brooklyn: 105 active parishes

1. St. James Cathedral Basilica, 1822   Baptisms and Marriages, 1829
250 Cathedral Pl., Brooklyn, NY 11201   (718) 852-4002
https://sites.google.com/a/brooklyncathedral.net/the-cathedral-basilica-of-st-james

**2. St. Paul Parish, 1838 (now called St. Paul and St. Agnes Parish; see no. 156)
St. Paul Baptisms and Marriages, 1837
St. Paul's parish merged with St. Peter–Our Lady of Pilar (no. 19 and no. 117) parish in 1975. St. Paul–St. Peter–Our Lady of Pilar parish merged with St. Agnes parish (no. 49) in 2007. See Chapter 7, Parish Publications for more information.

3. Ss. Peter and Paul Parish, 1840   Baptisms, Marriages, and Deaths, 1840
71 South 3rd St., Brooklyn, NY 11211   (718) 388-9576
The parish was called St. Mary's from 1840 to 1848. Its first boundaries were Hallett's Cove, Myrtle Ave., the East River and Middle Village. The church was first at North 8th and 1st streets and then at Wythe Ave. and 2nd St. When Epiphany parish (no. 94) was closed in 2007 it merged with Ss. Peter and Paul.

**4. Most Holy Trinity Parish, 1841 German (now called Most Holy Trinity–St. Mary Parish, see no. 155)
Baptisms and Marriages, 1841
Located in Williamsburg, Most Holy Trinity parish merged with Immaculate Conception of the Blessed Virgin Mary parish (no. 15) in 2007.

5. Assumption of the Blessed Virgin Mary Parish, 1842   Baptisms and Marriages, 1842
64 Middagh St., Brooklyn, NY 11201   (718) 625-1161
www.assumptionparishbrooklyn.org
The original church was on the corner of York and Jay streets.

6. Holy Cross Parish, 1843   Baptisms and Marriages, 1852
2530 Church Ave., Brooklyn, NY 11226   (718) 469-5900
This parish was a mission from St. Paul parish (no. 2) from 1843 to 1848 and from St. James parish (no. 1) from 1848 to 1852. The original church was located on Erasmus St. near Prospect St.

**7. St. Patrick Parish, 1843 (now called St. Lucy–St. Patrick Parish; see no. 150)
St. Patrick Baptisms and Marriages, 1845
St. Patrick parish merged with St. Lucy parish (no. 92) in 1974. The church was at Kent and Willoughby avenues in Fort Greene. Parish was known as St. Mary's from 1843-1856.

8. St. Patrick Parish, 1848   Baptisms and Marriages, 1854
9511 Fourth Ave., Brooklyn, NY 11209   (718) 238-2600

9. St. Charles Borromeo Parish, 1849   Baptisms and Marriage 1851
21 Sidney Pl., Brooklyn, NY 11201   (718) 625-1177
www.stcharlesbklyn.org

10. St. John the Evangelist Parish, 1849   Baptisms and Marriages, 1850
250 21st St., Brooklyn, NY 11215   (718) 768-3751

11. St. Joseph Parish, 1849   Baptisms and Marriages, 1853
856 Pacific St., Brooklyn, NY 11238   (718) 638-1071
www.stjosephbrooklyn.org

*12. St. Benedict Parish, 1852 German   Baptisms and Marriages, 1853
This parish closed in 1873. Before this parish was founded, local Catholics used to worship at Most Holy
Trinity parish (no. 4), in Williamsburg. Sacramental records prior to 1910 are at the Diocesan Archives,
and records after 1910 are at the Chancery Office. The church was at Fulton St. near Ralph Ave.

13. St. Boniface Parish, 1853 German   Baptisms and Marriages, 1853
109 Willoughby St., Brooklyn, NY 11201   (718) 875-2096

**14. St. Malachy Parish, 1853 (now called St. Michael–St. Malachy Parish; see no. 157)
Baptisms and Marriages, 1862
St. Malachy parish merged with St. Michael parish (no. 21) in 2007. Catholics had to go to mass in
Flatbush before St. Malachy's was founded. The original church was located on the east side of Van
Sicklen Ave., near the north side of Atlantic Ave.

**15. Immaculate Conception of the Blessed Virgin Mary Parish, 1853 (now called Most Holy Trinity–St.
Mary Parish; see no. 155)
Baptisms and Marriages, 1853
The parish was in Williamsburg and merged with Most Holy Trinity parish (no. 4) in 2007. The original
church was on the corner of Leonard and Maujer streets.

16. Visitation of the Blessed Virgin Mary Parish, 1854   Baptisms and Marriages, 1854
98 Richards St., Brooklyn, NY 11231   (718) 624-1572

17. St. Mary Star of the Sea Parish, 1855   Baptisms and Marriages, 1855
467 Court St., Brooklyn, NY 11231   (718) 625-2270

**18. St. Anthony Parish, 1858 (now called St. Anthony–St. Alphonsus Parish; see no. 151)
Baptisms and Marriages, 1858
St. Anthony parish merged with St. Alphonsus parish (no. 42) in 1975. The original church was on India
St. in Greenpoint. Later the church was on the corner of Manhattan Ave. opposite Milton St. The parish
was first called St. Anthony of Padua.

*&**19. St. Peter Parish, 1859 (now called St. Paul and St. Agnes Parish; see no. 156)
Baptisms and Marriages, 1859 / Deaths, 1935
St. Peter parish merged with Our Lady of Pilar (no. 117) parish in 1935. St. Peter–Our Lady of Pilar parish
merged with St. Paul parish (no. 2) in 1975. St. Paul–St. Peter–Our Lady of Pilar parish merged with St.
Agnes parish (no. 49) in 2007.

*20. St. Vincent de Paul Parish, 1860   Baptisms and Marriages, 1860
This parish closed in 2004. The church was on North 6th St. between Bedford and Driggs avenues in
Williamsburg.

**21. St. Michael Parish, 1860 German (now called St. Michael–St. Malachy Parish; see no. 157)
Baptisms and Marriages, 1860 / Deaths, 1897
St. Michael parish merged with St. Malachy parish (no. 14) in 2007. It was originally known as St. Michael
and Monastery parish. The church was on Jerome St. near Atlantic Ave.

*&**22. St. Ann Parish, 1860   St. Ann Baptisms and Marriages, 1861
St. Ann parish merged with St. George parish (no. 108) in 1986, and St. Ann–St. George parish closed in 2003. The original church was at the corner of Front and Gold streets, Fort Greene.

23. St. Mark Parish, 1861   Baptisms and Marriages, 1887
2609 East 19th St., Brooklyn, NY 11235   (718) 891-3100
www.stmarkparish.org
The parish was a mission from Holy Cross parish (no. 6) from 1861 to 1874, from St. Rose of Lima parish (no. 34) from 1875 to 1877, and from Guardian Angel parish (no. 54) from 1888 to 1889.

24. Annunciation of the Blessed Virgin Mary Parish, 1863 German   Baptisms and Marriages, 1863
275 North 8th St., Brooklyn, NY 11211   (718) 384-0223
In 1914 this became a Lithuanian parish.

25. St. Nicholas Parish, 1865 German   Baptisms, Marriages, and Deaths, 1866
26 Olive St., Brooklyn, NY 11211   (718) 388-1420

**26. St. Stephen Parish, 1866 (now called Sacred Hearts of Jesus and Mary–St. Stephen Parish; see no. 140)
Baptisms and Marriages, 1866
St. Stephen parish and Sacred Hearts of Jesus and Mary parish (no. 58) merged in 1941. The original church was on Smith and Hicks streets.

*27. St. Francis in the Fields Parish, 1866 German   Baptisms and Marriages, 1866
The parish closed in 1888. The originally church was located at Bedford Ave. near Madison St. and Putnam Ave. in Bedford–Stuyvesant. The parish records are held at the Chancery Office.

**28. All Saints Parish, 1867 German   Baptisms and Marriages, 1868
115 Throop St., Brooklyn, NY 11216   (718) 388-1951
The parish, still called All Saints, merged with St. Ambrose (no. 57) and Our Lady of Montserrate (no. 146) parishes in 2007. The original church was on Throop Ave. and Thornton St.

**29. St. John the Baptist Parish, 1868   Baptisms and Marriages, 1868
75 Lewis Ave., Brooklyn, NY 11206   (718) 455-6864
www.stjohnthebaptistrcc.org
St. John the Baptist parish merged with Our Lady of Good Counsel parish (no. 62) in 2007. The parish is still called St. John the Baptist.

*&**30. Our Lady of Victory Parish, 1868 (now called St. Martin de Porres Parish; see no. 160)
Baptisms and Marriages, 1868
St. Peter Claver parish (no. 122) merged with Nativity of the Blessed Lord parish (no. 36) in 1973. These parishes then merged with Our Lady of Victory parish and Holy Rosary parish (no. 68) in 2007 to form St. Martin de Porres parish (no. 160). The original church was located in Bedford–Stuyvesant on the corner of McDonagh St. and Throop Ave. and was predominantly African American since the 1930s.

*31. Our Lady of Mercy Parish, 1868   Baptisms and Marriages, 1868
The parish closed in 1930. The church was originally at DeKalb and Debevoise avenues. In 1908 a new church opened at Schemerhorn St. near Bond St. Sacramental records prior to 1910 are held at the Diocesan Archives and records after 1910 are at the Chancery Office.

*32. St. Louis Parish, 1869 French (now called St. Lucy-St. Patrick Parish; see no. 150)
Baptisms and Marriages, 1869
The parish closed in 1946. The original church was on Siegel St. near Ewan St. A church was then built on Ellery St. near Nostrand Ave. Many of the original French parishioners had connections with the Alsace-Lorraine area, but their numbers were greatly decreased by 1920. The former area of this parish is now covered by St. Lucy–St. Patrick parish.

33. St. Augustine Parish, 1870   Baptisms and Marriages, 1870
116 Sixth Ave., Brooklyn, NY 11217   (718) 783-3132
The original church was located near 5th Ave. and Bergen St.

34. St. Rose of Lima Parish, 1870   Baptisms and Marriages, 1874
269 Parkville Ave., Brooklyn, NY 11230   (718) 434-8040

35. St. Cecilia Parish, 1870   Baptisms and Marriages, 1874
84 Herbert St., Brooklyn, NY 11222   (718) 389-0010
Also known as the "gravedigger's chapel." It was a mission from Immaculate Conception of the Blessed Virgin Mary parish (no. 15) from 1871 to 1874.

*&**36. Nativity of the Blessed Lord Parish, 1871 (now called St. Martin De Porres Parish, see no. 160)
Baptisms and Marriages, 1871
Nativity of the Blessed Lord parish merged with St. Peter Claver parish (no. 122) in 1973. The parish was called Nativity–St. Peter Claver from 1973 to 1979 before reverting back to St. Peter Claver parish from 1979 onward. St. Peter Claver parish then merged with Our Lady of Victory parish (no. 30) and Holy Rosary parish (no. 68) in 2007 to form St. Martin de Porres parish (no. 160). Parishioners used to worship at St. Joseph (no. 29) or St. Patrick (no. 7) before Nativity of the Blessed Lord parish was founded. The parish was located in Bedford–Stuyvesant on Classon Ave. and Madison St. and was predominantly African American from the 1930s.

*37. St. Leonard of Port Maurice Parish, 1871 German (now called St. Joseph Patron of the Universal Church Parish; see no. 124)
Baptisms and Marriages, 1872
This parish closed in 1978 and was located in Bushwick. The Church was on Wilson Ave. and Jefferson St.

*38. St. Bernard Parish, 1871 German   Baptisms and Marriages, 1871
The parish closed in 1941. Originally the church was located at Hicks and Rapelyea streets in Carroll Gardens. Parishioners used to attend at St. Boniface parish (no. 13) before St. Bernard parish was created.

*&**39. Sacred Heart Parish, 1871 (now called Mary of Nazareth Parish; see no. 161)
Baptisms and Marriages, 1871
St. Edward parish merged with St. Michael the Archangel (no. 53) in 1942 to form St. Michael–St. Edward parish. St. Michael–St. Edward parish merged with Sacred Heart parish in 2008 to form Mary of Nazareth parish (no. 161). Sacred Heart parish was in Fort Greene on Park Ave. near Clermont Ave.

40. St. Frances de Chantal Parish, 1872   Baptisms and Marriages, 1892
1273 58th St., Brooklyn, NY 11219   (718) 436-6407
www.francesdechantal.org

*&**41. Our Lady of Lourdes Parish, 1872 (now called St. Martin of Tours parish; see no. 101)
Baptisms and Marriages, 1872
Fourteen Holy Martyrs parish (no. 63) merged with St. Martin of Tours parish (no. 101) in 1976. These parishes merged with Our Lady of Lourdes parish in 2007 to form St. Martin of Tours parish (no. 101). The original name of the parish was St. Francis de Sales until 1897. The church was located at Central Ave. and Covert St.

**42. St. Alphonsus Parish, 1873 German (now called St. Anthony–St. Alphonsus Parish; see no. 151)
Baptisms and Marriages, 1873
St. Alphonsus parish merged with St. Anthony parish (no. 18) in 1975. The original church was at Kent and Manhattan avenues.

43. Transfiguration Parish, 1874　　　　　　　　　Baptisms and Marriages, 1874
263 Marcy Ave., Brooklyn, NY 11211　　　　　　　　　(718) 388-8773

44. St. Teresa of Avila Parish, 1874　　　　　　　　Baptisms and Marriages, 1874
563 Sterling Pl., Brooklyn, NY 11238　　　　　　　　(718) 622-6500
The church name was changed to Holy Spirit parish in 1973 and then back to the original name in 1986. See Chapter 7, Parish Publications for more information.

45. St. Michael Parish, 1874　　　　　　　　　　　　Baptisms and Marriages, 1874
352 42nd St., Brooklyn, NY 11232　　　　　　　　　(718) 768-6065
Parishioners used to worship at the parishes of St. John the Evangelist (no. 10) and St. Patrick (no. 7) before St. Michael parish was founded.

**46. St. Casimir Parish, 1875 Polish (now called Our Lady of Czestochowa–St. Casimir Parish; see no. 153)
Baptisms and Marriages, 1875
St. Casimir parish and Our Lady of Czestochowa parish (no. 82) merged in 1980. The church was at Tillary and Laurence streets in the 1880s and later at Greene Ave. near Adelphi St.

47. Holy Name Parish, 1878　　　　　　　　　　　　Baptisms and Marriages, 1880
245 Prospect Park West, Brooklyn, NY 11215　　　　(718) 768-3071

*48. St. John's Chapel Parish, 1878　　　　　　　　Baptisms and Marriages, 1878
The parish closed in 1913. It was in Fort Greene with the church on the block formed by Green, Vanderbilt, Clermont, and Lafayette avenues.

**49. St. Agnes Parish, 1878 (now called St. Paul and St. Agnes Parish; see no. 156)
Baptisms and Marriages, 1878
The parish merged with St. Paul–St. Peter–Our Lady of Pilar parish in 2007. Previous to this, Our Lady of Pilar parish (no. 117) merged with St. Peter parish (no. 19) in 1935. St. Paul parish (no. 2) then merged with St. Peter–Our Lady of Pilar parish in 1975. The first masses were said in a building on Hoyt St. and the first church was built in 1881. The church was on Hoyt and Sackett streets.

50. Queen of All Saints Parish, 1879　　　　　　　　Baptisms and Marriages, 1879
300 Vanderbilt Ave., Brooklyn, NY 11205　　　　　　(718) 638-7625
The parish was known as St. John's Chapel until 1913.

**51. Holy Family Parish, 1880 German (now called Holy Family–St. Thomas Aquinas Parish; see no. 162)
Baptisms and Marriages, 1880
Holy Family parish absorbed St. Stanislaus Martyr parish (no. 71) in 1979 and then merged with St. Thomas Aquinas parish (no. 59) in 2008. The Church was located at Fourth Ave. and 27th St. until the early 1890s.

52. St. Finbar Parish, 1880   Baptisms and Marriages, 1880 / Deaths, 1936
138 Bay 20th St., Brooklyn, NY 11214   (718) 236-3312

*&**53. St. Michael the Archangel Parish, 1880 Polish (now called Mary of Nazareth Parish, see no. 161)
Baptisms and Marriages, 1891
St. Michael the Archangel parish merged with St. Edward parish (no. 73) in 1942 to form St. Michael–St. Edward parish. St. Michael–St. Edward parish merged with Sacred Heart parish (no. 39) in 2008 to form Mary of Nazareth parish (no. 161). St. Michael the Archangel church was in Fort Greene on Price and Concord streets and then moved to Tillary and Laurence streets. Although Polish when it was first formed in the early 1890s, it became an Italian parish when many Italian families moved to the area.

54. Guardian Angel Parish, 1880   Baptisms and Marriages, 1881
2978 Ocean Parkway, Brooklyn, NY 11235   (718) 266-1561
The parish was attended as a mission from St. Mary Star of the Sea parish (no. 17) from 1880 to 1888.

55. St. Brigid Parish, 1882   Baptisms and Marriages, 1886
409 Linden St., Brooklyn, NY 11237   (718) 821-1690

56. St. Thomas Aquinas Parish, 1882   Baptisms, Marriages, and Deaths, 1885
1550 Hendrickson St., Brooklyn, NY 11234   (718) 253-4404
The church was a mission from Holy Cross parish (no. 6) from 1884 to 1887 and from St. Rose of Lima parish (no. 34) from 1887 to 1891. See Chapter 7, Parish Publications for more information.

*&**57. St. Ambrose Parish, 1883 (now called All Saints Parish; see no. 28)
Baptisms and Marriages, 1883
St. Ambrose parish merged with Our Lady of Montserrate (no. 146) in 1978. These two parishes then merged with All Saints parish (no. 28) in 2007. The original St. Ambrose parish was created between St. Patrick's parish (no. 7) and St. John the Baptist parish (no. 29). The original church was on the corner of Tomkins and DeKalb avenues.

**58. Sacred Hearts of Jesus and Mary Parish, 1884 Italian (now called Sacred Hearts of Jesus and Mary–St. Stephen parish; see no. 140)
Baptisms, 1883 / Marriages, 1884
Sacred Hearts of Jesus and Mary parish and St. Stephen parish (no. 26) merged in 1941. It was a mission from 1882 to 1884 from St. Peter parish (no. 19). The church was at Van Brunt and Presidents streets and later at Degraw and Hicks streets.

**59. St. Thomas Aquinas Parish, 1884 (now called Holy Family–St. Thomas Aquinas Parish; see no. 162)
Baptisms and Marriages, 1904
St. Thomas Aquinas merged with Hold Family parish (no. 51) in 2008. The Church was at 4th Ave. and 9th St.

**60. St. Matthew Parish, 1885
1123 Eastern Parkway, Brooklyn, NY 11213
Baptisms, Marriages, and Deaths, 1886
(718) 774-6747
The parish, which merged with Our Lady of Charity parish (no. 106) in 2007, is still called St. Matthew parish. The original church was on Schenectady Ave. near Montgomery St.

61. St. Francis Xavier Parish, 1886
225 Sixth Ave., Brooklyn, NY 11215
www.stfxbrooklyn.org
Baptisms and Marriages, 1886
(718) 638-1880

*&**62. Our Lady of Good Counsel Parish, 1886 (now called St. John the Baptist Parish, see no. 29)
Our Lady of Good Counsel Baptisms and Marriages, 1886
Our Lady of Good Counsel parish merged with St. John the Baptist parish (no. 29) in 2007. The parish was in Bedford–Stuyvesant, with the original church on Madison St.

*&**63. Fourteen Holy Martyrs Parish, 1887 German (now called St. Martin of Tours Parish; see no. 101)
Baptisms and Marriages, 1888
Fourteen Holy Martyrs parish merged with St. Martin of Tours parish (no. 101) in 1976. St. Martin of Tours–Fourteen Holy Martyrs parish merged with Our Lady of Lourdes parish (no. 41) in 2007 to form St. Martin of Tours parish (no. 101). The church was at Central Ave. and Covert St. in Bushwick.

64. Our Lady of Mount Carmel Parish, 1887 Italian
275 North 8th St., Brooklyn, NY 11211
Baptisms and Marriages, 1887 / Deaths, 1893
(718) 384-0223

**65. Our Lady of the Presentation Parish, 1887 (Our Lady of the Presentation–Our Lady of Loreto Parish; see no. 159)
Baptisms and Marriages, 1887
Our Lady of Loreto parish (no. 82) merged with Our Lady of the Presentation parish in 2008. Since the 1930s onward it has been an African American parish. The original church was on St. Mark Ave.

*&**66. Our Lady of Sorrows Parish, 1889 German (now called St. Joseph Patron of the Universal Church Parish; see no. 124)
Baptisms and Marriages, 1890
This parish closed in 1942, merging with St. Joseph Patron of the Universal Church parish. It was located at Morgan and Harrison streets.

67. St. Mary Mother of Jesus Parish, 1889
2326 84th St., Brooklyn, NY 11214
Baptisms and Marriages, 1890
(718) 372-4000

*&**68. Holy Rosary Parish, 1889 (now called St. Martin de Porres Parish; see no. 160)
Baptisms and Marriages, 1889
Nativity of the Blessed Lord parish (no. 36) merged with St. Peter Claver parish (no. 122) in 1973. St. Peter Claver parish then merged with Our Lady of Victory parish (no. 30) and Holy Rosary parish (no. 68) in 2007 to form St. Martin de Porres parish (no. 160). The original church was in Bedford–Stuyvesant on Chauncey St. between Stuyvesant and Reid avenues. Since the 1930s it has been a predominantly African American parish. The parish was known as Our Lady of the Holy Rosary in the 1890s.

*69. St. Mary of the Angels Parish, 1891 Lithuanian
Baptisms and Marriages, 1888
The parish closed in 1981. Originally named St. George, it was located on North 10th St., Williamsburg, until 1894. It then moved to South 4th and Roebling streets until 1981. Sacramental records prior to 1910 are held at the Diocesan Archives and records after 1910 are at the Chancery Office.

70. Blessed Sacrament Parish, 1891   Baptisms and Marriages, 1904
198 Euclid Ave., Brooklyn, NY 11208   (718) 827-1200
Local Catholics attended St. Malachy's (no. 14) before Blessed Sacrament parish was founded.

*71. St. Stanislaus Martyr Parish, 1891 Scandinavian   Baptisms, Marriages, and Deaths, 1891
The parish closed in 1979 and was absorbed into Holy Family parish (no. 51); this parish then merged with St. Thomas Aquinas parish (no. 59) in 2008 to form Holy Family–St. Thomas Aquinas parish (no. 162). The first masses were said at 299 15th St. and the first church was at 328 14th St., which is now the parish church for Resurrection Coptic Catholic Church (no. 154).

72. Our Lady of Angels Parish, 1891   Baptisms and Marriages, 1892
7320 Fourth Ave., Brooklyn, NY 11209   (718) 836-7200

*&**73. St. Edward Parish, 1891 (now called Mary of Nazareth Parish; see no. 161)
Baptisms and Marriages, 1891
St. Edward parish merged with St. Michael the Archangel (no. 53) in 1942 to form St. Michael–St. Edward parish. This parish then merged with Sacred Heart parish (no. 39) in 2008 to form Mary of Nazareth parish (no. 161). Located in Fort Greene, St. Edward parish was originally formed from sections of St. James parish (no. 1), Our Lady of Mercy parish (no. 31), and Sacred Heart parish (no. 39). The original church was located on the corner of old Canton and Division streets.

74. St. Elias Parish, 1891 Greek Ruthenian / Eastern Rite Byzantine   Baptisms, 1910 / Marriages, 1898
145 Kent St., Brooklyn, NY 11222   (212) 677-0516

75. St. Catherine of Alexandria Parish, 1892   Baptisms and Marriages, 1902
1119 41st St., Brooklyn, NY 11218   (718) 436-5917
The parish was created from St. Michael's parish (no. 45). The original boundary was from Seventh to Sixteenth avenues and from Chester Ave. to 49th St.

76. Our Lady of Perpetual Help Parish, 1893   Baptisms and Marriages, 1893
526 59th St., Brooklyn, NY 11220   (718) 492-9200

77. St. Barbara Parish, 1893 German   Baptisms, Marriages, and Deaths, 1893
138 Bleecker St., Brooklyn, NY 11221   (718) 452-3660

78. Ss. Simon & Jude Parish, 1893   Baptisms and Marriages, 1908
185 Van Sicklen St., Brooklyn, NY 11223   (718) 375-9600

79. Immaculate Heart of Mary Parish, 1893   Baptisms, Marriages, and Deaths, 1893
2805 Fort Hamilton Pkwy., Brooklyn, NY 11218   (718) 871-1310
The parish was formed from Holy Name parish (no. 47) and St. Rose of Lima parish (no. 34).

80. Holy Family Parish, 1895   Baptisms and Marriages, 1895
9719 Flatlands Ave., Brooklyn, NY 11236   (718) 257-4423

**81. Our Lady of Czestochowa Parish, 1896 Polish (now called Our Lady of Czestochowa-St. Casimir Parish; see no. 153)
Baptisms and Marriages, 1896
Our Lady of Czestochowa parish and St. Casimir parish (no. 46) merged in 1980. The parish was located in Bush Terminal (now known as Industry City), which is in the Greenwood Heights area of Brooklyn.

**82. Our Lady of Loreto Parish, 1896 Italian (Our Lady of the Presentation–Our Lady of Loreto Parish, see no. 159)
Baptisms and Marriages, 1894
Our Lady of Loreto parish merged with Our Lady of the Presentation parish (no. 65) in 2008. The church was located at Pacific and Sackman streets.

**83. St. Francis of Assisi Parish, 1898 (now called St. Francis of Assisi–St. Blaise Parish; see no. 152)
Baptisms and Marriages, 1898
St. Francis of Assisi parish merged with St. Blaise parish (no. 97) in 1980. The church was located at 319 Maple Ave. in Crown Heights.

84. St. Stanislaus Kostka Parish, 1898 Polish   Baptisms and Marriages, 1896
607 Humboldt St., Brooklyn, NY 11222   (718) 388-0170
http://ststanskostka.org
Local Catholic worshiped at St. Casimir's (no. 46) before this parish opened.

85. Our Lady of Peace Parish, 1899 Italian   Baptisms and Marriages, 1899
522 Carroll St., Brooklyn, NY 11215   (718) 624-5122

86. Our Lady of Solace Parish, 1901   Baptisms and Marriages, 1901
2866 West 17th St., Brooklyn, NY 11224   (718) 266-1612

*&**87. St. Gabriel Parish, 1901 (now called Mary Mother of the Church Parish, see no. 158)
Baptisms and Marriages, 1901
St. Gabriel parish merged with St. John Cantius parish (no. 90) in 2007 to become Mary Mother of the Church parish (no. 158). It was known as St. Gabriel the Archangel parish from 1984 to 2007. The parish was founded from St. Malachy (no. 14) and Blessed Sacrament parishes (no. 70). The original church was first located at Blake and New Jersey avenues then on New Lots Ave. and Linwood St.

88. St. Jerome Parish, 1901   Baptisms and Marriages, 1901
2900 Newkirk Ave., Brooklyn, NY 11226   (718) 462-0223
Parishioners of St. Jerome had previously attended Holy Cross parish (no. 6) and St. Thomas Aquinas parish (no. 56).

89. Our Lady of the Rosary of the Pompeii Parish, 1901 Italian   Baptisms and Marriages, 1900
225 Seigel St., Brooklyn NY 11206   (718) 497-0614

*&**90. St. John Cantius Parish, 1902 Polish (now called Mary Mother of the Church Parish; see no. 158)
Baptisms and Marriages, 1902
St. John Cantius merged with St. Gabriel parish (no. 87) in 2007 to become Mary Mother of the Church parish. It was originally known as St. John of Kenty from 1901 to 1905. The church was located on Blake and New Jersey avenues.

91. Holy Family Parish, 1903 Slovak   Baptisms and Marriages, 1905
21 Nassau Ave., Brooklyn, NY 11222   (718) 388-5145
Masses were held at St. Vincent de Paul parish (no. 20) until 1911.

**92. St. Lucy Parish, 1903 Italian (now called St. Lucy-St. Patrick parish, see no. 150)
Baptisms, Marriages, and Deaths, 1904
Local Catholics had worshiped at St. Patrick's parish (no. 7) before St. Lucy's was founded. St. Lucy parish merged with St. Patrick parish (no. 7) in 1974. The church was in Fort Greene at Kent Ave. near Park Ave.

93. St. Saviour Parish, 1905 — Baptisms and Marriages, 1905
611 Eighth Ave., Brooklyn, NY 11215 — (718) 768-4055

*&**94. Epiphany Parish, 1905 (now called Sts. Peter and Paul Parish; see no. 3)
Baptisms, Marriages, and Deaths, 1905
Local Catholics had worshiped at Sts. Peter and Paul parish (no. 3) and St. Patrick parish (no. 7) before Epiphany parish was found. Epiphany parish closed and merged with Sts. Peter and Paul parish (no. 3) in 2007. The church was at South 9th St. near Bedford Ave. in Williamsburg.

95. St. Rocco Parish, 1905 — Baptisms and Marriages, 1902 / Deaths, 1904
216 27th St., Brooklyn, NY 11232 — (718) 768-9798
The original parish boundaries were 10th and 40th streets and from Seventh Ave. to Gowanus Bay. The parish was also known locally as St. Roch's.

96. St. Rosalia (Regina Pacis) Parish, 1905 — Baptisms and Marriages, 1904
1230 65th St., Brooklyn, NY 11219 — (718) 236-0909
www.reginaparish.org
St. Rosalia parish took on the supplementary name of Regina Pacis in 1963 and is now called St. Rosalia–Regina Pacis.

**97. St. Blaise Parish, 1905 Italian (now called St. Francis of Assisi–St. Blaise Parish, see no. 152)
Baptisms and Marriages, 1905
St. Blaise parish merged with St. Francis of Assisi parish (no. 83) in 1980. The church was located in Crown Heights at 526 Kingston Ave.

98. Our Lady of Guadalupe Parish, 1906 — Baptisms and Marriages, 1906
7201 15th Ave., Brooklyn, NY 11228 — (718) 236-8300

99. Our Lady of Lebanon Cathedral Parish, 1906 Eastern Rite Maronite — Baptisms and Marriages, 1906
113 Remsen St., Brooklyn, NY 11201 — (718) 624-7228
The parish was created by Syrians who had worshiped at the Church of St. Joseph (Manhattan, no. 70) in Manhattan.

100. St. Gregory the Great Parish, 1906 — Baptisms and Marriages, 1906
224 Brooklyn Ave., Brooklyn, NY 11213 — (718) 773-0100
St. Gregory the Great parish was formed from St. Teresa of Avila (no. 60), St. Matthew (no. 44), and Our Lady of Victory (no. 30) parishes.

**101. St. Martin of Tours Parish, 1906 — Baptisms and Marriages, 1906
1288 Hancock St., Brooklyn, NY 11221 — (718) 443-8484
www.stmartinbrooklyn.parishesonline.com
Fourteen Holy Martyrs parish (no. 63) merged with St. Martin of Tours parish in 1976. This parish merged with Our Lady of Lourdes parish (no. 41) in 2007 to form St. Martin of Tours parish. Originally, St. Martin of Tours parish was founded from sections of St. Brigid's (no. 55), Our Lady of Good Counsel (no. 62) and Our Lady of Lourdes (no. 41) parishes. It is still called St. Martin of Tours.

102. St. Brendan Parish, 1907 — Baptisms and Marriages, 1907
1525 East 12th St., Brooklyn, NY 11230 — (718) 339-2828
The parish was formed from sections of St. Rose of Lima (no. 34), SS. Simon and Jude (no. 78), St. Mark's (no. 23), and Holy Cross (no. 6) parishes.

*&**103. St. Columbkille Parish, 1908 (now called SS. Cyril and Methodius Parish; see no. 119)
Baptisms and Marriages, 1916
The parish, which closed in 1950, was located at 140 Dupont St. in Greenpoint. It was originally formed to accommodate some of the excess parishioners of St. Anthony's parish (no. 18). It reverted back to being a mission church from SS. Cyril and Methodius parish (no. 119) in 1939 and it was absorbed into that parish in 1950. Consult with SS. Cyril and Methodius parish (no. 119) for parish register information.

*104. Sacred Heart Parish, 1908 Polish   Baptisms and Marriages, 1908
The parish closed in 1942. Its original name was St. Andrew, which it kept until 1910. It then reverted back to being a mission church from St. John Cantius parish (no. 90) from 1914 to 1939 and from St. Thomas Aquinas (no. 56) parish from 1939 to 1942. The parish was located where Floyd Bennett Field now is.

105. St. Ignatius Parish, 1908   Baptisms and Marriages, 1908
1101 Carroll St., Brooklyn, NY 11225   (718) 774-2102
Also known as St. Ignatius Loyola parish. See Chapter 7, Parish Publications for more information.

*&**106. Our Lady of Charity Parish, 1908 Italian (now called St. Matthew Parish; see no. 60)
Baptisms, Marriages, and Deaths, 1904
Our Lady of Charity merged with St. Matthew parish (no. 60) in 2007. Since the 1960s the parish has been predominantly African American. The church was located at 1665 Dean St.

107. Holy Innocents Parish, 1909   Baptisms and Marriages, 1909
279 East 17th St., Brooklyn, NY 11226   (718) 469-9500

*&**108. St. George Parish, 1909 Lithuanian   Baptisms, 1909 / Marriages, and Deaths, 1910
St. George parish merged with St. Ann parish (no. 22) in 1986, and then St. Ann–St. George parish closed in 2003. The original church was located in Fort Greene at York St. near Gold St.

109. Our Lady of Consolation Parish, 1909 Polish   Baptisms and Marriages, 1909
184 Metropolitan Ave., Brooklyn, NY 11211   (718) 388-1942
This parish was formed from St. Stanislaus Kostka parish (no. 84).

110. Church of the Virgin Mary Parish, 1910 Syrian   Baptisms, Marriages, and Deaths, 1911
216 Eighth Ave., Brooklyn, NY 11215   (718) 788-5454

111. Our Lady of Refuge Church, 1911   Baptisms and Marriages, 1911
2020 Foster Ave., Brooklyn, NY 11210   (718) 434-2090

112. St. Catherine of Genoa Parish, 1911   Baptisms and Marriages, 1911
520 Linden Blvd., Brooklyn, NY 11203   (718) 282-7162
www.stcatherinegenoabrooklyn.com
The parish was created from Holy Cross parish (no. 6), Flatbush. The original boundaries were from Clarkson St. to Snyder Ave. and from East 52nd St to East 36th St.

113. St. Agatha Parish, 1912   Baptisms and Marriages, 1912
702 48th St., Brooklyn, NY 11220   (718) 4267-1080

114. Holy Ghost Ukrainian Catholic Parish, 1913 Ukrainian   Births, Marriages, and Deaths, 1913
161 North 5th St., Brooklyn, NY 11211   (718) 782-9592

115. St. Athanasius Parish, 1913
2154 61st St., Brooklyn, NY 11204

Births, Marriages, and Deaths, 1913
(718) 236-0124

116. St. Rita Parish, 1913 Italian
275 Shepherd Ave., Brooklyn, NY 11208

Baptisms and Marriages, 1913
(718) 647-4910

*&**117. Our Lady of Pilar Parish, 1916 Puerto Rican (now called St. Paul and St. Agnes Parish; see no. 156)
Baptisms and Marriages, 1916
Our Lady of Pilar parish merged with St. Peter parish (no. 19) in 1935. St. Peter–Our Lady of Pilar parish merged with St. Paul parish (no. 2) in 1975. St. Paul–St. Peter–Our Lady of Pilar parish merged with St. Agnes parish (no. 49) in 2007. The original church was located at 264 Cumberland St.

118. St. Nicholas Ukrainian Catholic Parish, 1916 Ukranian
261 19th St., Brooklyn, NY 11215

Baptisms and Marriages, 1916
(718) 768-0628

119. SS. Cyril and Methodius Parish, 1917 Polish
150 Dupont St., Brooklyn, NY 11222

Baptisms, Marriages, and Deaths, 1917
(718) 389-4424

This parish absorbed the closed parish of St. Columbkille (no. 103) in 1950.

120. St. Francis of Paola Parish, 1918 Italian
219 Conselyea St., Brooklyn, NY 11211

Baptisms, Marriages, and Deaths, 1918
(718) 387-0526

121. St. Margaret Mary Parish, 1920
215 Exeter St., Brooklyn, NY 11235

Baptisms, Marriages, and Deaths, 1920
(718) 743-1824

*&**122. St. Peter Claver Parish 1920 African American (now called St. Martin de Porres parish; see no. 160)
Baptisms, and Marriages, 1919
St. Peter de Claver parish merged with Nativity of the Blessed Lord parish (no. 36) in 1973. The parish was called Nativity–St. Peter Claver from 1973 to 1979; it was then called St. Peter Claver parish from 1979 on. St. Peter Claver parish merged with Our Lady of Victory parish (no. 30) and Holy Rosary parish (no. 68) in 2007 to form St. Martin de Porres parish (no. 160). The church was located at 29 Claver Pl. in Bedford-Stuyvesant. See Chapter 7, Parish Publications for more information.

123. St. Ephrem Parish, 1921
929 Bay Ridge Parkway, Brooklyn, NY 11228
www.stephremparish.com

Baptisms and Marriages, 1921
(718) 833-1010

124. St. Joseph Patron of the Universal Church Parish, 1921
185 Suydam St., Brooklyn, NY 11221

Baptisms and Marriages, 1922
(718) 386-0175

The parish was a mission of Our Lady of the Rosary of Pompeii parish (no. 89) from 1921 to 1924. It absorbed Our Lady of Sorrows parish (no. 66) in 1942 and St. Leonard of Port Maurice (no. 37) parish in 1978.

125. St. Anselm Parish, 1922
356 82nd St., Brooklyn, NY 11209
http://starcc.net/stanselm/home.html

Baptisms and Marriages, 1922
(718) 238-2900

126. Holy Spirit Parish, 1922
1712 45th St., Brooklyn, NY 11204
The parish was called Holy Ghost parish until 1981.

Baptisms and Marriages, 1920
(718) 436-5565

127. St. Edmund Parish, 1922
2460 Ocean Ave., Brooklyn, NY 11229

Baptisms and Marriages, 1922
(718) 743-0102

128. St. Sylvester Parish, 1923
416 Grant Ave., Brooklyn, NY 11208

Baptisms and Marriages, 1923
(718) 647-1995

129. St. Vincent Ferrer Parish, 1923
1603 Brooklyn Ave., Brooklyn, NY 11210

Baptisms, Marriages, and Deaths, 1923
(718) 859-9009

130. Resurrection Parish, 1924
2331 Gerritsen Ave., Brooklyn, NY 11229

Baptisms and Marriages, 1924
(718) 743-7234

131. St. Therese of Lisieux Parish, 1926
1281 Troy Ave., Brooklyn, NY 11203
www.stthereseoflisieuxchurch.org

Baptisms and Marriages, 1926
(718) 451-1500

132. Good Shepherd Parish, 1927
1950 Batchelder St., Brooklyn, NY 11229
www.goodshepherdrcc.com

Baptisms and Marriages, 1927
(718) 998-2800

133. Our Lady Help of Christians Parish, 1927
1315 East 28th St., Brooklyn, NY 11210

Baptisms and Marriages, 1927
(718) 338-5242

134. Precious Blood Parish, 1927 Italian
70 Bay 47th St., Brooklyn, NY 11214

Baptisms and Marriages, 1928
(718) 372-8022

135. Mary Queen of Heaven Parish, 1927
1395 East 56th St., Brooklyn, NY 11234
www.mqhchurch.net

Baptisms and Marriages, 1927
(718) 763-2330

136. St. Fortunata Parish, 1934
2609 Linden Blvd., Brooklyn, NY 11208
The parish was a mission from Nativity of the Blessed Virgin Mary parish (Queens, no. 31), in Ozone Park, from 1922 to 1934.

Baptisms and Marriages, 1924
(718) 647-2632

137. St. Bernadette Parish, 1935 Italian
8201 13th Ave., Brooklyn, NY 11228

Baptisms and Marriages, 1935
(718) 837-3400

138. Our Lady of Grace Parish, 1935 Italian
430 Ave. W, Brooklyn, NY 11223

Baptisms and Marriages, 1935
(718) 627-2020

139. Our Lady of Miracles Parish, 1939 Italian
757 East 86th St., Brooklyn, NY 11236
The parish was a mission from Holy Family parish (no. 80) from 1936 to 1939.

Baptisms and Marriages, 1938
(718) 257-2400

140. Sacred Hearts of Jesus and Mary–St. Stephen Parish, 1941　　　Baptisms and Marriages, 1941
108 Carroll St., Brooklyn, NY 11231　　　　　　　　　　　　　　　　(718) 596-7750
Sacred Hearts of Jesus and Mary parish (no. 58) and St. Stephen parish (no. 26) merged in 1941.

141. St. Bernard Parish, 1961　　　　　　　Baptisms and Marriages, 1961 / Deaths, unknown
2055 East 69th St., Brooklyn, NY 11234　　　　　　　　　　　　　　(718) 763-5533

142. St. Frances Cabrini Parish, 1961　　　　Baptisms and Marriages, 1961 / Deaths, unknown
1562 86th St., Brooklyn, NY 11228　　　　　　　　　　　　　　　　(718) 236-9165

143. St. Jude Parish, 1961　　　　　　　　Baptisms and Marriages, 1961 / Deaths, unknown
1677 Canarsie Road, Brooklyn, NY 11236　　　　　　　　　　　　　(718) 763-6300

144. St. Laurence Parish, 1964　　　　　　Baptisms and Marriages, 1964 / Deaths, unknown
1020 Van Siclen Ave., Brooklyn, NY 11207　　　　　　　　　　　　(718) 649-0545

145. Our Lady of Mercy Parish, 1965　　　　Baptisms and Marriages, 1965 / Deaths, unknown
680 Mother Gaston Blvd., Brooklyn, NY 11212　　　　　　　　　　(718) 346-3166
This parish was as a mission from Our Lady of the Presentation parish (no. 65) from 1961 to 1965.

*&**146. Our Lady of Montserrate Parish, 1966 Spanish (now called All Saints parish; see no. 28)
Baptisms and Marriages, 1966 / Deaths, Unknown
Our Lady of Montserrate parish merged with St. Ambrose parish (no. 57) in 1978. These two parishes
then merged with All Saints parish (no. 28) in 2007. It was a mission of St. Peter–Our Lady of Pilar (no.
156, now St. Paul–St. Agnes parish) from 1965 to 1966.

147. St. Columba Parish, 1967　　　　　　Baptisms and Marriages, 1967 / Deaths, unknown
2245 Kimball St., Brooklyn, NY 11234　　　　　　　　　　　　　　(718) 338-6265

148. St. Dominic Parish, 1972　　　　　　Baptisms and Marriages, 1972 / Deaths, unknown
2001 Bay Ridge Parkway, Brooklyn, NY 11204　　　　　　　　　　(718) 259-4636

149. St. Andrew the Apostle Parish, 1972　　Baptisms and Marriages, 1972 / Deaths, unknown
6713 Ridge Blvd., Brooklyn, NY 11220　　　　　　　　　　　　　(718) 680-1010
www.standrewtheapostle.net

150. St. Lucy–St. Patrick Parish, 1974
285 Willoughby Ave. Brooklyn, NY 11205　　　　　　　　　　　　(718) 622-8748
St. Lucy parish (no. 92) merged with St. Patrick parish (no. 7) in 1974. The territory of St. Louis parish
(no. 32), which was closed in 1946, is included in this parish.

151. St. Anthony–St. Alphonsus Parish, 1975
862 Manhattan Ave., Brooklyn, NY 11222　　　　　　　　　　　　(718) 383-3339
St. Anthony parish (no. 18) merged with St. Alphonsus parish (no. 42) in 1975.

152. St. Francis of Assisi–St. Blaise Parish, 1980
319 Maple St., Brooklyn, NY 11225　　　　　　　　　　　　　　　(718) 756-2015
St. Francis of Assisi parish (no. 83) merged with St. Blaise parish (no. 97) in 1980.

153. Our Lady of Czestochowa–St. Casimir Parish, 1980
183 25th St., Brooklyn, NY 11232   (718) 768-5724
Our Lady of Czestochowa parish (no. 81) merged with St. Casimir parish (no. 46) in 1980.

154. Resurrection Coptic Catholic Church Parish, 1985
328 14th St., Brooklyn, NY 11215   (718) 499-6946
The church building had originally housed St. Stanislaus Martyr parish (no. 71).

155. Most Holy Trinity–St. Mary Parish, 2007
138 Montrose Ave., Brooklyn, NY 11201   (718) 384-0215
Most Holy Trinity parish (no. 4) merged with Immaculate Conception Blessed Virgin Mary parish (no. 115) in 2007.
www.mhtbrooklyn.org

156. St. Paul and St. Agnes Parish, 2007
234 Congress St., Brooklyn, NY 11201   (718) 624-3425
St. Agnes parish (no. 49) merged with St. Paul–St. Peter–Our Lady of Pilar (nos. 2, 19 and 117) parish in 2007.

157. St. Michael–St. Malachy Parish, 2007
225 Jerome St., Brooklyn, NY 11207   (718) 647-1818
St. Malachy parish (no. 14) merged with St. Michael parish (no. 21) in 2007.

158. Mary Mother of the Church Parish, 2007
749 Linwood St., Brooklyn, NY 11208   (718) 257-0612
St. Gabriel parish (no. 87) merged with St. John Cantius parish (no. 90) in 2007 to become Mary Mother of the Church parish.

159. Our Lady of the Presentation–Our Lady of Loreto Parish, 2008
1661 St. Marks Ave., Brooklyn, NY 11233   (718) 345-2604
Our Lady of the Presentation parish (no. 65) merged with Our Lady of Loreto parish (no. 82) in 2008.

160. St. Martin de Porres Parish, 2008
29 Claver Pl., Brooklyn, NY 11238   (718) 622-4647
St. Peter Claver parish (no. 122) merged with Nativity of the Blessed Lord parish (no. 36) in 1973. The parish was called Nativity–St. Peter Claver from 1973 to 1979, after which it was called St. Peter Claver parish. It then merged with Our Lady of Victory parish (no. 30) and Holy Rosary parish (no. 68) in 2007 to form St. Martin de Porres parish.

161. Mary of Nazareth Parish, 2008
41 Adelphi St., Brooklyn, NY 11205   (718) 625-5115
St. Edward parish (no. 73) merged with St. Michael Archangel parish (no. 53) in 1942. St. Michael–St. Edward parish merged with Sacred Heart parish (no. 39) in 2008 to form Mary of Nazareth parish.

162. Holy Family–St. Thomas Aquinas Parish, 2008
249 9th St., Brooklyn, NY 11215   (718) 768-9471
www.stthomasaquinaschurch.org
Holy Family parish (no. 51) absorbed St. Stanislaus Martyr parish (no. 71) in 1979 and then merged with St. Thomas Aquinas parish (no. 59) in 2008.

*Sacred Heart Chapel

This chapel was in Carroll Gardens and closed in 1995. Chapels are places of worship for Catholics that never attained the status of a parish. The year of establishment is unknown. Contact St. Mary Star of the Sea (no. 17) for more information.

*Frances Cabrini Chapel

This chapel was in Carroll Gardens and closed in 1996. Chapels are places of worship for Catholics that never attained the status of a parish. The year of establishment is unknown. Contact Sacred Hearts of Jesus and Mary–St. Stephen (no. 140) for more information.

Queens
Diocese of Brooklyn: 96 active parishes

**1. Our Lady of Mount Carmel Parish, 1841 (now called Our Lady of Mount Carmel–St. Margaret Mary parish, see no. 102)
Baptisms, 1848 / Marriages, 1853
Our Lady of Mount Carmel parish merged with St. Margaret Mary parish (no. 95) in 2007. Originally named Blessed Virgin of Mount Carmel, it was renamed Blessed Virgin Mary of Mount Carmel in 1865. The parish changed to its long running name, Our Lady of Mount Carmel, in 1893. Our Lady of Mount Carmel–St. Margaret Mary parish has also had a mission chapel:

> Our Lady of Mount Carmel Chapel Parish
> 103-56 52nd Ave., Corona, NY, 11368   (718) 592-7569
> A mission of the Diocese of Brooklyn

2. St. Michael Parish, 1843   Baptisms and Marriages, 1843
136-76 41st Ave., Flushing, NY 11355   (718) 961-0295/961-0182
www.stmichaels-flushing.org

*3. St. Monica Parish, 1848   Baptisms and Marriage 1859
The church, located at 94-120 160th St., Jamaica, closed in 1973. Sacramental records prior to 1910 are held at Diocesan Archives. For records after 1910, contact the Chancery Office.

4. Blessed Virgin Mary Help of Christians Parish, 1854   Baptisms and Marriages, 1858
70-31 48th Ave., Woodside, NY 11377   (718) 672-4848
Also known as St. Mary's, Winfield, because Woodside was called Winfield until 1949.

5. St. Fidelis Parish, 1856 German   Baptisms and Marriages, 1856
123-06 14th Ave., College Point, NY 11356   (718) 445-6164
See Chapter 7, Parish Publications for more information.

6. St. Margaret Parish, 1860 German   Baptisms and Marriages, 1861
66-05 79th Pl., Middle Village, NY 11379   (718) 326-1911

7. St. Raphael Parish, 1865   Baptisms, 1868 / Marriages, 1879
35-20 Greenpoint Ave., Long Island City, NY 11101   (718) 729-8957
The parish was a mission church from Blessed Virgin Mary Help of Christians parish (no. 4), in Winfield (Woodside), beginning in 1857.

**8. St. Mary Star of the Sea Parish, 1868 (now called St. Mary Star of the Sea–St. Gertrude Parish, see no. 104)
Baptisms and Marriages, 1868
St. Mary Star of the Sea merged with St. Gertrude parish (no. 57) in 2008. It was a mission church from a parish in Jamaica, probably St. Monica's (no. 3), from at least 1844.

9. St. Patrick Parish, 1868   Baptisms and Marriage, 1869
39-38 29th St., Long Island City, NY 11101   (718) 729-6060

10. St. Mary Parish, 1868   Baptisms, 1889 / Marriages, 1893
10-08 49th Ave., Long Island City, NY 11101   (718) 786-0705
This was a mission church from St. Anthony of Padua (no. 82), in Greenpoint, from 1865 to 1868.

11. St. Luke Parish, 1870
16-34 Clintonville St., Whitestone, NY 11357

Baptisms and Marriages, 1870
(718) 746-8102

12. St. Stanislaus Kostka Parish, 1872
57-15 61st St., Maspeth, NY 11378

Baptisms, 1877 / Marriages, 1876
(718) 326-2185

13. St. Elizabeth Parish, 1873 German
94-20 85th St., Ozone Park, NY 11416

Baptisms and Marriage, 1877
(718) 296-4900

The parish originally comprised Woodhaven, Union Course, Clarenceville, Aqueduct, and Brooklyn Hills.

14. Our Lady of Sorrows Parish, 1876
104-11 37th Ave., Corona, NY 11368

Baptisms and Marriages, 1872
(718) 424-7554

This parish was a mission from Blessed Virgin Mary Help of Christians parish (no. 4), Winfield (Woodside), from 1870 to 1876. Before Our Lady of Sorrows was created Catholics in this area went to Flushing or Woodside for mass.

15. St. Joseph Parish, 1877 German
43-19 30th Ave., Astoria, NY 11103

Baptisms and Marriages, 1879
(718) 278-1611

The first mass was said in a hall at Schutzen Park and the parish was a mission from Blessed Virgin Mary Help of Christians (no. 4), until 1879.

16. Sacred Heart Parish, 1878
215-35 38th Ave., Bayside, NY 11362

Baptisms and Marriages, 1893
(718) 428-2200

The parish was a mission from St. Fidelis parish (no. 5), in College Point from 1870 to 1878.

17. St. Rose of Lima Parish, 1884
130 Beach 84th St., Rockaway Beach, NY 11693
www.stroseoflimarb.org

Baptisms and Marriages, 1886
(718) 634-7394

For the first two years after this parish was founded Mass was said at an old schoolhouse.

18. Presentation of the Blessed Virgin Mary Parish, 1886 German
88-19 Parsons Blvd., Jamaica, NY 11432

Baptisms and Marriages, 1886
(718) 739-0241

The parish was created out of St. Monica's (no. 3) for German-speaking worshippers.

19. St. Adalbert Parish, 1891 Polish
52-29 83rd St., Elmhurst, NY 11373

Baptisms, 1891 / Marriages, 1892
(718) 639-0212

This was the first territorial Polish parish in Queens.

20. St. Aloysius Parish, 1892
382 Onderdonk Ave., Ridgewood, NY 11385

Baptisms and Marriages, 1892
(718) 821-0231

21. St. Benedict Joseph Labre Parish, 1892
94-40 118th St., Richmond Hill, NY 11419

Baptisms and Marriages, 1892
(718) 849-4048

The area in which this church is located was called Morris Park until 1938.

22. St. Sebastian Parish, 1894
39-63 57th St., Woodside, NY 11377
www.stsebastianwoodside.org

Baptisms, 1908 / Marriages, 1894
(718) 429-4442

Local Catholics went to Mass in Blissville or Woodside before this parish was created.

23. SS. Joachim and Anne Parish, 1896 German
218-26 105 Ave., Queens Village, NY 11429

Baptisms and Marriages, 1896
(718) 465-0124

24. St. Leo Church, 1903 Italian
104-05 49th Ave., Corona, NY 11368
This was the first territorial Italian parish founded in Queens.

Baptisms and Marriages, 1903
(718) 592-7569

25. St. Joseph Church, 1904 Polish
108-43 Sutphin Blvd., Jamaica, NY 11435

Baptisms and Marriages, 1904
(718) 739-4781

26. St. Pancras Parish, 1904
72-22 68th St., Glendale, NY 11385
www.saintpancras.org

Baptisms and Marriages, 1904
(718) 821-2323

St. Pancras parish was a mission from St. Brigid's (Brooklyn, no. 55), in Middle Village (1898–1899) and from St. Margaret's (no. 6), in Middle Village (1899–1904).The parish was founded to provide for those who lived far from these churches.

27. St. Mary Gate of Heaven Parish, 1904
101-25 104th St., Ozone Park, NY 11416

Baptisms, 1904 / Marriages, 1905
(718) 847-5957

28. St. Rita Parish, 1904 Italian
36-25 11th St., Long Island City, NY 11106

Baptisms, 1902 / Marriages, 1904
(718) 786-4573

The parish was a mission from St. Patrick's (no. 9), in Long Island City from 1894 to 1904.

29. St. Francis de Sales Parish, 1906
129-16 Rockaway Beach Blvd., Belle Harbor, NY 11356
www.stfrancisdesalesparish.org

Baptisms and Marriages, 1906
(718) 634-6464

This parish was a mission from St. Rose of Lima parish (no. 17), in Hammels, Rockaway Beach from 1903 to 1906.

30. St. Bartholomew Parish, 1906
43-22 Ithaca St., Elmhurst, NY 11373

Baptisms and Marriages, 1906
(718) 424-5400

31. Nativity of the Blessed Virgin Mary Parish, 1906
101-41 91st St., Ozone Park, NY 11416

Baptisms, 1906 / Marriages, 1907 / Deaths, 1923
(718) 845-3691

The parish was named Nativity of our Blessed Lady until 1939. The area was known as Woodhaven until 1924.

32. St. Gerard Majella Church, 1907
188-16 91st Ave., Hollis, NY 11423

Baptisms and Marriages, 1907
(718) 468-6565

This parish was a mission from St. Monica's parish (no. 3), Jamaica, from 1901 to 1907.

33. Transfiguration Parish, 1908 Lithuanian
64-14 Clinton Ave., Maspeth, NY 11378

Baptisms, Marriages, and Deaths, 1908
(718) 326-2236

The parish was created from St. Mary Queen of Angels parish (Brooklyn, no. 69) in Brooklyn, which at the time was the only Lithuanian parish in the diocese. It was the first territorial Lithuanian parish in Queens.

34. St. Matthias Parish, 1908 German   Baptisms, Marriages, and Deaths, 1909
58-15 Catalpa Ave., Ridgewood, NY 11385   (718) 821-6447
www.saintmatthiaschurch.net
The parish was formed from sections of St. Brigid's (Brooklyn, no. 55) in Brooklyn and St. Aloysius (no. 20) parish.

35. St. Pius V Parish, 1908 Italian   Baptisms, Marriages, and Deaths, 1908
106-12 Liverpool St., Jamaica, NY 11435   (718) 739-7086
This parish was created from St. Monica's parish (no. 3). In the 1970s and 1980s the parish had a substantial Portuguese-speaking population.

36. St. Mary Magdalene Parish, 1909   Baptisms and Marriages, 1907
218-12 136th Ave., Springfield Gardens, NY 11413   (718) 949-4311
The parish was a mission from St. Monica's parish (no. 3) from 1901 to 1909.

37. St. Thomas the Apostle Parish, 1909   Baptisms and Marriages, 1909
87-19 88th Ave., Woodhaven, NY 11421   (718) 849-3776
www.stawoodhaven.org

38. Holy Child Jesus Parish, 1910   Baptisms and Marriages, 1911
111-11 86th Ave., Richmond Hill, NY 11418   (718) 847-1860
The parish was created out of St. Benedict Joseph Labre parish (no. 21), in Benedict Hill (Morris Park).

39. St. Josaphat Parish, 1910 Polish   Baptisms and Marriages, 1910
34-32 210th St., Bayside, NY 11361   (718) 229-1663

40. Holy Cross Parish, 1912 Polish   Baptisms and Marriages, 1913
61-21 56th Road, Maspeth, NY 11378   (718) 894-1387
Parishioners used St. Stanislaus Kosta's (no. 12) church building for the first year until their church was built. Before that, they attended St. Adelbert parish (no. 19), in Elmhurst.

41. St. Camillus Parish, 1912   Baptisms and Marriages, 1912 / Deaths, 1911
99-15 Rockaway Beach Blvd., Rockaway Park, NY 11694   (718) 634-8229
http://stcstv.com
The parish was a mission from St. Rose of Lima parish (no. 17) from 1904 to 1912.

42. Our Lady Queen of Martyrs Parish, 1912   Baptisms and Marriages, 1917
110-06 Queens Blvd., Forest Hills, NY 11375   (718) 268-6251
www.ourladyqueenofmartyrs.org

43. St. Virgilius Parish, 1912   Baptisms and Marriages, 1912
16 Noel Road, Broad Channel, NY 11693   (718) 634-5680
http://stcstv.com

44. St. Clement Pope Parish, 1913   Baptisms and Marriages, 1913
141-11 123rd Ave., South Ozone Park, NY 11436   (718) 529-0273
The parishioners attended St. Monica's parish (no. 3), Jamaica, from 1908 to 1913.

45. St. Andrew Avellino Parish, 1914   Baptisms and Marriages, 1914
35-60 158th St., Flushing, NY 11358   (718) 359-0417

46. St. Anastasia Parish, 1915
45-14 245th St., Douglaston-Little Neck, NY 11362
www.stanastasia.info

Baptisms, 1915 / Marriages, 1916
(718) 631-4454

47. Our Lady of the Miraculous Medal Parish, 1917 German
62-81 60th Pl., Ridgewood, NY 11385

Baptisms and Marriages, 1917
(718) 366-3360

48. St. Nicholas of Tolentine Parish, 1917
150-75 Goethals Ave., Jamaica, NY 11432
http://iamsnt.org

Baptisms and Marriages, 1917
(718) 969-3226

49. St. Joan of Arc Parish, 1920
82-00 35th Ave., Jackson Heights, NY 11372

Baptisms and Marriages, 1920
(718) 429-2333

50. Our Lady of Grace Parish, 1922
100-05 159th Ave., Howard Beach, NY 11414

Baptisms and Marriages, 1922 / Deaths, 1925
(718) 843-6218

51. Most Precious Blood Parish, 1922
32-23 36th St., Long Island City, NY 11106
The parish was named Precious Blood until 1977.

Baptisms and Marriages, 1922
(718) 278-3337

52. Our Lady of the Cenacle Parish, 1922
136-06 87th Ave., Richmond Hill, NY 11418

Baptisms and Marriages, 1922 / Deaths, 1932
(718) 291-2540

*&**53. St. Catherine of Siena Parish, 1922 (now called Our Lady of Light Parish; see no. 104)
Baptisms, 1922 / Marriages, 1922
St. Catherine of Siena parish merged with St. Pascal Baylon parish (no. 72) in 2008 to form Our Lady of
Light Parish (no. 103). St. Catherine of Siena parish was in St. Albans.

54. St. Gabriel Parish, 1923
26-26 98th St., East Elmhurst, NY 11369

Baptisms, Marriages, and Deaths, 1923
(718) 639-0474

55. St. Stanislaus Bishop and Martyr Church Parish, 1923
88-10 102nd Ave., Ozone Park, NY 11416

Baptisms and Marriages, 1923
(718) 845-6206

56. Our Lady of Perpetual Help Parish, 1923
111-50 115th St., South Ozone Park, NY 11420

Baptisms, Marriages, and Death 1923
(718) 843-1212

**57. St. Gertrude Parish, 1923 (now called St. Mary Star of the Sea–St. Gertrude Parish; see no. 104)
Baptisms and Marriages, 1923
St. Gertrude parish merged with St. Mary Star of the Sea parish (no. 8) in 2008. The original church was
at 336 Beach 38th St., in the Edgemere section of Queens.

58. Immaculate Conception Parish, 1924
21-47 29th St., Astoria, NY, 11105
www.immaculateconceptionastoria.net

Baptisms and Marriages, 1924
(718) 728-1613

59. Immaculate Conception Parish, 1924
86-45 Edgerton Blvd., Jamaica, NY 11432

Baptisms and Marriages, 1925
(718) 739-0880

60. St. Clare Parish, 1924
137-35 Brookville Blvd., Rosedale, NY 11422

Baptisms and Marriages, 1924
(718) 341-1018

61. Our Lady of Lourdes Parish, 1924
92-96 220th St., Queens Village, NY 11428

Baptisms, Marriages, and Deaths, 1924
(718) 479-5111

62. St. Kevin Parish, 1926
45-21 194th St., Flushing, NY 11358

Baptisms, 1926 / Marriages, 1927
(718) 357-8888

63. Resurrection–Ascension Parish, 1926
61-11 85th St., Rego Park, NY 11374

Baptisms and Marriages, 1926 / Deaths, 1937
(718) 424-5212

64. Mary's Nativity Church Parish, 1926
46-02 Parsons Blvd., Flushing, NY 11355

Baptisms and Marriages, 1926
(718) 359-5996

65. St. Ann Church Parish, 1927
142-30 58th Ave., Flushing, NY 11355

Baptisms and Marriages, 1927
(718) 886-3890

66. Incarnation Parish, 1927
89-43 Francis Lewis Blvd., Queens Village, NY 11427
www.incrcc.org
The area where this parish is located was known as Bellaire until 1975.

Baptisms and Marriages, 1927
(718) 465-8534

67. St. Teresa Church, 1928
50-20 45th St., Woodside, NY 11377

Baptisms and Marriages, 1928
(718) 784-2123

68. Sacred Heart Parish, 1929
83-17 78th Ave., East Glendale, NY 11385

Baptisms and Marriages, 1929
(718) 821-6434

69. St. Teresa of Avila Parish, 1929
109-26 130th St., South Ozone Park, NY 11420

Baptisms and Marriages, 1929
(718) 529-3587

70. Blessed Sacrament Parish, 1929
34-43 93rd St., Jackson Heights, NY 11372
www.blessedsacramentjacksonheightsny.com

Baptisms and Marriages, 1929 / Deaths, 1934
(718) 639-3888

71. St. Bonaventure Parish, 1930
114-58 170th St., Jamaica, NY 11434

Baptisms, Marriages, and Deaths, 1930
(718) 526-0040

*&**72. St. Pascal Baylon Parish, 1930 (now called Our Lady of Light Parish; see no. 104)
Births, Marriages, and Deaths, 1930
St. Catherine of Siena parish (no. 53) merged with St. Pascal Baylon parish in 2008 to form Our Lady of Light parish (no. 103). St. Pascal Balyon parish was in St. Albans.

73. St. Francis of Assisi Parish, 1930
21-17 45th St., Astoria, NY 11105

Baptisms and Marriages, 1930
(718) 728-7801

74. Our Lady of Mercy Parish, 1930
70-01 Kessel St., Forest Hills, NY 11375

Baptisms and Marriages, 1930
(718) 268-6143

75. Our Lady of the Blessed Sacrament Parish, 1930
Baptisms and Marriages, 1930 / Burials 1930 to 1936
34-24 203rd St., Bayside, NY 11361 (718) 229-5929

76. St. Benedict the Moor Parish, 1932 African American Baptisms and Marriages, 1933
171-17 110th Ave., Jamaica, NY 11433 (718) 526-4018

77. Christ the King Parish, 1933 Baptisms and Marriages, 1933
145-39 Farmers Blvd., Springfield Gardens, NY 11434 (718) 528-6010
www.christthekingsg.org

78. St. Gregory the Great Parish, 1936 Baptisms, Marriages, and Deaths, 1936
242-20 88th Ave., Bellerose, NY 11426 (718) 347-3707

79. Sacred Heart Parish, 1936 Baptisms, 1936 / Marriages, 1938
115-58 222nd St., Cambria Heights, NY 11411 (718) 528-0577

80. Corpus Christi Parish, 1937 Baptisms, Marriages, and Deaths, 1937
31-30 61st St., Woodside, NY 11377 (718) 278-8114

*&**81. St. Thomas More–St. Edmund Parish, 1937 (now called Blessed Trinity Parish; see no. 105)
Baptisms and Marriages, 1937
St. Thomas More–St. Edmund parish merged with St. Genevieve parish (no. 92) to form Blessed Trinity
parish (no. 106) in 2008. The parish, located in Breezy Point, was originally called St. Thomas More until
its name was changed to St. Thomas More-St. Edmund parish in 1954.

82. St. Anthony of Padua Parish, 1937 Italian Baptisms and Marriages, 1937
133-25 128th St., South Ozone Park, NY 11420 (718) 843-7410

83. Our Lady of the Angelus Parish, 1938 Baptisms and Marriages, 1938
63-63 98th St., Rego Park, NY 11374 (718) 897-4444

84. Queen of Peace Parish, 1939 Baptisms and Marriages, 1939
141-36 77th Ave., Kew Gardens, NY 11367 (718) 380-5031

85. St. Robert Bellarmine Parish, 1939 Baptisms and Marriages, 1939
56-15 213 St., Bayside, NY 11364 (718) 229-6465
www.stroberts.org

86. St. Mel Parish, 1941 Baptisms and Marriages, 1941
26-15 154th St., Flushing, NY 11354 (718) 886-0201

87. Holy Family Parish, 1941 Baptisms and Marriages, 1941
175-20 74th Ave., Flushing, NY 11366 (718) 969-2448

88. Ascension Paris, 1945 Baptisms and Marriages, 1945 / Deaths, unknown
86-13 55th Ave., Elmhurst, NY 11373 (718) 335-2626
www.churchoftheascension.org

89. American Martyrs Parish, 1948
79-43 Bell Boulevard, Bayside, NY 11364
http://americanmartyrsbayside.com

Baptisms and Marriages, 1948 / Deaths, unknown
(718) 464-4582

90. Our Lady of the Snows Parish, 1948
258-15 80th Ave., Floral Park, NY 11004
www.olsnows.org

Baptisms and Marriages, 1948 / Deaths, unknown
(718) 347-6070

91. Our Lady of Fatima Parish, 1948
25-02 80th St., East Elmhurst, NY 11370

Baptisms and Marriages, 1948 / Deaths, unknown
(718) 899-2801

*&**92. St. Genevieve Parish, 1950 (now called Blessed Trinity Parish; no. 106)
Baptisms and Marriages, 1950 / Deaths, Unknown
St. Thomas More–St. Edmund parish (no. 81) merged with St. Genevieve parish to form Blessed Trinity parish (no. 105) in 2008. St. Genevieve parish was in Roxbury.

93. Our Lady of Hope Parish, 1960
61-27 71st St., Middle Village, NY 11379

Baptisms and Marriages, 1960 / Deaths, unknown
(718) 429-5438

94. St. Pius X Parish, 1960
148-10 249th St., Rosedale, NY 11422

Baptisms and Marriages, 1960 / Deaths, unknown
(718) 525-9099

**95. St. Margaret Mary Parish, 1961 (now called Our Lady of Mount Carmel-St. Margaret Mary Parish, see no. 102)
Baptisms and Marriages, 1961 / Deaths, unknown
St. Margaret Mary parish, located in Long Island City, merged with Our Lady of Mount Carmel parish (no. 1) in 2007.

96. St. Paul the Apostle Parish, 1964
98-16 55th Ave., Corona, NY 11378
www.stpaulcorona.com

Baptisms and Marriages, 1964 / Deaths, unknown
(718) 271-1100

97. Holy Trinity Parish, 1965
14-51 143rd St., Whitestone, NY 11357

Baptisms and Marriages, 1965 / Deaths, unknown
(718) 746-7730

98. Queen of Angels Parish, 1966
44-04 Skillman Ave., Sunnyside, NY 11104
http://queenofangelsnyc.org

Baptisms and Marriages, 1966 / Deaths, unknown
(718) 472-2625

99. St. Helen Parish, 1966
157-10 83rd St., Howard Beach, NY 11414

Baptisms and Marriages, 1966 / Deaths, Unknown
(718) 738-1616

100. St. John Vianney Parish, 1967
140-10 34th Ave., Flushing, NY 11354

Baptisms and Marriages, 1967 / Deaths, unknown
(718) 762-7920

101. St. Paul Chong Ha Sang Parish, 2007 Korean
32-15 Parsons Blvd., Flushing Park, NY 11354

Baptisms and Marriages, 2007 / Deaths, unknown
(718) 321-7676

102. Our Lady of Mount Carmel–St. Margaret Mary Parish, 2007
23-25 Newtown Ave., Astoria, NY 11102   (718) 278-1834
www.mountcarmelastoria.org
Our Lady of Mount Carmel parish (no. 1) merged with St. Margaret Mary parish (no. 95) in 2007.

103. Our Lady of Light Parish, 2008
118-22 Riverton St., St. Albans, NY 11412   (718) 528-1220
St. Catherine of Siena parish (no. 53) merged with St. Pascal Baylon parish (no. 72) in 2008 to form Our Lady of Light parish.

104. St. Mary Star of the Sea –St. Gertrude Parish, 2008
1920 New Haven Ave., Far Rockaway, NY 11691   (718) 327-1133
St. Mary Star of the Sea parish (no. 8) merged with St. Gertrude parish (no. 57) in 2008.

105. Blessed Trinity Parish, 2008
204-25 Rockaway Point Blvd., Rockaway Point, NY 11697   (718) 634-6357
St. Thomas More–St. Edmund parish (no. 81) merged with St. Genevieve parish (no. 92) in 2008 to form Blessed Trinity Parish in 2008.

Holy Cross Parish
31-120th St., Long Island City, NY 11106   (718) 932-4060
This church is in Queens but does not belong to the Diocese of Brooklyn. Instead, it is a parish of the Ukrainian Catholic Eparchy of Stamford

Annunciation of the Blessed Virgin Mary Parish
48-26 171st St., Fresh Meadows, NY 11365   (718) 939-4116
This church is in Queens but does not belong to the Diocese of Brooklyn. Instead, it is a parish of the Ukrainian Catholic Eparchy of Stamford

Our Lady of the Skies Chapel, 1966
JFK International Airport, Terminal 4 - 4th Floor, Jamaica, NY 11430   (718) 656-5348
www.jfkchapel.org
Chapels are places of worship for Catholics that never attained the status of a parish.

Our Lady of China Chapel, 1978
54-09 92nd St., Elmhurst, NY 11373   (718) 699-1929
www.olc.faithweb.com
Chapels are places of worship for Catholics that never attained the status of a parish.

St. Augustine Yu Chin-Gil Chapel
2115 61st St., Brooklyn, NY 11204   (718) 259-5424
Chapels are places of worship for Catholics that never attained the status of a parish. The year of establishment is unknown.

St. Raphael's Korean Martyrs Apostolate Chapel
35-20 Greenpoint Avenue, Long Island City, NY 11101   (718) 729-2220
Chapels are places of worship for Catholics that never attained the status of a parish. The year of establishment is unknown.

Bronx
Archdiocese of New York: 67 active parishes

1. Church of St. Raymond, 1835   Baptisms, 1842 / Marriages, 1847
1759 Castle Hill Ave., Bronx, NY 10462   (718) 792-4044 b258@archny.org
www.straymondparish.org
Church of St. Raymond was the first Catholic church erected in Westchester/Bronx.

2. Church of St. Augustine, 1849   Baptisms and Marriages, 1852
1183 Franklin Ave., Bronx, NY 10456   (718) 893-0072 b228@archny.org
The parish initially included Melrose, Mott Haven, East and West Morrisania, Tremont, West Farms,
Central Morrisania, Highbridge, and Westock.

3. Church of Our Lady of Mercy, 1852   Baptisms and Marriages, 1855
2496 Marion Ave., Bronx, NY 10458   (718) 933-4400 b258@archny.org
www.ourladyofmercyny.org
See Chapter 7, Parish Publications for more information.

4. Church of the Immaculate Conception, 1853 German   Baptisms and Marriages, 1853
389 East 150th St., Bronx, NY 10455   (718) 292-6970 b206@archny.org

5. Church of St. Jerome, 1869   Baptisms and Marriages, 1869
230 Alexander Ave., Bronx, NY 10454   (718) 665-5533 b240@archny.org
The parish centered on Mott Haven. The original parish limits were Bronx Kills and 128th St. to 4th Ave.,
Park Ave. to 163rd St., then east to Long Island Sound.

6. Church of St. Joseph, 1873 German   Baptisms and Marriages, 1873
1949 Bathgate Ave., Bronx, NY 10457   (718) 731-2504 b245@archny.org

7. Church of the Sacred Heart, 1875   Baptisms and Marriages, 1875
1253 Shakespeare Ave., Bronx, NY 10452   (718) 293-2766 b219@archny.org
Church of the Sacred Heart parish was created out of St. Augustine parish (no. 2). St. Francis of Assisi
(no. 58) parish became a mission of this parish in 2007.

8. Church of St. Mary Star of the Sea, 1887   Baptisms and Marriages, 1897
595 Minneford Ave., Bronx, NY 10464   (718) 885-1440 b252@archny.org

9. Church of St. Mary, 1886   Baptisms and Marriages, 1886
650 East 226th St., Bronx, NY 10466   (718) 547-8000 b251@archny.org

10. Church of St. John, 1886   Baptisms and Marriages, 1886
3021 Kingsbridge Ave., Bronx, NY 10463   (718) 548-1221 b242@archny.org

11. Church of St. Thomas Aquinas, 1890   Baptisms and Marriages, 1889
1900 Crotona Parkway, Bronx, NY 10460   (718) 589-5235 b263@archny.org

12. Church of St. Margaret of Cortona, 1890   Baptisms and Marriages, 1890
6000 Riverdale Ave., Bronx, NY 10471   (718) 549-8053 b248@archny.org

13. Church of St. Anselm, 1891   Baptisms and Marriages, 1891
673 Tinton Ave., Bronx, NY 10455   (718) 585-8666 b223@archny.org

*14. Church of St. Valentine, 1891   Baptisms and Marriages, 1891
This parish closed in the mid-1990s. The church was located at 810 East 221th St.

15. Church of the Holy Family, 1896   Baptisms and Marriages, 1896
2158 Watson Ave., Bronx, NY 10472   (718) 863-9156 b203@archny.org
Church of Holy Family created out of St. Raymond's parish (no. 1).

16. Church of Sts. Peter and Paul, 1897   Baptisms and Marriages, 1897
833 St. Ann's Ave., Bronx, NY 10456   (718) 665-3924 b254@archny.org

17. Church of St. Luke, 1897   Baptisms and Marriages, 1897
623 East 138th St., Bronx, NY 10454   (718) 665-6677 b247@archny.org
Church of St. Luke was created out of St. Jerome's parish (no. 5).

18. Church of St. Martin of Tours, 1897   Baptisms and Marriages, 1897
664 Grote St., Bronx, NY 10457   (718) 295-0913 b250@archny.org

19. Church of St. Philip Neri, 1898   Baptisms and Marriages, 1898
3025 Grand Concourse, Bronx, NY 10468   (718) 733-3200 b256@archny.org
See Chapter 7, Parish Publications for more information.

*20. Church of St. Adalbert, 1898 Polish   Baptisms and Marriages, 1898
This parish closed in the 1980s. The church was at 150th St. and Robbins Ave. and then moved to 422 East 156th St. in 1899.

21. Church of St. Frances of Rome, 1898   Baptisms and Marriages, 1898
4307 Barnes Ave., Bronx, NY 10466   (718) 324-5340/41 b236@archny.org
http://sfrbx.org

22. Church of St. John Chrysostom, 1899   Baptisms and Marriages, 1899
985 East 167th St., Bronx, NY 10459   (718) 542-6164/5 b243@archny.org
The parish was created out of St. Augustine parish (no. 2).

23. Church of St. Angela Merici, 1899   Baptisms and Marriages, 1899
917 Morris Ave., Bronx, NY 10451   (718) 293-0984 b221@archny.org
www.saintangelamerici.net

24. Church of St. Roch, 1899   Baptisms and Marriages, 1900
525 Wales Ave., Bronx, NY 10455   (718) 292-3834 b260@archny.org

25. Church of St. Rita of Cascia, 1900   Baptisms and Marriages, 1900
448 College Ave., Bronx, NY 10451   (718) 585-5900 b259@archny.org

26. Church of the Holy Spirit, 1901   Baptisms and Marriages, 1901
1940 University Ave., Bronx, NY 10453   (718) 583-0120 b205@archny.org

27. Church of the Immaculate Conception, 1903 Italian   Baptisms and Marriages, 1903
754 Gun Hill Road, Bronx, NY 10467   (718) 653-2200 b207@archny.org

28. Church of Our Lady of Solace, 1903
731 Morris Park Ave., Bronx, NY 10462
This parish was created out of St. Raymond's parish (no. 1).

Baptisms and Marriages, 1903
(718) 863-3282 b216@archny.org

29. Church of St. Anthony of Padua, 1903 German
832 East 166th St., Bronx, NY 10459

Baptisms and Marriages, 1903
(718) 542-7293 b226@archny.org

30. Church of Our Lady of Mount Carmel, 1906 Italian
627 East 187th St., Bronx, NY 10458
www.ourladymtcarmelbx.org

Baptisms and Marriages, 1906
(718) 295-3770 b213@archny.org

31. Church of St. Pius V, 1906
420 East 145th St., Bronx, NY 10454

Baptisms and Marriages, 1907
(718) 665-6642 b257@archny.org

32. Church of St. Nicholas of Tolentine, 1906
2345 University Ave., Bronx, NY 10468

Baptisms and Marriages, 1906
(718) 295-6800/1 b253@archny.org

33. Church of St. Athanasius, 1907
878 Tiffany St., Bronx, NY 10459

Baptisms and Marriages, 1907
(718) 328-2558 b227@archny.org

*34. Church of Our Lady of Suffrage, 1908 Italian
Baptisms and Marriages, 1908
This parish closed in 2007. Also known as Our Lady of Pity, it was originally located at 276 East 151st St.

35. Church of St. Anthony, 1908 Italian
1496 Commonwealth Ave., Bronx, NY 10460

Baptisms and Marriages, 1908
(718) 931-4040 b224@archny.org

36. Church of St. Brendan, 1908
333 East 206th St., Bronx, NY 10467
www.saintbrendanchurch.org

Baptisms and Marriages, 1908
(718) 547-6655 b231@archny.org

The parish was created out of St. Mary's parish (no. 9), Williamsbridge. The initial boundaries were the New Haven Railroad and Bronx Park to the east, Van Cortland Park and Jerome Ave. to the west, Woodlawn Cemetery to the north, and Moshulu Parkway to the south.

37. Church of Our Lady of Victory, 1909
1512 Webster Ave., Bronx, NY 10457

Baptisms and Marriages, 1909
(718) 583-4044 b217@archny.org

This parish was created out of St. Joseph (no. 6) and St. Augustine (no. 2) parishes.

38. Church of St. Barnabas, 1910
409 East 241st St., Bronx, NY 10470

Baptisms and Marriages, 1910
(718) 324-1478 b229@archny.org

The parish was created out of St. Francis of Rome parish (no. 21).

39. Church of Our Savior, 1912
2317 Washington Ave., Bronx, NY 10458
http://churchoursaviour.org

Baptisms and Marriages, 1912
(718) 295-9600 b218@archny.org

This parish was created out of parishes in the Fordham, Belmont and Tremont sections of the Bronx.

40. Church of St. Anthony, 1919
4505 Richardson Ave., Bronx, NY 10470
http://sfrbx.org

Baptisms and Marriages, 1919
(718) 324-5340 b225@archny.org

The parish office and records are at St. Frances of Rome parish (no. 21).

41. Church of St. Simon Stock, 1919
2191 Valentine Ave., Bronx, NY 10457

Baptisms and Marriages, 1919
(718) 367-1251 b261@archny.org

42. Church of the Holy Cross, 1921
600 Soundview Ave., Bronx, NY 10473
www.holycrossbronx.org

Baptisms and Marriages, 1921
(718) 893-5550 holycross@holycrossbronx.org

43. Church of Our Lady of Refuge, 1922
290 East 196th St., Bronx, NY 10458
www.ourladyofrefuge.com

Baptisms and Marriages, 1922
(718) 367-4690 b215@archny.org

Our Lady of Refuge parish was created out of the southern part of St. Philip Neri parish (no. 19) and the northern part of Our Lady of Mercy parish (no. 3), encompassing the area from East 194th St. north to East 198th St.

44. Church of St. Benedict, 1923
2969 Otis Ave., Bronx, NY 10465
http://stbenedictchurchnyc.clubspaces.com

Baptisms and Marriages, 1923
(718) 828-3403 b230@archny.org

45. Church of St. Margaret Mary, 1923
1914 Morris Ave., Bronx, NY 10453

Baptisms and Marriages, 1923
(718) 299-4233 b249@archny.org

46. Church of Our Lady of the Assumption, 1923
1634 Mahan Ave., Bronx, NY 10461

Baptisms and Marriages, 1923
(718) 824-5454 b210@archny.org

47. Church of the Nativity of Our Blessed Lady, 1924
1531 East 233rd St., Bronx, NY 10466
http://nativityofourblessedlady.org

Baptisms and Marriages, 1924
(718) 324-3531 b208@archny.org

48. Church of Our Lady of Angels, 1924
2860 Webb Ave., Bronx, NY 10468

Baptisms and Marriages, 1924
(718) 548-3005 b209@archny.org

49. Church of Our Lady of Grace, 1924
3985 Bronxwood Ave., Bronx, NY 10466

Baptisms and Marriages, 1924
(718) 652-4817 b211@archny.org

50. Church of St. Dominic, 1924
1739 Unionport Road, Bronx, NY 10462

Baptisms and Marriages, 1924
(718) 828-2424 b233@archny.org

51. Church of the Holy Rosary, 1925
1510 Adee Ave., Bronx, NY 10469

Baptisms and Marriages, 1925
(718) 379-4432 b204@archny.org

52. Church of Christ the King, 1926
141 Marcy Place, Bronx, NY 10452

Baptisms and Marriages, 1926
(718) 538-5546 b201@archny.org

53. Church of St. Frances de Chantal, 1927
190 Hollywood Ave., Bronx, NY 10465
www.sfdchantal.org

Baptisms and Marriages, 1927
(718) 792-5500 b235@archny.org

54. Church of the Blessed Sacrament, 1927
1170 Beach Ave., Bronx, NY 10472

Baptisms and Marriages, 1927
(718) 892-3214 b200@archny.org

55. Church of St. Ann, 1927
3519 Bainbridge Ave., Bronx, NY 10467

Baptisms and Marriages, 1927
(718) 547-9350 b222@archny.org

56. Church of St. Lucy, 1927
833 Mace Ave., Bronx, NY 10467

Baptisms and Marriages, 1927
(718) 882-0710 b222@archny.org

57. Church of St. Theresa of the Infant Jesus, 1927 Italian
2855 St. Theresa Ave., Bronx, NY 10461

Baptisms and Marriages, 1927
(718) 892-1900 b262@archny.org

**58. Church of St. Francis of Assisi, 1928 (now called Church of the Sacred Heart; see no. 7)
Baptisms and Marriages, 1928   (718) 731-6840 b234@archny.org
The church, located at 1546 Shakespeare Ave., became a mission of Church of the Sacred Heart in 2007.
For information about sacramental records, write to P.O. Box 520013, Bronx, NY 10452.

59. Church of Santa Maria, 1928
2352 St. Raymond Ave., Bronx, NY 10462

Baptisms and Marriages, 1928
(718) 828-2380 b265@archny.org

60. Church of St. Francis Xavier, 1928
1703 Lurting Ave., Bronx, NY 10461

Baptisms and Marriages, 1928
(718) 892-3330 b237@archny.org

61. Church of the Visitation, 1928
160 Van Cortlandt Park South, Bronx, NY 10463

Baptisms and Marriages, 1928
(718) 548-1455 b266@archny.org

62. Church of St. Clare of Assisi, 1929
1918 Paulding Ave., Bronx, NY 10462
www.rc.net/newyork/stclare

Baptisms and Marriages, 1929
(718) 863-8974 b232@archny.org

63. Church of St. Gabriel, 1939
3250 Arlington Ave., Bronx, NY 10463

Baptisms and Marriages, 1939
(718) 548-4470 b238@archny.org

64. Church of St. Helena, 1940
1315 Olmstead Ave., Bronx, NY 10462
www.sthelenabronxny.org

Baptisms and Marriages, 1940
(718) 892-3232 b239@archny.org

65. Church of Sts. Philip and James, 1949
1160 East 213th St., Bronx, NY 10469

Baptisms and Marriages, 1949
(718) 547-2203 b255@archny.org

66. Church of St. Joan of Arc, 1949
1372 Stratford Ave., Bronx, NY 10472

Baptisms and Marriages, 1949
(718) 842-2233 b241@archny.org

67. Church of St. John Vianney, Cure of Ars, 1949
715 Castle Hill Ave., Bronx, NY 10473

Baptisms and Marriages, 1949
(718) 863-4411 b244@archny.org

68. Church of St. Francis of Assisi, 1949
4343 Baychester Ave., Bronx, NY 10466

Baptisms and Marriages, 1949
(718) 324-5340 b268@archny.org
The parish merged with Church of St. Frances of Rome (no. 21) in 2007 but remains a mission parish.
Office and church records are at Church of St. Frances of Rome.

69. Church of St. Michael, 1969
765 Co-op City Boulevard, Bronx, NY 10475

Baptisms and Marriages, 1969
(718) 671-8057 b267@archny.org

70. Church of St. John Nam, 1989 Korean
3663 White Plains Road, Bronx, NY 10467

Baptisms and Marriages, 1989
(718) 231-2414 b271@archny.org

Staten Island
Archdiocese of New York: 34 active parishes

1. Church of St. Peter, 1839
53 St. Mark's Place, Staten Island, NY 10301

Baptisms and Marriages, 1839
(718) 727-2672 i327@archny.org

2. Church of St. Mary, 1852
1101 Bay St., Staten Island, NY 10305
http://stmaryschurchrosebank.org
Many Italian immigrants moved to this parish in the 1880s and 1890s.

Baptisms, Marriages, and Deaths, 1852
(718) 727-0671 i322@archny.org

3. Church of St. Joseph and St. Thomas, 1855
6097 Amboy Rd, Staten Island, NY 10309
http://sjstparish.org
The parish, a mission from Church of St. Peter's (Manhattan, no. 1) from 1848 to 1855, was originally called Church of St. Joseph.

Baptisms and Marriages, 1855
(718) 984-4572 i320@archny.org

4. Church of St. Patrick, 1862
53 St. Patrick's Place, Staten Island, NY 10306

Baptisms and Marriages, 1862
(718) 979-4227 or (718) 351-0044 i325@archny.org

5. Church of Sacred Heart, 1875
981 Castleton Ave., Staten Island, NY 10310
The parish was previously known as St. Rose of Lima. Its name was changed to Church of Sacred Heart in 1899.

Baptisms, 1875 / Marriages, 1876
(718) 442-0058 i310@archny.org

6. Church of St. Mary of the Assumption, 1877
2230 Richmond Terrace, Staten Island, NY 10302
http://simarycarmel.info

Baptisms, 1854 / Marriages, 1877
(718) 442-6372 i323@archny.org

7. Church of the Immaculate Conception, 1887 Irish and German
128 Targee St., Staten Island, NY 10304

Baptisms and Marriages, 1877
(718) 447-2165 i303@archny.org

8. Church of Our Lady Help of Christians, 1890
7396 Amboy Road, Staten Island, NY 10307
www.olhcparish.org
Before the parish was founded, Catholics residing in Tottenville attended the Church of St. Joseph and St. Thomas at Rosville (no. 3).

Baptisms and Marriages, 1898
(718) 317-9772 i305@archny.org

*9. Church of St. Joachim and St. Anne, 1891
This parish is closed, probably in 1977. A fire completely destroyed the church in 1973.

Baptisms and Marriages, 1891

10. Church of Our Lady of Good Counsel, 1899
Ten Austin Place, Staten Island, NY 10304
www.ologc.catholicweb.com

Baptisms and Marriages, 1899
(718) 447-1503 i304@archny.org

11. Church of St. Adalbert, 1901 Polish
337 Morningstar Road, Staten Island, NY 10303

Baptisms, Marriages, and Deaths, 1901
(718) 442-8476 i311@archny.org

12. Church of St. John Baptist de la Salle, 1901 German
128 Targee St., Staten Island, NY 10304

Baptisms and Marriages, 1900
(718) 447-2165 i318@archny.org

13. Church of St. Joseph, 1902 Italian
171 St. Mary's Ave., Staten Island, NY 10305

Baptisms and Marriages, 1902
(718) 816-0047 i319@archny.org

14. Church of St. Anthony of Padua, 1910
24 Shelly Ave., Staten Island, NY 10314

Baptisms, Marriages, and Deaths, 1908
(718) 761-6660 i313@archny.org

15. Church of the Blessed Sacrament, 1910
30 Manor Road, Staten Island, NY 10310
www.blessedsacramentchurchsi.com

Baptisms, Marriages, and Deaths, 1910
(718) 442-1581 i301@archny.org

This parish was created out of Sacred Heart (no. 5) and St. Mary's (no. 2). It merged with Church of Our Lady of Mount Carmel (no. 17) in the 1930s, but they were separated again in 1949.

**16. Church of St. Clement, 1910 (now called Church of St. Clement–St. Michael; see no. 36)
Baptisms, Marriages, and Deaths, 1910
Church of St. Clement merged with Church of St. Michael (no. 25) in 1945. The Church is located at 126 Van Pelt Ave.

**17. Church of Our Lady of Mount Carmel, 1913 Italian (now called Church of Our Lady of Mount Carmel–St. Benedicta, see no. 37)
Baptisms and Marriages, 1913
Church of Our Lady of Mount Carmel merged with Church of the Blessed Sacrament (no. 15) in 1936 and was a mission parish before the two again became separate parishes in 1949. In 1957 Church of Our Lady of Mount Carmel and Church of St. Benedicta (no. 30) merged.

18. Church of St. Ann, 1914
101 Cromwell Ave., Staten Island, NY 10304

Baptisms and Marriages, 1914
(718) 351-0270 i312@archny.org

19. Church of Our Lady Star of the Sea, 1916
5371 Amboy Road, Staten Island, NY 10312
http://olssparish.org

Baptisms and Marriages, 1916
(718) 984-0593 i309@archny.org

20. Church of St. Rita, 1921
281 Bradley Ave., Staten Island, NY 10314
www.churchofstrita.com

Baptisms, Marriages, and Deaths, 1921
(718) 698-3746 i328@archny.org

21. Church of St. Sylvester, 1921
854 Targee St., Staten Island, NY 10304

Baptisms, Marriages, and Deaths, 1921
(718) 727-4639/89 i331@archny.org

22. Church of St. Clare, 1921
110 Nelson Ave., Staten Island, NY 10308
www.stclaresi.com

Baptisms and Marriages, 1924
(718) 984-7873 i316@archny.org

23. Church of Our Lady Queen of Peace, 1922
90 Third St., Staten Island, NY 10306

Baptisms and Marriages, 1922
(718) 351-1093 i307@archny.org

24. Church of St. Roch, 1922
602 Richmond Ave., Staten Island, NY 10302

Baptisms and Marriages, 1922
(718) 442-4755 i329@archny.org

**25. Church of St. Michael, 1922 (now called Church of St. Clement–St. Michael; see no. 36)
Baptisms, Marriages, and Deaths, 1922
Church of St. Michael merged with Church of St. Clement (no. 16) in 1945. The church is located at 211 Harbor Road.

**26. Church of the Assumption, 1922 (now called Church of the Assumption–St. Paul; see no. 42)
Baptisms, Marriages, and Deaths, 1921
The parish was created out of Church of Our Lady of Mount Carmel (no. 17). The Church of the Assumption merged with Church of St. Paul parish (no. 27) in 2007.

**27. Church of St. Paul, 1923 (now called Church of the Assumption–St. Paul; see no. 42)
Baptisms and Marriages, 1923
Church of St. Paul merged with Church of the Assumption (no. 26) in 2007.

28. Church of Our Lady of Pity, 1923   Baptisms and Marriages, 1923
1616 Richmond Ave., Staten Island, NY 10314   (718) 761-5421 i308@archny.org

29. Church of St. Stanislaus Kostka, 1923   Baptisms, Marriages, and Deaths, 1923
109 York Ave., Staten Island, NY 10301   (718) 447-3937 i330@archny.org
www.stkostka.org

**30. Church of St. Benedicta, 1924 (now called Church of Our Lady of Mount Carmel–St. Benedicta; see no. 37)
Baptisms, Marriages, and Deaths, 1925
Church of St. Benedicta merged with Church of Our Lady of Mount Carmel (no. 15) in 1957. St. Benedicta was a mission from Church of Our Lady of Mount Carmel from 1922 to 1924.

31. Church of St. Margaret Mary, 1926   Baptisms, Marriages, and Deaths, 1926
560 Lincoln Ave., Staten Island, NY 10306   (718) 351-2612 i321@archny.org

32. Church of St. Teresa, 1926   Baptisms, 1925 / Marriages, 1926
1634 Victory Boulevard, Staten Island, NY 10314   (718) 442-5412 i332@archny.org
www.saintteresasi.org

33. Church of St. Christopher, 1926   Baptisms and Marriages, 1926
130 Midland Ave., Staten Island, NY 10306   (718) 351-2452 i315@archny.org

34. Church of the Holy Rosary, 1927   Baptisms, Marriages, and Deaths, 1927
80 Jerome Ave., Staten Island, NY 10305   (718) 727-3360 i302@archny.org
www.hrosarychurch.com

**35. Church of Christ the King, 1928   Baptisms and Marriages, 1928
This is now a mission church from Church of St. Mary of the Assumption (no. 7). Church of Christ the King is located at 180 Park Ave in Port Richmond.

36. Church of St. Clement–St. Michael, 1945
207 Harbor Road, Staten Island, NY 10303   (718) 442-1688 i324@archny.org
Church of St. Clement (no. 16) merged with Church of St. Michael (no. 25) in 1945.

37. Church of Our Lady of Mount Carmel–St. Benedicta, 1957
1265 Castleton Ave., Staten Island, NY 10310   (718) 442-3411 i306@archny.org
http://simarycarmel.info
Church of Our Lady of Mount Carmel (no. 15) and Church of St. Benedicta (no. 30) merged in 1957.

38. Church of St. Charles Borromeo, 1960   Baptisms and Marriages, 1960
644 Clawson St., Staten Island, NY 10306   (718) 987-2670 or 7950 i314@archny.org

39. Church of the Holy Child, 1966   Baptisms and Marriages, 1966
4747 Amboy Road, Staten Island, NY 10312   (718) 356-5890 i333@archny.org

40. Church of the Holy Family, 1966   Baptisms and Marriages, 1966
366 Watchogue Road, Staten Island, NY 10314   (718) 761-6663 i334@archny.org
www.holyfamily-staten-island.4lpi.com

41. Church of St. John Neumann, 1982   Baptisms and Marriages, 1982
1380 Arthur Kill Road, Staten Island, NY 10312   (718) 984-8535 SJNeumann@archny.org

42. Church of the Assumption–St. Paul, 2007
145 Clinton Ave., Staten Island, NY 10301   (718) 727-4594 i300@archny.org
www.assumption-stpaul.org
Church of the Assumption (no. 26) merged with Church of St. Paul (no. 27) in 2007.

9 Cemeteries

The early history of Catholic cemeteries in New York City is tied to the building of the first churches. When land was purchased for the first Catholic church, St. Peter's in 1785, the area around the boundaries of the plot was used for burials. Before this, the few Catholics who died in Manhattan were usually buried in the Episcopal Trinity Church graveyard. Those who were less fortunate were buried in one of the public graveyards or potter's fields.

The next plot of land purchased by the Catholic Church for burials was at Mott St. on the grounds of Old St. Patrick's Cathedral in 1801, where the first cathedral was built between 1809 and 1815. Despite the cemetery opening at the beginning of the 19th century, interments were not officially recorded until 25 May 1813. Old St. Patrick's cemetery closed in 1833, with the total number of burials standing at 32,153.[116]

The growing Catholic population in New York City led to a pressing need for a larger cemetery. Land was identified in the current-day East Village, bordered by First Ave., Avenue, A, East 11th and 12th streets. This cemetery, known as the 11th Street cemetery, was used until August 1848; the total number of interments was 41,016.[117] This was the last Catholic cemetery founded in Manhattan as the 1847 Rural Cemetery Act prohibited the building of new cemeteries on the island. In 1909, between 3000 and 5000 bodies were reinterred in Calvary Cemetery. Unfortunately, no records were kept when the reburials occurred, and the identities of the deceased are not known.

Catholic cemeteries were founded on the open lands of the other boroughs, beginning in the 1820s in Brooklyn and the 1840s elsewhere. In Brooklyn, burials in the grounds of St. James Cathedral Basilica began in 1823. The first Catholic cemeteries in the other boroughs were Our Lady of Mount Carmel in Queens in 1841, Old St. Raymond's in the Bronx c.1845, and St. Peter's in Staten Island in 1848. Before then, as occurred in Manhattan, members of the small Catholic population were buried in an Episcopal or public cemetery, or potter's field. While these and other cemeteries grew in size and number of interments, the largest Catholic cemetery in New York City, Calvary in Queens, opened in 1848. It is now the largest cemetery in the United States.

To date there have been over three million interments in Calvary. The cemetery is divided into four sections. First Calvary, or St. Calixtus division, sold burial plots until 1867, Second Calvary, or St. Agnes division, until 1888; Third Calvary, or St. Sebastian division, until 1900. Fourth Calvary, or St. Domitilla division, is still selling plots. It is important to remember that interments took taken place in each section for many years and decades after plots were no longer sold.

Don't discount areas outside the five boroughs in your search for the burial places of those who lived and died in New York City. Before the bridges and tunnels that link Manhattan to the rest of the city were built, it was almost the same distance to New Jersey by ferry as it was to Queens or Brooklyn. Therefore, burials in cemeteries in Jersey City, Bayonne, and Newark should not be overlooked, especially if your ancestors lived on the west side of Manhattan. One example is the New York Bay Cemetery in Jersey City. Your ancestors may also have lived outside the five boroughs, in places such as Westchester County or on Long Island, before moving to the city and dying there. There could have been a family cemetery plot, or special affinity with, an area outside the city, and so burials may have taken place there.

There are two types of cemetery records that are valuable to the genealogist: interment lists that give details of each person buried in a grave, and information engraved on the headstone. The list and the headstone provide overlapping but not identical information, so it is important to try obtain both. For example, an interment list from Calvary invariably gives Ireland as a place of birth, but the headstones might provide the actual county or parish. Also, the interment list often includes names of people who are not memorialized on the headstone.

There are many websites dedicated to information transcribed from headstones, as well as digital photographs of the monuments. The three biggest are Interment (www.interment.net), Find-a-Grave (www.findagrave.com), and Billion Graves (www.billiongraves.com). Along with these three, there are many other smaller websites and webpages that provide headstone information and digital images. Chapter 6, Sources for the Place of Origin in Ireland gives details about publications of New York City cemetery headstone transcriptions that give a place of birth/origin in Ireland.

In the rest of this chapter you will find the names of all the Catholic cemeteries known to have existed in New York City. They are arranged by the date from which they began accepting burials. This will help genealogists trying to work out which cemeteries existed when their ancestor died. A separate section provides information about public, nondenominational, and institutional cemeteries.[118]

Conflicting dates are given for the beginning of interments in some of the cemeteries. Every effort has been made here to present the correct dates.

Catholic Cemeteries
Manhattan
St. Peter's Roman Catholic Churchyard
1785–1836
16 Barclay St., New York, NY 10007.
(212) 233-8355
See the introductory paragraphs of this chapter for more information. For more information, write to Saint Peter's Rectory, at the preceding address.

Old St. Patrick's
1801–1833
See the introductory paragraphs of this chapter for more information. An 1866 fire destroyed many church and burial records, but Calvary Cemetery in Queens has the surviving burial records. In January 2013 cremation interments began at this cemetery.
http://oldcathedral.org/cemetery

St. Patrick and St. Peter
In 1828 land was bought at a site that today is bounded by 49th and 50th streets and Park and 5th avenues. A cemetery was to be located here; however, the ground was too rocky for burials and was never used for this purpose. In 1842, a church was erected on this site but it was later demolished. The present-day St. Patrick's Cathedral was built here.

11th Street Cemetery
1833–1848
See the introductory paragraphs of this chapter for more information.

Seventh Ave. between West 123rd and 124th streets
A Catholic cemetery is believed to have been at this location, but no further information is available.

Brooklyn

St. James Cathedral Basilica Churchyard
1823–1849
Located at St. James Cathedral Basilica, 240 Jay St., Brooklyn, NY 11201
(718) 852-4002
About a thousand people were buried in this cemetery. Burial records are kept at St. John's Cemetery, 80-01 Metropolitan Ave., Flushing, NY 11379. The number for St. John's Cemetery is (718) 894-4888.

St. Mary's Churchyard
1837–c.1850
The cemetery was located at North 8th St. and Kent Ave., Brooklyn. The property was sold in 1890, and the bodies were reinterred in St. John's Cemetery. Burial records are kept at St. John's Cemetery, 80-01 Metropolitan Ave., Flushing, NY 11379. The number for St. John's Cemetery is (718) 894-4888.

Holy Cross
1849–Present
3620 Tilden Ave., Brooklyn, NY 11203
(718) 284-4520
Burials records are available at the cemetery.

Most Holy Trinity
1851–Present
675 Central Avenue, Brooklyn, NY 11207
(718) 894-4888
This cemetery has traditionally been for German immigrants and their descendants. Burial records are kept at St. John's Cemetery, 80-01 Metropolitan Ave., Flushing, NY 11379. The number for St. John's Cemetery is (718) 894-4888.

St. Charles
A Catholic cemetery is believed to have been in the area of St. Charles Borromeo church, but no further information is known.

Queens

Our Lady of Mount Carmel
1841–1926
21st St. and 26th Ave., Astoria, NY 11102
This cemetery is sometimes referred to as the Famine Cemetery because burials from 1850 to 1880 were exclusively Irish. Burial records are kept at St. John's Cemetery, 80-01 Metropolitan Ave., Flushing, NY 11379. The number for St. John's Cemetery is (718) 894-4888. For headstone transcriptions, images, and more information, see www.pefagan.com/gen/astoria/mtcarm/mtcframe.htm. See the "Headstone Transcriptions" section in Chapter 6 for more information about records for this cemetery.

Calvary
1848–Present
49-01 Laurel Hills Blvd., Woodside, NY 11377
(718) 786-8000
See the introductory paragraphs of this chapter for more information. Burials records are available at the cemetery.
www.calvarycemeteryqueens.com

St. Fidelis
1856–1894
The cemetery was located at 124th St. between 14th and 15th avenues, Flushing, NY 11316.
(718) 445-6164
For more information contact the St. Fidelis Parish, 123-06 14th Ave., Flushing, NY 11316 (Queens, no.5 in Chapter 8).

St. John
1880–Present
80-01 Metropolitan Ave., Middle Village, NY 11379
(718) 894-4888
Burial records are available at the cemetery.

Mount St. Mary
1900–Present
172-02 Booth Memorial Ave., Flushing, NY 11365
(718) 353-1560
Burial records are kept at St. John's Cemetery, 80-01 Metropolitan Ave., Flushing, NY 11379. The number for St. John's Cemetery is (718) 894-4888.

St. Monica
c.1901–1910
The cemetery was located at 160th St. and Liberty Ave., Jamaica, NY 11433.
Burial records are kept at St. John's Cemetery, 80-01 Metropolitan Ave., Flushing, NY 11379. The number for St. John's Cemetery is (718) 894-4888.

Bronx
Old St. Raymond
1842–1875
1759 Castle Hill Avenue, Bronx, NY 10462
(718) 792-4044
For more information, write to St. Raymond's Church (Bronx, no. 1 in Chapter 8) at the preceding address.

Fordham University Chapel Cemetery
1848–1909
Fordham University, Rose Hill Campus, 441 East Fordham Rd., Bronx, NY 10458
(718) 817-3560
This burial place contains the remains of about 150 Jesuit priests who worked at the university.

St. Augustine
1850–c.1865
This cemetery was in Morrisania on East 170th St. In 1865 the city built a street through the cemetery, and the deceased were reinterred at Old St. Raymond's Cemetery. For more information write to St. Raymond's Church, 1759 Castle Hill Avenue, Bronx, NY 10462 (Bronx, no. 1 in Chapter 8).

Mount St. Vincent
c.1856–1956
College of Mount Saint Vincent, 6301 Riverdale Ave., Bronx, NY 10471
(718) 549-8000
The cemetery contains the remains of 150 nuns from the Sisters of Charity of Mount Saint Vincent.

St. Raymond's (New)
1875–Present
1201 Balcom Ave., Bronx, NY 10462
(718) 792-1133
The cemetery is divided in two by a highway. Burial records are available at the cemetery; write to 2600 Lafayette Ave, Bronx NY 10465.

Staten Island
St Peter
1848–Present
893 Clove Rd., Staten Island, NY 10301
(718) 442-2363
Burial records are available at the cemetery; mailing address is 52 Tyler Avenue, Staten Island, NY 10310.

St. Mary of the Assumption
1854–Present
160 Walker St., Staten Island, NY 10302
(718) 442-6372
For more information, write to St. Mary of the Assumption Church, 2230 Richmond Terrace, Staten Island, NY 10302 (Staten Island, no. 6 in Chapter 8).

St. Joseph
1860–1934
The cemetery is located at Barry St.
For more information write to Church of Saint Joseph and Thomas, 6135 Amboy Road, Staten Island, NY 10309 (Staten Island, no. 3 in Chapter 8). The contact number is (718) 984-4572.

St. Mary / Mount St. Mary
1862–Present
155 Parkinson's Ave., Staten Island, NY 10305
(718) 447-0598
Burial records are available at the cemetery.

Mount Loreto Home Cemetery
c.1880–1910
Mission of the Immaculate Virgin, 6581 Hylan Blvd., Staten Island, NY 10309
(718) 984-1500
This burial ground is part of an institution that was founded to take in homeless and disabled children. Children were buried here if no relative came forward to claim the remains.

Polish National Catholic Cemetery
1904–Present
50 Willowbrook Rd., Staten Island, NY 10302
(201) 858-4320
This cemetery is owned by Heart of Jesus Polish National Catholic Church in Bayonne, New Jersey.

Resurrection
1979–Present
361 Sharonton Rd., Staten Island, NY 10309
(718) 356-7738
Burials records are available at the cemetery.

St. Michael's Home
Years unknown
419 Woodrow Rd., Staten Island, NY 10312
(718) 356-2121
This is a private cemetery used by the Presentation Sisters. For more information, write to Presentation Sisters, 419 Woodrow Rd., Staten Island, NY 10312.

Further Information
For further information about any Roman Catholic cemetery, you can contact the relevant diocesan authorities, as follows.

Archdiocese of New York–Calvary and Allied Cemeteries
Contact: George Borrero
1011 First Ave., 17th Floor, New York, NY 10022
(212) 371-1011, ext. 2789
www.archny.org/departments/?i=856
George.Borrero@archny.org

Diocese of Brooklyn–Diocesan Offices
310 Prospect Park West
Brooklyn, NY 11215
(718) 965-7300
http://dioceseofbrooklyn.org

Public, Nondenominational, and Institutional
Most Catholic Irish were buried in one of the city's Catholic cemeteries. However, it is possible some were buried in public, nondenominational, or institutional cemeteries because, for example, there was no Catholic cemetery nearby, or they died destitute. Catholics were sometimes buried in individual consecrated graves within these cemeteries. With this in mind, this section presents a list of public, nondenominational, and institutional cemeteries. They are arranged in chronological order by year of first interment.

Madison Square Cemetery–Manhattan
1794–1797, public
This cemetery was located on the site of the current Madison Square Park in Manhattan. It was used to bury those who died at Bellevue Hospital and the city almshouse. No known records exist.

Tompkinsville Quarantine Hospital Cemetery–Staten Island
1799–1858, institutional
This cemetery was used for those who died of infectious diseases in the quarantine hospitals. Many Famine Irish were treated here, died, and were buried. No known records exist. The bodies were removed to Silver Mount Cemetery sometime in the second half of the 19th century after the hospitals were burned down by locals in 1858. A list of those who died between 1 June 1849 and 31 May 1850 was published in the *Newsletter of Friends of Abandoned Cemeteries of Staten Island* (Vol. 15, Issue 3, Fall 1998). For more information on the Famine Irish buried here, see: McPartland, Kevin. "The Forgotten Burial Ground." *New York Irish History*. Vol. 18. 2009. pp. 49–53.

Bryant Park Cemetery–Manhattan
1823–1840, public
This cemetery was located between 40th and 42nd streets and Fifth and Sixth avenues. This land is now occupied by Bryant Park and the New York Public Library. The cemetery was used as a public burial ground for the city. The remains of the deceased were most likely moved to Wards Island after the burial site was decommissioned. No known records exist.

Wallabout Cemetery–Brooklyn
1825–1857, public
This cemetery was located at North Portland Ave. between Auburn Pl. and Park Ave. It was the public cemetery for the town of Brooklyn, and all churches, including Catholic ones, buried their dead here. The Catholics were removed to Holy Cross Cemetery when Wallabout closed.

Brooklyn Village Cemetery–Brooklyn
1830s, public
This cemetery was located on Boerum Pl., between Schermerhorn St. and Livingston St. It is now a store. The Brooklyn Historical Society has transcriptions of headstones from the cemetery. For more information, write to the Brooklyn Historical Society. See the "Institutions" section in Chapter 1 for contact details.

Flatland Town Cemetery–Brooklyn
c.1832–c.1902, public
This cemetery was located on Avenue J between Remsen Ave. and East 92nd St. The area now makes up four commercial city blocks. Headstone transcriptions can be found in: Eardley, William Appleby. *Cemeteries in Kings and Queens Counties, Long Island, New York: 1793 to 1902*. New York, NY: Self-published. 1916.

Fiftieth Street Cemetery–Manhattan
1836–1843, public
This cemetery was located between 49th and 50th streets and Third and Park avenues. Over 100,000 bodies were moved to the Wards Island public cemetery in 1858. No known records exist.

Green-wood Cemetery–Brooklyn
1840–Present, nonsectarian
Green-wood's website has a search facility for almost all burials, and all burial records are available at the cemetery.
500 25th St., Brooklyn, NY 11232
(718) 768–7300
www.green–wood.com
info@greenwoodcemetery.org

Forty-fifth Street Cemetery–Manhattan
1845–1851, public
This cemetery was located on the north side of West 45th St. between 10th and 11th avenues. It might have been used to bury those who died at Bellevue Hospital. No known records exist.

Morrisania Cemetery–Bronx
1848–1868, public
This cemetery was once the Morrisania town burial ground. It was located in St. Mary's Park where St. Mary's Ave. and 149th St. intersect in the Mott Haven area of the Bronx. When it closed, remains were moved to Woodlawn Cemetery and Green–wood Cemetery.

Cypress Hills Cemetery–Brooklyn
1848–Present, nonsectarian
Burial records are available at the cemetery.
833 Jamaica Ave,, Brooklyn, NY 11208
(718) 277–2900
http://cypresshillscemetery.net

Cemetery of the Evergreens–Brooklyn
1851–Present, nonsectarian
This cemetery has over 100,000 burials, with many transferred from various cemeteries in Manhattan. Burial records are available at the cemetery.
1629 Bushwick Ave., Brooklyn, NY 11207
(718) 455–5300
www.theevergreenscemetery.com
info@theevergreenscemetery.com

Wards Island Cemetery
1852–c.1880, public
This cemetery was located on Wards Island, which is in the East River, between Manhattan, Bronx and Queens. Many burials would have come from the city's almshouses. The cemetery received 100,000 bodies when the Fiftieth Street Cemetery closed. Wards Island is now part of Randall's Island as the two were merged in the 1930s. No known records exist.

Flushing Cemetery–Queens
1853–Current, nonsectarian
Burial records are available at the cemetery.
163–06 46th Ave., Flushing, NY 11358
(718) 359–0100
www.flushingcemetery.com

Woodlawn Cemetery–Bronx
1865–Present, public
Burial records are available at the cemetery.
Webster Ave. and East 233rd St., Bronx, NY 10470
(718) 920–0500 or toll-free (877) 496–6352
www.thewoodlawncemetery.org
research@thewoodlawncemetery.org

Hart Island Cemetery
1869–Present, public
This cemetery, in Long Island Sound, used to bury those who died in city almshouses and bodies that were unidentified. It was known as City Cemetery in the 19th and 20th centuries. Today, it is the largest potter's field in the United States. Some of the records are located at the Municipal Archives. See Chapter 3, Underutilized Records for more information.
Hart Island is located in Long Island Sound
http://hartisland.net

Silver Mount Cemetery–Staten Island
c.1875–Present, nonsectarian
Burial records from 1900 onwards are available at the cemetery. Records for burials before 1900 no longer exist.
918 Victory Blvd., Staten Island, NY 10301
(718) 727–7020

Woodland Cemetery–Staten Island
c.1875–Present, public
Burial records are available at the cemetery.
982 Victory Blvd., Staten Island, NY 10301
(718) 727–0222

Maple Grove Cemetery–Queens
1875–Present, nonsectarian
Burial records are available at the cemetery.
127–15 Kew Gardens Rd., PO Box 150086, Kew Gardens, NY 11415
(718) 544–3600
www.maplegrove.biz
info@maplegrovecenter.org

Canarsie Cemetery–Brooklyn
1888–Present, nonsectarian
Burial records are available at the cemetery. Originally used by the town of Flatlands, the cemetery is now owned and operated by Cypress Hills Cemetery.
1370 Remsen Ave., Brooklyn, NY 11236
(718)251–6934
For more information, write to Canarsie Cemetery Administration Office at the preceding address.
http://canarsiecemetery.homestead.com

Fairview Cemetery–Staten Island
c.1889–Present, nonsectarian
Burial records are available at the cemetery.
1852 Victory Blvd., Staten Island, NY 10314
(718) 448–9140

10 Periodicals

Periodicals are a source that is often overlooked by those conducting family history research. However, genealogical periodicals have existed since the mid-19th century in the United States, and historical publications go back even further. As a result, they can be a valuable resource for information about ancestors, specific areas, or Irish immigration and settlement in the United States. They can also help researchers learn more about genealogical methodologies, case studies, and little-known or complex record sources.

In this chapter you will find almost five hundred articles in sixteen periodicals relevant to Irish genealogical research in New York City and its environs. The vast majority of these articles are to be found in PERSI, the Periodical Source Index. The others come from the respective periodical websites, where available; the index provides the most recent article titles. All of the periodicals are, or have been, published in the United States, Ireland, and Northern Ireland.

PERSI, which is maintained by the Allen County Public Library in Fort Wayne, Indiana, contains almost two million citations from over 6500 genealogy and history periodicals. One of the services the library provides is to photocopy any article in PERSI that a researcher is interested in. You can find more about this service and the library at www.genealogycenter.org. The titles indexed in PERSI do not correspond exactly to the titles in the periodicals. Some words are abbreviated and geographic locations and time periods are sometimes added to provide clarify what the article is about. Despite this, finding an article is a simple process.

Articles in this chapter are arranged alphabetically by surname, part of New York City (e.g., Harlem, Brooklyn), or keyword, such as migration, Catholic Church, and policemen. Some of the articles overlap with other locations and so will also be relevant to places outside New York City. Many of the articles are concerned with Irish immigration before the Famine, biographies of prominent Irishmen in early America, early 20th-century obituaries, and Irish pioneers.

When you find an article of interest in the following list go to "Periodical Abbreviations" in the second section of this chapter to get the full name of the periodical. Then go to the third section, "Periodicals", where you will find full details about the publication. For each periodical the years of publication are listed. You can get a copy of any article in this list from the Allen County Public Library or other libraries if listed in the "Periodicals" section.

Periodical Index

Keyword	Article Title	Periodical
Abolitionists	American Irish abolitionists, 1830–60	NYIH Vol. 11 (1997)
Adams	Samuel Adams, New Brunswick and NY	JAIHS Vol. 27 (1928)
Ambrose–Doyle	David Ambrose Doyle, NY	JAIHS Vol. 12 (1913)
Bannin	Michael E. Bannin, NY	JAIHS Vol. 12 (1913)
Barry	John E. Barry (Rev.), 1836–1900, NY	JAIHS Vol. 4 (1904)
Benevolent	St. John's/Benevolent Irish society	JAIHS Vol. 28 (1930)
Bennett	William Bennett, 1860–1931, NY	JAIHS Vol. 30 (1930)
Biggane	Martin L. Biggane, NY	JAIHS Vol. 25 (1926)
Bourke	William Bourke Cockran, NY	JAIHS Vol. 23 (1924)
Boyel	Michael Boyel, NY	JAIHS Vol. 16 Is.2 (1917)
Boyles	Boyles–Goldsmith–Rawlings fam., MO, NY	IAG Issue 7 (1976)
Boyton	Paul Boyton bio., 1848–1924, Ire., NY	IR Issue 2 (2002)

Brady	Daniel M. Brady, NY	JAIHS Vol. 25 (1926)
	Jas. B. "Diamond Jim" Brady bio., 1856–1917, NY	IR Issue 2 (2002)
	Nicholas F. Brady, NY	JAIHS Vol. 29 (1931)
	Peter J. Brady, 1881–1931, NY	JAIHS Vol. 30 (1932)
Brann	Henry A. Brann (Rev.), NY	JAIHS Vol. 28 (1930)
Brennan	Michael Brennan, 1832–1905, NY	JAIHS Vol. 5 (1905)
Briggs	Francis, Wm. and Joseph Briggs, Ire., NY	NYIH Vol. 9 (1995)
Britt	John Gabriel Britt, NY	JAIHS Vol. 14 (1915)
	Philip J. Britt, NY	JAIHS Vol. 30 (1932)
Brooklyn	Brooklyn area map, 1894	TIHA Vol. 3, Is. 4 (1995)
	Brooklyn families, index, n.d.	IFHFN Vol. 10,Is.3(2001)
Burke	John H. Burke, NY	JAIHS Vol. 15 (1916)
Burns	George Henry Burns, 1868–1931, NY	JAIHS Vol. 30 (1932)
	James Burns (Capt.), Long Island Railroad	JAIHS Vol. 21 (1922)
	Michael F. Burns, NY	JAIHS Vol. 23 (1924)
Burr	William P. Burr, NY	JAIHS Vol. 29 (1931)
Butler	John Paul Butler, NY	JAIHS Vol. 17 (1918)
	Thomas Vincent Butler, NY	JAIHS Vol. 13 (1914)
Byrne	James J. Byrne, NY	JAIHS Vol. 29 (1931)
	Thomas F. Byrne, 1866–1911, NY	JAIHS Vol. 11 (1912)
Cahill	James Cahill, police officer, d. 1854, NY	NYIH Vol. 15 (2001)
	John H. Cahill, NY	JAIHS Vol. 16,Is.3 (1917)
Caldwell	John Caldwell, Irishman exiled to NY	NYIH Vol. 13 (1999)
Carroll	Carroll's in old New York	JAIHS Vol. 26 (1927)
Casey	John J. Casey, NY	JAIHS Vol. 29 (1931)
Cassidy	Charles A. Cassidy (Rev.), NY	JAIHS Vol. 29 (1931)
Catholic Church	Nursing sisters of New York City	NYIH Vol. 13 (1999)
	Franciscan brothers in Ire. and Brooklyn, 1426+	NYIH Vol. 14 (2000)
	Franciscan brothers in Ire. and Brooklyn, 1829+	NYIH Vol. 14 (2000)
	Saint Francis Academy and others, 1849+	NYIH Vol. 14 (2000)
	Manhattan Catholic church maps	IFHFN Vol. 6, Is.1 (1996)
	Roman Catholic parishes in Manhattan	IFHFN Vol. 6, Is.1 (1996)
	Brooklyn Roman Catholic parishes	IFHFN Vol. 6, Is.4 (1996)
	Roman Catholic parishes in Queens, list and map	IFHFN Vol. 8, Is.1 (1998)
	Roman Catholic parishes in Bronx, list and map	IFHFN Vol. 8, Is.4 (1999)
	Roman Catholic parishes of Staten Island	IFHFN Vol. 8, Is.6 (1999)
	De La Salle Christian brothers in NY, 1848–1914	NYIH Vol. 7 (1992)
Cemetery	The Irish in old New York—The Irish dead in Trinity and St. Paul's Churchyards	JAIHS Vol. 25 (1926)
	Catholic Cemeteries in NYC overview	TIHA Vol. 3, Is. 2 (1995)
	A Bit of New York History	JAIHS Vol. 7 (1907)
	Irish gravesites in New York	NYIH Vol. 2, Is. 1 (1987)
	Cemetery of the Holy Cross history, Brooklyn	NYIH Vol. 6 (1991)
	Saint Raymond's Cemetery, Bronx	NYIH Vol. 7 (1992)
	Tompkinsville Quarantine and its forgotten burial ground of Irish immigrants, 1799–1858	NYIH Vol. 18 (2004)
	Cemetery of the Holy Road, sel. Irish stones	IFHFN Vol. 5, Is.7 (1996)
	Location of Riker cem., Astoria	IFHFN Vol. 9, Is.1 (2000)
	Green–wood Cemetery history, 1838+	IFHFN Vol.17,Is.3 (2007)
	Holy Cross cemetery, Brooklyn, Irish–born, note	DIFHR Issue 17 (1994)

Cemetery, Calvary	Calvary Cemetery: some research strategies	TIHA Vol. 3, Iss.3 (1995)
	Calvary Cemetery, NYC	TS Vol. 15, No.1 (1994)
	Calvary Cemetery, Woodside, NY	TS Vol. 16, No.1 (1995)
	Calvary Cemetery, Woodside, NY	TS Vol. 16, No.2 (1995)
	Calvary cemetery history, Long Island	NYIH Vol. 11 (1997)
	Old Calvary cemetery note	IFHFN Vol.3, Is.10(1994)
Census	State census records overview, 1855–1925	TIHA Vol. 3, Iss.3 (1995)
Clark	Eugene P. Clark, 1871–1931, NY	JAIHS Vol. 30 (1932)
Clarke	Joseph I. C. Clarke, NY	JAIHS Vol. 24 (1925)
Cline	Maggie Cline bio., 1857–1934, MA, NY	IR Issue 2 (2002)
Clinton	Clinton, famous Irish family in NY	JAIHS Vol. 28 (1930)
Cochrane	John Cochrane (Gen.), d. 1897, NY	JAIHS Vol. 2 (1899)
Cohalan	Michael J. Cohalan, NY	JAIHS Vol. 25 (1926)
Coleman	James S. Coleman, d. 1906, NY	JAIHS Vol. 6 (1906)
Collins	John Collins, granary foreman, d. 1913, NY	IFHFN Vol. 7, Is.4 (1998)
Colton	Charles H. Colton (Rev.), NY	JAIHS Vol. 14 (1915)
Conley	Louis D. Conley, NY	JAIHS Vol. 29 (1931)
Connor	Francis Connor, NY	JAIHS Vol. 28 (1930)
Cork	County Cork Association history	NYIH Vol. 3 (1988)
Cornbury	Lord Cornbury, NY governor & transvestite, 1702+	IFH Vol. 16 (2000)
Corr	John J. Corr, NY, 1865–1923	JAIHS Vol. 23 (1924)
Coughlin	John H. Coughlin (Dr.), NY	JAIHS Vol. 29 (1931)
Cox–Brady	James Cox Brady, NY	JAIHS Vol. 26 (1927)
Coyle	John G. Coyle (Dr.), 1868–1931, NY	JAIHS Vol. 30 (1932)
Crimmins	Clarence P. Crimmins, 1888–1931, NY	JAIHS Vol. 30 (1932)
Crimmons	Cyril Crimmons, NY	JAIHS Vol. 28 (1930)
Culleton–Henry	Agnes Patricia Culleton Henry family piano, a family	
	history artifact, b. 1873, NY	IFHFN Vol.15,Is.5 (2005)
Cunnion	James J. Cunnion, NY	JAIHS Vol. 29 (1931)
Daly	Joseph F. Daly, NY state supreme court justice	JAIHS Vol. 16 Is.2 (1917)
Delaney	John J. Delany, NY	JAIHS Vol. 15 (1916)
de Valera	Eamon de Valera fam., 1882–1932; Ire., NY	IR Issue 1 (2000)
	Vivian de Valera, search for recs., NY	IR Issue 4 (1999)
	Vivian de Valera search continues,	NY IR Issue 2 (2004)
Dillon	Gregory Dillon, EISB's 1st pres., 1782–1854	NYIHRN Fall (2000)
	Luke Dillon, England, PA, NY	JAIHS Vol. 29 (1931)
Donaher	Franklin M. Donaher (Hon.), NY	JAIHS Vol. 20 (1921)
Dongan	Thomas Dongan	JAIHS Vol. 2 (1899)
	Thomas Dongan, colonial governor of NY	JAIHS Vol. 16 Is.1 (1917)
	Dongan (Gov.) and religious liberty, 1683, NY	JAIHS Vol. 28 (1930)
Donnelly	Eugene J. Donnelly (Msgr.), NY	JAIHS Vol. 29 (1931)
	Eugene J. Donnelly (Rev.), NY	JAIHS Vol. 30 (1932)
Dow	C. H. Dow and Wm. D. Jones, Wall Street Journal, NY	ISGB Is. 17 (1997)
Dowling	Bernard Downing (Sen.), NY	JAIHS Vol. 30 (1932)
Doyle	John F. Doyle, 1837–1911, NY	JAIHS Vol. 11 (1912)
Draft Riots	Draft riots, Irish dead, 1863	IFHFN Vol. 4, Is.9 (1995)
	Draft riots of 1863 dead	IFHFN Vol. 5, Is.5 (1996)
	Dead from draft riots, 1863	IFHFN Vol. 5, Is.6 (1996)
	NYC draft riot deaths, list	IFHFN Vol. 6, Is.6 (1997)
	Wounded police officers, draft riots	IFHFN Vol. 6, Is.7 (1997)
Driscoll	John T. Driscoll (Rev.), NY	JAIHS Vol. 15 (1916)

Drum	John Drum (Capt.), 1840–98, NY	JAIHS Vol. 2 (1899)
Duane	James Duane, NY	JAIHS Vol. 16 Is.2 (1917)
	James Duane, mayor of NY, 1784	JAIHS Vol. 32 (1941)
Duffy	Edward L. Duffy (Col.), NY	JAIHS Vol. 26 (1927)
	Chaplain Duffy of 69th regt., NY	JAIHS Vol. 31 (1937)
	Francis Patrick Duffy (Rev.), NY	JAIHS Vol. 31 (1937)
Dunn	John Dunn (Capt.) bio., d. 1863, Ire., NY	IR Issue 2 (2002)
Edwards	James Edwards fam., Ire., NY	IHL Vol. 3, Is. 10 (1990)
Egan	Brigid Egan, Immigrant, 1888, Ire., New York City	NYIHRN Spring (2007)
Ellis Island	Ellis Island, gateway to America	IR Issue 4 (1992)
	Ellis Island database resource	IT Vol. 5, Is. 8 (2001)
Ellsworth	Elmer Ellsworth, first Union casualty of Civil War, biographical notes, 1837–1861, IL, WI, NY, VA	IGQ Vol. 18, Is.1 (2009)
Emigrant Savings Bank	Emigrant Industrial Savings Bank, 1850–2000	NYIHRN Fall (2000)
	Emigrant Savings Bank records	NYIH Vol. 9 (1995)
	Emigrant Savings Bank records note	IFHFN Vol.5,Is.3 (1995)
	Tully McDonnell–Ann Kelly Emigrant Savings Bank records explained, 1849–1856, Ireland, NY	IFHFN Vol.19,Is.2 (2009)
	Emigrant savings bank records	IGQ Vol. 9, Is. 1 (2000)
	Emigrant Industrial Savings Bank depositor index	IR Issue 1 (2002)
	Emigrant Industrial Savings Bank recs., tips	IR Issue 1 (2002)
	Emigrant Industrial Sav. Bank recs., note, 1850+	ISGB Issue 11 (1995)
Emmet	Thomas Addis Emmet, NY	JAIHS Vol. 18 (1919)
	Thos. A. Emmet bio., 1764–1828, NY	NYIHRN Fall (1998)
Emmet–Jennings	Robert Emmet Jennings, NY	JAIHS Vol. 28 (1930)
Eustace	Alexander C. Eustace, NY	JAIHS Vol. 12 (1913)
Exton	Thomas Exton, NY	JAIHS Vol. 16 Is.2 (1917)
Fallon	Joseph P. Fallon, NY	JAIHS Vol. 15 (1916)
Famine	Famine survivors in NY	NYIH Vol. 9 (1995)
Farrell	B. Farrell (Mgr.), NY	JAHS Vol. 29 (1931)
Fearons	George H. Fearons, NY	JAIHS Vol. 29 (1931)
Fermanagh	The Records Speak: Fermanagh Association	NYIH Vol. 4 (1989)
Ferrymen	Pre–Revolutionary ferrymen	JAIHS Vol. 15 (1916)
Firemen	Fires and firemen of old NYC, hist. notes	NYIHRN Fall (2002)
Fitzgerald	James Fitzgerald (Hon.), NY	JAIHS Vol. 23 (1924)
	Thomas and Hannah Fitzgerald, NY	IF Vol. 7, Is. 1 (1991)
	William Fitzgerald, NY	JAIHS Vol. 29 (1931)
	Charles Mansfield, Daniel Fitzpatrick family, NY, 19th C.	IFHFN Vol.14,Is.2 (2004)
Fitzpatrick	Frederick F. Fitzpatrick, NY	JAIHS Vol. 26 (1927)
Fitzsimmons	Owen Oakes–Alice Fitzsimmons family, 1827+, Ire.; NY	IFH Vol. 18 (2002)
Fitzsimons	Thomas P. Fitzsimons, NY	JAIHS Vol. 14 (1915)
Fleming	John C. Fleming (Capt.), 1850–1910, NY	JAIHS Vol. 10 (1911)
Ford	Patrick Ford bio., 1834–1952, Ire.; NY; Chn.	IR Issue 2 (2002)
	Thomas Ford, NY	JAIHS Vol. 28 (1930)
Fraternal	Ancient Order of Hibernians in Greenpoint	NYIH Vol. 10 (1996)
	Society of the Friendly Sons of St. Patrick	JAIHS Vol. 8 (1909)
	County Associations in Irish New York, 1945–1965	NYIH Vol. 22 (2008)
	Emerald Association of Brooklyn	JAIHS Vol. 28 (1930)
Freemen	Irish freemen of NY, list	JAIHS Vol. 17 (1918)
Gaffney	James Gaffney–Mary Quail family research, Kinsella connection, pre–1858+, Ire.; NY	IFH Vol. 21 (2005)

Gallagher	Michael D. Gallagher, 1849–1931, NY	JAIHS Vol. 30 (1932)
	Patrick Gallagher, NY	JAIHS Vol. 27 (1928)
	Thomas Gallagher (Dr.), Ire.; NY	NYIH Vol. 2, Is. 1 (1987)
	Catherine O'Connor O'Neil, James Gallagher, NY	TR Vol. 134, Is. 4 (2003)
Gavan	Joseph W. Gavan obit., 1935, NYC	NYIH Vol. 7 (1992)
Gaynor	Patrick A. Gaynor, NY	JAIHS Vol. 26 (1927)
Gibbons-Huneker	James Gibbons Huneker, NY	JAIHS Vol. 20 (1921)
Gilbert	Maria Gilbert aka Lola Montez, 1818–61, NY	IR Issue 3 (2000)
Gilliland	William Gilliland, Champlain Valley, NY	JAIHS Vol. 14 (1915)
Gilmore	Patrick Gilmore bio., 1829–92, NY	NYIH Vol. 12 (1998)
Gilroy	Thomas F. Gilroy, 1839–1911, NY	JAIHS Vol. 11 (1912)
Gleason	Matthew C. Gleason (Rev.), NY	JAIHS Vol. 26 (1927)
	Last Mayor of Long Island City: Patrick Jerome Gleason	NYIH Vol. 1 (1986)
Glynn	Martin H. Glynn, governor of NY, 1913	JAIHS Vol. 24 (1925)
Godkin	Lawrence Godkin, NY	JAIHS Vol. 28 (1930)
Goff	John W. Goff, NY	JAIHS Vol. 24 (1925)
Grant	Hugh J. Grant (Mayor), 1910, NY	JAIHS Vol. 10 (1911)
Greenpoint (Brklyn)	When Williamsport and Greenpoint were Irish	NYIH Vol. 10 (1996)
Griffin	Patrick Francis Griffin, NY	JAIHS Vol. 15 (1916)
Griffith–Mancini	Pat Griffith Mancini fam., 1841+; Can., NY	IFHFN Vol. 8, Is.5 (1999)
Grogan	Anthony J. Grogan (Rev.), NY; Ireland	JAIHS Vol. 29 (1931)
Halloran	John H. Halloran, NY	JAIHS Vol. 28 (1930)
Hannan	John Hannan, NY	JAIHS Vol. 15 (1916)
Harrington	John C. Harrington (Rev.), NY, MA	JAIHS Vol. 12 (1913)
	Josie Shea–Richard Harrington family info. and photo, m. 1903, MT, NY	IGQ Vol. 17, Is. 3 (2008)
Harlem (M'hattan)	Battle of Harlem Heights	JAIHS Vol. 11 (1912)
	Battle of Harlem Heights, 1776	JAIHS Vol. 10 (1911)
Harris	Charles N. Harris, AL, NY	JAIHS Vol. 28 (1930)
Harson	M. Joseph Harson, NY	JAIHS Vol. 29 (1931)
Haven	Mrs. Mott Haven death notice, 1854, NY	ISGB Vol. 11, Is.4 (2003)
Haynes	Timothy J. Haynes, NY	JAIHS Vol. 25 (1926)
Healy	Edmund J. Healy, NY	JAIHS Vol. 27 (1928)
Heath	Elizabeth Heath, Irish immigrant, 1913, Ireland; NY	NYIH Vol. 15 (2001)
Heeney	Cornelius Heeney, NY	JAIHS Vol. 17 (1918)
Hicks	Michael Hicks, 1832–1905, NY	JAIHS Vol. 5 (1905)
Higgins	Charles M. Higgins, NY	JAIHS Vol. 28 (1930)
	Francis Higgins, NY	JAIHS Vol. 13 (1914)
Highbridge (Bronx)	Crossing Highbridge	NYIH Vol. 7 (1992)
	The best air in the city: Socioeconomics of the Irish in Highbridge, 1920–1960	NYIH Vol. 24 (2010)
Hughes	William F. Hughes (Rev.), NY	JAIHS Vol. 28 (1930)
Hynes	Thomas W. Hynes, NY	JAIHS Vol. 25 (1926)
Immigrant Girls Home	Our Lady of the Rosary Protection of Irish Immigrant Girls ledger found, brief, 1883–1926	NYIHRN Spring (2006)
	Womens employment & Ir. Immig. Girls Home, c.1879+	NYIH Vo. 14 (2000)
	Irish Immigrant Girls Home, c. 1883–1940s	NYIH Vol. 15 (2001)
	Irish Immigrant Girls Home Titanic survivors, 1912	NYIH Vol. 15 (2001)
	Pete Halpin and Irish Immigrant girls, 1906, NY	NYIH Vol. 15 (2001)
Innd	Thomas C. Innd, NY	JAIHS Vol. 14 (1915)
Institutions	New York Soc. for Prevention of Cruelty to Child.	IFHFN Vol.5, Is. 4 (1995)

Jackson	Andrew Jackson Shipman, NY	JAIHS Vol. 15 (1916)
	New York port ship arrivals, 1750–58	JAIHS Vol. 13 (1914)
Jones	C.H. Dow & Wm. D. Jones, Wall St. Journal, NY	ISGB Issue 17 (1997)
Journalism	Distinct Irish in American journalism	JAIHS Vol. 4 (1904)
Joy	Edward Joy, NY	JAIHS Vol. 29 (1931)
Joyce	Henry L. Joyce, NY	JAIHS Vol. 30 (1932)
	John Jay Joyce, 1861–1911, NY	JAIHS Vol. 11 (1912)
Kearny	Philip Kearny (Gen.), NY	JAIHS Vol. 14 (1915)
Keeley	Patrick C. Keeley bio., 1816–96, Ire.; NY	IR Issue 2 (2002)
Keena	Mary A. Keena, NY	JAIHS Vol. 20 (1921)
Kelley	A.W. Kelley, NY	JAIHS Vol. 29 (1931)
Kelly	Jerome Kelly, NY	JAIHS Vol. 17 (1918)
	Thomas P. Kelly, 1851–1911, NY	JAIHS Vol. 11 (1912)
	James Edward Kelly bio., 1855–1933, NY	NYIHRN Fall (2006)
	James Edward Kelly, 1855–1933, NY	JAIHS Vol. 31 (1937)
	William J. Kelly, NY	JAIHS Vol. 29 (1931)
Kenedy	P. J. Kenedy, 1843–1906, NY	JAIHS Vol. 6 (1906)
Kennedy	Thomas F. Kennedy, NY	JAIHS Vol. 27 (1928)
Kenney	John Jerome Kenney, NY	JAIHS Vol. 13 (1914)
Keogh	Martin J. Keogh, NY	JAIHS Vol. 27 (1928)
Kerry	New York and County Kerry, 1851–1930	NYIH Vol. 23 (2009)
Kiernan	John J. Kiernan, financial news, 1868, NY	ISGB Issue 17 (1997)
Kinsella	William C. Kinsella, Brooklyn bridge engineer	JAIHS Vol. 21 (1922)
	James Gaffney–Mary Quail family research, Kinsella connection, pre–1858+, Ire.; NY	IFH Vol. 21 (2005)
Kinsley	William Joseph Kinsley, NY	JAIHS Vol. 15 (1916)
Land	Land grants to Irish settlers, NY province	JAIHS Vol. 14 (1915)
	Land grants to Irish settlers in colony and state	JAIHS Vol. 24 (1925)
	Irish settlers in 17th and 18th centuries	JAIHS Vol. 24 (1925)
Langley	John T. Langley, NY	JAIHS Vol. 29 (1931)
Leary	Leary family, early NY	JAIHS Vol. 15 (1916)
Lee–Morrell	Robert Lee Morrell, NY	JAIHS Vol. 28 (1930)
Legal	Irish ancestry at the Bench and Bar of NY	JAIHS Vol. 23 (1924)
	Irish in the surrogate's records	JAIHS Vol. 26 (1927)
	Irish in probate records	JAIHS Vol. 27 (1928)
	Capital punishment and NY Irish, 1700s+	NYIH Vol. 12 (1998)
	Legal executions in NY state, 1756–1916	NYIH Vol. 12 (1998)
	Wills, 1750–1815 (sel.)	JAIHS Vol. 29 (1931)
	Marriage license bonds	JAIHS Vol. 30 (1932)
Lenehan	B. C. Lenehan (Mgr.), 1843–1910, NY	JAIHS Vol. 9 (1910)
Longford	County Longford colony in New York, emigration from Ireland, 1729–1926	NYIH Vol. 17 (2003)
	County Longford colony in New York City, 1800s–1930s	NYIH Vol. 18 (2004)
Lower East Side (M'tn)	Researching your Irish ancestors on the lower east side	IFHFN Vol.18,Is.6 (2008)
Lynch	Dominick Lynch and his family, 1786, NY	JAIHS Vol. 7 (1907)
	James E. Lynch, NY	JAIHS Vol. 29 (1931)
Lyon	James B. Lyon, NY	JAIHS Vol. 29 (1931)
Lyons	Richard J. Lyons, NY	JAIHS Vol. 15 (1916)
MacCarthy	Charles MacCarthy, E. Greenwich, NY	JAIHS Vol. 3 (1900)
MacGuire	Constantine J. MacGuire (Dr.), NY	JAIHS Vol. 29 (1931)
	James Clark MacGuire, MD, NY	JAIHS Vol. 29 (1931)

MacNeven	William James MacNeven, 1763–1841, NY	JAIHS Vol. 32 (1941)
MacNevin	William MacNevin Purdy, NY	JAIHS Vol. 28 (1930)
Magrath	Patrick Francis Magrath, NY	JAIHS Vol. 20 (1921)
Mahoney	Cornelius Mahoney, teacher and inventor, NY	JAIHS Vol. 21 (1922)
	Michael J. Mahoney, NY	JAIHS Vol. 17 (1918)
Malone	Sylvestor Malone (Rev.), NY	JAIHS Vol. 20 (1921)
Manhattan	Areas of Manhattan heavily settled by Irish immigrants	IFHFN Vol.18,Is.3 (2008)
Manion	John C. Manion, NY	JAIHS Vol. 16,Is.3 (1917)
Manning	John J. Manning, NY	JAIHS Vol. 16 Is.3 (1917)
	William Manning (Lt.), Brooklyn, NY	JAIHS Vol. 23 (1924)
Mansfield	Charles Mansfield, Daniel Fitzpatrick family, NY, 19th C.	IFHFN Vol.14,Is.2 (2004)
	Patricia Mansfield Phelan recalls Mary J. Mansfield, 1800s, NY	IFHF Vol. 19 (2003)
McAlareny	John J. Young–Ellen E. McAlareny family, c. 1860+, NY	NYIH Vol. 15 (2001)
McBride	Denis H. McBride, PA, NY	JAIHS Vol. 25 (1926)
McCabe	James J. McCabe, NY	JAIHS Vol. 29 (1931)
McCarthy	John McCarthy, 1856–1931, NY	JAIHS Vol. 30 (1932)
	Michael McCarthy: The Family History of a Hero	NYIH Vol. 23 (2009)
McCartney	Catherine McCartney, Immigrant, 1888, Ireland, NY	NYIH Vol. 15 (2001)
McClure	David McClure, NY	JAIHS Vol. 12 (1913)
McCormack	Charles J. McCormack, NY	JAIHS Vol. 15 (1916)
	James W. McCormick, 1862–1910, NY	JAIHS Vol. 10 (1911)
McCormick	John G. McCormick (Rev.), NY	JAIHS Vol. 25 (1926)
McCready	Charles McCready (Rev.), NY	JAIHS Vol. 14 (1915)
McDonald	John B. McDonald, 1844–1911, NY	JAIHS Vol. 10 (1911)
McDonnell	Joseph Pat. McDonnell bio., 1847–1906	NYIH Vol. 14 (2000)
	Peter McDonnell, 1905, NY	JAIHS Vol. 7 (1907)
McElligot	Peter P. McElligott, NY	JAIHS Vol. 30 (1932)
McElroy	Ross O. McElroy, NY	JAIHS Vo. 29 (1931)
McFarland	Myles McFarland aka Brother David, NY	JAIHS Vol. 25 (1926)
	Stephen McFarland, NY	JAIHS Vol. 28 (1930)
McGinnis	Daniel J. McGinnis, NY	JAIHS Vol. 12 (1913)
McGinnity	Joseph J. McGinnity, NY	IF Vol. 9, Is. 3 (1993)
McGlynn	Doctor Edward McGlynn biography, 1837–1900, NY	NYIH Vol. 21 (2007)
McGowan	John McGowan (Adm.), NY	JAIHS Vol. 15 (1916)
McGuire	Peter James McGuire biography, 1852–1906, NY, NJ	NYIH Vol. 16 (2002)
	Patrick Francis McGowan, NY	JAIHS Vol. 12 (1913)
McKenna	Charles Francis McKenna (Dr.), NY	JAIHS Vol. 29 (1931)
	Edward McKenna (Monsignor), NY	JAIHS Vol. 30 (1932)
McLaughlin	Hugh McLaughlin bio., 1826–1904, NY	IR Issue 2 (2002)
McLoughlin	John J. McLoughlin (Monsignor), NY, NJ	JAIHS Vol. 27 (1928)
McMahon	James McMahon, NY	JAIHS Vol. 13 (1914)
McManus	Mary McManus, Co. Leitrim, Ire., NYC	NYIH Vol.3 (1988)
McNally	James McNally, Flatbush note, d. 1850, Ire.	IR Issue 2 (2002)
McNevin	McNevin fam., Ire., NY	IFH Vol. 12 (1996)
McPartland	Stephen McPartland, 1844–1912, NY	JAIHS Vol. 11 (1912)
McTighe	Patrick J. McTighe, 1840–1908, NY	JAIHS Vol. 8 (1909)
McTigue	John G. McTigue, NY	JAIHS Vol. 27 (1928)
Meagher	Thomas Francis Meagher (Gen.), letters	JAIHS Vol. 30 (1932)
Medical	Physicians of Manhattan and Brooklyn, early 1900s	NYIH Vol. 15 (2001)

Newspaper	Information wanted, ads as research aid, 1850–71	IFHFN Vol.10,Is.2 (2001)
	Irish Echo, history	NYIH Vol. 8 (1993–94)
	Irish–American newspapers in 19th century	NYIH Vol. 8 (1993–94)
	Irish World newspaper, FDR and the Great Depression, 1870–1930s	NYIH Vol. 17 (2003)
	Lists published in Irish Chronicle, 1811	JAIHS Vol. 28 (1930)
	Newspaper obit. notices, 1762–1825	JAIHS Vol. 25 (1926)
	New York Gazette advertisements by Irish business	JAIHS Vol. 14 (1915)
	The Gael, Irish magazine of NY, 1881–1904	NYIH Vol. 2, Is. 1 (1987)
	Shamrock of New York, first Irish–Amer. Newspaper	NYIH Vol. 4 (1989)
	Using index to marriages and deaths in the NY Herald	IFHFN Vol.12,Is.1 (2003)
	Truth Teller information wanted ads, 1825–1844	IR Issue 56 (2005)
Nicholson	John T. Nicholson, NY	JAIHS Vol. 30 (1932)
Nielson	Samuel Nielson, Co. Down, Ire.	NYIH Vol. 2, Is. 1 (1987)
Norwood	Norwood, sampling in Irish neighborhood	NYIH Vol. 2, Is. 1 (1987)
Oakes	Owen Oakes–Alice Fitzsimmons family, 1827+, Ire.; NY	IFH Vol. 18 (2002)
O'Beirne	James R. O'Beirne (Gen.), NY	JAIHS Vol. 16 Is.2 (1917)
O'Brien	Denis Richard O'Brien, NY	JAIHS Vol. 28 (1930)
	Fitz–James O'Brien, writer in NYC, and 7th NY, d. 1862	NYIH Vol. 20 (2006)
	Michael C. O'Brien (Dr.), NY	JAIHS Vol. 26 (1927)
	Morgan J. O'Brien (Judge), NY	JAIHS Vol. 32 (1941)
	Thomas O'Brien (Hon.), NY	JAIHS Vol. 21 (1922)
O'Byrne	Michael A. O'Byrne, NY	JAIHS Vol. 27 (1928)
O'Connor	Catherine O'Connor O'Neil, James Gallagher, NY	TR Vol. 134, Is. 4 (2003)
	Charles O'Connor, 1804–84, NY	JAIHS Vol. 27 (1928)
	Denis O'Connor, priest, Our Lady of the Scapular	NYIH Vol. 20 (2006)
	Joseph O'Connor, 1908, NY	JAIHS Vol. 8 (1909)
O'Connor–Stine	Nora O'Connor Stine, Ireland to NY, 1906	NYIH Vol. 13 (1999)
O'Conor	John Michael O'Conor (Lt.), 1812, NY	JAIHS Vol. 7 (1907)
O'Donoghue	Joseph J. O'Donohue, 1834–97, NY	JAIHS Vol. 32 (1941)
O'Donovan Rossa	Jeremiah O'Donovan Rossa memoir excerpt, 1860s, NY	NYIHRN Fall (2006)
O'Dwyer	Daniel H. O'Dwyer (Rev.), 1862–1909, NY	JAIHS Vol. 9 (1910)
	Edward F. O'Dwyer, NY	JAIHS Vol. 21 (1922)
	William O'Dwyer, New York City mayor, 1940s	NYIH Vol. 16 (2002)
O'Flynn	Denis P. O'Flynn (Rev.), 1847–1906, NY	JAIHS Vol. 6 (1906)
O'Herin	William O'Herin, NY, MO	JAIHS Vol. 14 (1915)
O'Hern	Lewis J. O'Hern (Rev.), DC, NY	JAIHS Vol. 29 (1931)
O'Keefe	Gerald Joseph O'Keefe, NY	JAIHS Vol. 29 (1931)
O'Keffee	Alfred J. O'Keffee, NY	JAIHS Vol. 29 (1931)
O'Leary	Major Jeremiah O'Leary bio. note, 1910s, NY	NYIHRN Fall (2005)
	Michael J. O'Leary, NY	JAIHS Vol. 17 (1918)
	John Stratton O'Leary and the O'Leary Flats	NYIH Vol. 4 (1989)
O'Lenahan	Michael J. O'Lenahan, 1863+, Ire.; NY	NYIHRN Spring (2000)
O'Meara	Maurice O'Meara, 1843–1910, NY	JAIHS Vol. 9 (1910)
O'Neale	Peggy O'Neale, famous innkeeper's daughter	JAIHS Vol. 28 (1930)
O'Neil	Catherine O'Connor O'Neil, James Gallagher, NY	TR Vol. 134, Is. 4 (2003)
	Chas. O'Neil will, d.1887, NY; Ire.	IR Issue 3 (2002)
	James O'Neil, NY	JAIHS Vol. 17 (1918)
O'Neill	O'Neill allied fam., from Ire. to Brooklyn	TR Vol. 134, Is. 1 (2003)
O'Shea	James O'Shea, NY	JAIHS Vol. 15 (1916)

Saville	Richard Saville Newcoombe, NY	JAIHS Vol. 29 (1931)
Scotch–Irish	Scotch–Irish and Anglo–Saxon fallacies	JAIHS Vol. 2 (1899)
Scott	Catherine Scott, Co. Cavan, Ire.; NY	NYIH Vol.8 (1993–94)
Shanley	The Shanleys of Broadway	NYIH Vol.5 (1990)
	Detective Mary Shanley, NYC, 1941, photo	NYIH Vol. 20 (2006)
Shea	John B. Shea, 1835–1907, NY	JAIHS Vol. 7 (1907)
	Josie Shea–Richard Harrington family info. and photo, m. 1903, MT, NY	IGQ Vol. 17, Is. 3 (2008)
Sheahan	Denis B. Sheahan, famed sculptor, NY	JAIHS Vol. 23 (1924)
Sheehan	William F. Sheehan (Hon.), NY	JAIHS Vol. 16 Is.2 (1917)
Shely	Terence J. Shealy (Rev.), NY	JAIHS Vol. 21 (1922)
Sloane	Charles William Sloane, NY	JAIHS Vol. 28 (1930)
Smith	Josephine Smith, Ireland; NY	NYIH Vol.6 (1991)
Soldiers	New York Irish soldiers	JAIHS Vol. 10 (1911)
Sport	New York Gaelic Athletic assn.	NYIH Vol. 3 (1988)
	Hurling in 18th century NY	NYIH Vol. 11 (1997)
St. Patrick's Day	Saint Patrick's Day in New York City, 1762–88	JAIHS Vol. 5 (1905)
Staten Island	Staten Island Irish, 1680s+	NYIH Vol. 12 (1998)
Stewart	M. E. Ryan, J. F. A. Stewart, Brooklyn note	IFHFN Vol.10,Is.3 (2001)
	David Stewart family notes, 1792+, Ireland; NY	IFHFN Vol.17,Is.3 (2007)
Stuart	Joseph Stuart, EISBs 2nd pres., 1803–74	NYIHRN Fall (2000)
Sullivan	James F. Sullivan, PA, NY	JAIHS Vol. 29 (1931)
	Big Tim Sullivan, King of the Bowery, 1862–1913	NYIH Vol. 20 (2006)
Sweeney	John F. Sweeney, NY	JAIHS Vol. 13 (1914)
	Thomas W. Sweeny (Brig.–Gen.), NY	JAIHS Vol. 2 (1899)
Teachers	Irish Schoolmastes in Early New York City	NYIH Vol. 23 (2009)
Teevan	Bernard Teevan, Ireland; NYC	NYIH Vol. 5 (1990)
Tracy	John Tracy, NY	JAIHS Vol. 30 (1932)
	Michael Tracy, NY	JAIHS Vol. 26 (1927)
	Thomas Ward–Marg. Tracy family, m. 1890, NY; Ire.	IFH Vol. 18 (2002)
Travers	Ambrose F. Travers, 1851–1906, NY	JAIHS Vol. 6 (1906)
	Francis C. Travers, d.1905, NY	JAIHS Vol. 5 (1905)
Tyrone	County Tyrone Society of New York	NYIH Vol. 5 (1990)
Union	New York City's TWU labor movement, 1930s–1940s	NYIH Vol. 15 (2001)
	Organizing Transit: The Irish and the TWU	NYIH Vol. 23 (2009)
	The Controversial History of the TWU	NYIH Vol. 1 (1986)
Waller	Thomas M. Waller (Hon.), NY	JAIHS Vol. 23 (1924)
Walsh	John Walsh biography and career as fireman, 1884–1962, Ireland; NY	NYIH Vol. 18 (2005)
	Simon J. Walsh (Dr.), NY, MA	JAIHS Vol. 27 (1928)
	Doctor William J. Walsh murdered by John William Wilson, NY, 1932	NYIH Vol. 20 (2006)
Ward	Thomas Ward–Marg. Tracy family, m. 1890, NY; Ire.	IFH Vol. 18 (2002)
Waters	Frank J. Waters, NY	JAIHS Vol. 23 (1924)
Whalen	John S. Whalen, NY	JAIHS Vol. 12 (1913)
White	Andrew J. White, 1845–1900, NY	JAIHS Vol. 4 (1904)
	John B. White, NY	JAIHS Vol. 28 (1930)
Whitney	Patrick A. Whitney, NY	JAIHS Vol. 29 (1931)
Williamsburg (Brklyn)	When Williamsport and Greenpoint were Irish	NYIH Vol. 10 (1996)
Wood	Benjamin Wood (Mrs.), NY	JAIHS Vol. 31 (1937)
Woodside (Queens)	Jack Doherty recalls Woodside, c. 1909+	NYIH Vol. 15 (2001)

Worsam–Meade	Richard Worsam Meade, 3rd, 1837–97, NY	JAIHS Vol. 1 (1898)
	Richard Worsam Meade (R.Admr.), 1837–97, NY	JAIHS Vol. 2 (1899)
Wright	Henry P. Wright, 1836–1910, NY	JAIHS Vol. 10 (1911)
Young	John J. Young–Ellen E. McAlareny family, c. 1860+, NY	NYIH Vol. 15 (2001)

Periodical Abbreviations

DIFHR	*Directory of Irish Family History Research*
IAG	*Irish American Genealogist* (formerly the *Irish Genealogical Helper*)
IF	*Irish Families*
IFH	*Irish Family History*
IFHFN	*Irish Family History Forum Newsletter*
IGQ	*Irish Genealogical Quarterly*
IHL	*Irish Heritage Links*
IR	*Irish Roots*
ISGB	*Irish/Scottish Gaelic Bulletin*
IT	*Irish Tree*
JAIHS	*The Recorder: Journal of the American Irish Historical Society*
NYIH	*New York Irish History*
NYIHRN	*New York Irish History Roundtable Newsletter*
TIHA	*The Irish at Home and Abroad*
TR	*The New York Genealogical and Biographical Record*
TS	*The Septs*

Periodicals

Directory of Irish Family History Research
Published by Ulster Genealogical and Historical Guild
www.ancestryireland.com
Years of publication: 1991–Present
Address: 12 College Square East, Belfast, BT1 6DD Northern Ireland
At: Ulster Genealogical and Historical Guild / Allen County Public Library / Los Angeles California Family History Library

Irish American Genealogist (formerly *Irish Genealogical Helper*)
Published by Augustan Society
http://augustansociety.org
Years of publication: 1973–1996
Address: Augustan Society, PO Box 75, Daggett, CA 92327
At: Augustan Society / Allen County Public Library / Dallas Public Library / Family History Library, Salt Lake City / Library of Congress / New York Public Library / Public Library of Cincinnati & Hamilton Co.

Irish Families
Published by Irish Genealogical Foundation
www.irishroots.com
Years of publication: 1986–2003
Address: O'Lochlainn's Journal of Irish Families, Box 7575 Dept. HPA, Kansas City, MO 64116
At: Irish Genealogical Foundation / Allen County Public Library / Family History Library, Salt Lake City

Irish Family History
Published by Irish Family History Society
www.ifhs.ie
Years of publication: 1985–2009
Address: Secretary, PO Box 36, Naas, Co. Kildare, Ireland
At: Irish Family History Society / Allen County Public Library / Family History Library, Salt Lake City

Irish Family History Forum Newsletter
Published by Irish Family History Forum
www.ifhf.org
Years of publication: 1993–Present
Address: PO Box 67, Plainview, NY 11803–0067
At: Irish Family History Forum / Allen County Public Library / New York Public Library / Family History Library, Salt Lake City

Irish Genealogical Quarterly
Published by Irish Genealogical Society of Wisconsin
www.igswonline.com
Years of publication: 1992–2010 Vol. 19 Is. 4
Address: PO Box 13766, Wauwatosa, WI 53213–0766
At: Irish Genealogical Society of Wisconsin /Allen County Public Library / Family History Library, Salt Lake City / New York Public Library

Irish Heritage Links
Published by Irish Heritage Association
No longer in existence
Years of publication: 1984–?
Address: 164 Kingsway, Dunmurry, Belfast, BT17 9AD, Northern Ireland and Old Engine House, Portview, 310 Newtownards Rd., Belfast BT4 1HE
At: Allen County Public Library / Family History Library, Salt Lake City

Irish Roots
Published by Irish Roots Media
www.irishrootsmedia.com
Years of publication: 1992–Present
Address: Irish Roots Media Ltd., Blackrock, Blessington, Co. Wicklow, Ireland
At: Irish Roots Media / Allen County Public Library / Family History Library, Salt Lake City / New York Public Library

Irish/Scottish Gaelic Bulletin
Published by Orange County California Genealogical Society
http://occgs.com
Years of publication: 1993–?
Address: OCCGS, c/o Huntington Beach Central Library, 7111 Talbert Ave., Huntington Beach, CA 92648
At: Orange County California Genealogical Society / Allen County Public Library

Irish Tree
Published by Irish Genealogical Society of Michigan
www.rootsweb.ancestry.com/~miigsm
Years of publication: 1998–?
Address: Irish Genealogical Society of Michigan, c/o The Gaelic League, 2068 Michigan Ave., Detroit, MI 48216
At: Irish Genealogical Society of Michigan / Allen County Public Library / Family History Library, Salt Lake City

The Recorder: Journal of the American Irish Historical Society
Published by American Irish Historical Society
http://aihs.org
Years of publication: 1898–1900, 1904–1907, 1909–1928, 1930–1932, 1937, 1941–Present (possibly with gaps)
Address: 991 Fifth Ave. New York, NY 10028
At: American Irish Historical Society / Library of Congress / New York Public Library / Allen County Public Library / Family History Library, Salt Lake City / Google Books

New York Irish History
Published by New York Irish History Roundtable
www.irishnyhistory.org
Years of publication: 1986–Present
Address: PO Box 2087, Church Street Station, New York, NY 10008–2087
At: New York Irish History Roundtable / New York Public Library / Allen County Public Library / Family History Library, Salt Lake City

New York Irish History Roundtable Newsletter
Published by New York Irish History Roundtable
www.irishnyhistory.org
Years of publication: 1994–Present
Address: PO Box 2087, Church Street Station, New York, NY 10008–2087
At: New York Irish History Roundtable / New York Public Library / Allen County Public Library / Family History Library, Salt Lake City

The Irish at Home and Abroad
No longer published
Years of publication: 1993–1999
At: Allen County Public Library / New York Public Library / Family History Library, Salt Lake City

The New York Genealogical and Biographical Record
Published by New York Genealogical and Biographical Society
http://newyorkfamilyhistory.org
Years of publication: 1870–Present
Address: 36 West 44th St., 7th Floor, New York, NY 10036–8105
At: New York Genealogical and Biographical Society / Allen County Public Library / Atlanta–Fulton Public Library / Dallas Public Library / Family History Library, Salt Lake City / Library of Congress / Los Angeles Public Library / New England Historic Genealogical Society Library / New York Genealogical and Biographical Society / New York Public Library / Newberry Library, Chicago / Public Library of Cincinnati & Hamilton Co. / State Historical Society of Wisconsin Library

The Septs
Published by Irish Genealogical Society International
http://irishgenealogical.org
Years of publication: 1980–2012
Address: 1185 Concord St. N., Suite 218, South St. Paul, MN 55075
At: Irish Genealogical Society International / Allen County Public Library / Family History Library, Salt Lake City

11 Websites and Publications to Compliment Your Research

In this chapter websites and publications that deal with the Irish in New York City are listed. It is hoped that they will aid and supplement your genealogical research. They cover such areas as history, culture, politics, sociology, religion, employment, and many more. Countless publications exist that document the immigration of the Irish to America, and many refer specifically to the Irish in New York City. Two standout publications are *Making the Irish American: History and Heritage of the Irish in the United States* (2006), edited by Joseph Lee and Marion Casey, and *Emigrants and Exiles: Ireland and the Irish Exodus to North America* (1985) by Kerby Miller.

A comprehensive compilation of publications concerning the Irish in New York City was published in 1995 by the New York Irish History Roundtable (NYIHR). *The Irish Experience in New York City* by Ann M. Shea and Marion Casey contains almost 700 bibliographic references to various publications and visual media. In particular, it has a thorough selection of master's theses and doctoral dissertations that were written either about the Irish in New York City or on subjects where the Irish are heavily featured. These works are not always thought of as potential source material by those conducting genealogical research. Many of the publications listed in this chapter can be found in the Shea and Casey publication.

In addition to genealogical information, many of the websites and books can provide information about the social history of your ancestors, such as their employment, the industries they worked in, and their position on the social class-ladder in New York City.

Websites
Academic
- Archives of Irish America at New York University www.nyu.edu/library/bobst/research/aia
- CUNY Institute for Irish American Studies http://irishamericanstudies.com
- Hofstra University Irish Studies
  www.hofstra.edu/academics/colleges/hclas/irish/irish_faculty.html
- Institute of Irish Studies, Fordham University
  www.fordham.edu/academics/programs_at_fordham_/irish_studies_instit
- Lehman College Irish Studies www.lehman.edu/lehman/irishamericanstudies
- Molloy College Irish Studies
  http://alumni.molloy.edu/s/869/index.aspx?sid=869&gid=1&pgid=469
- New York University Ireland House http://irelandhouse.fas.nyu.edu
- Queens College Irish Studies
  www.qc.cuny.edu/Academics/Degrees/DSS/IrishStudies/Pages/default.aspx

Catholic Church
- Archdiocese of New York www.archny.org
- Bronx Catholic http://bronxcatholic.blogspot.com
- Brooklyn Catholic http://brooklyncatholic.blogspot.com
- Catholic Churches of Manhattan http://catholicmanhattan.blogspot.com
- *Catholic New York* newspaper www.cny.org
- Catholics in New York 1808-1946 Museum Exhibit
  www.mcny.org/exhibitions/past/catholics-in-new-york-1808-1946.html
- Diocese of Brooklyn http://dioceseofbrooklyn.org
- Diocese of Brooklyn Cemeteries www.cathcemetery-bklyn.org
- New York City Cemetery Project http://nycemetery.wordpress.com

County Associations

- Armagh http://countyarmaghny.com
- Carlow http://carlownyc.com
- Cavan www.cavannewyork.com
- Cork www.nycorkassociation.org
- Donegal www.donegalny.org
- Down www.facebook.com/countydownny
- Galway www.facebook.com/GalwayAssociationofNewYork
- Kerry www.kerrymen.com
- Kildare http://countykildare.org
- Laois www.nylaoisassociation.blogspot.com
- Leitrim http://leitrimsocietyofny.com
- Longford www.countylongfordny.com
- Mayo www.mayosocietyofny.org
- Monaghan http://monaghansociety.org
- Roscommon http://countyroscommonsocietyofnewyork.com
- Sligo www.sligoassociationnyc.com
- Tipperary www.facebook.com/Tipperary.NY
- Waterford http://countywaterford.org
- Wexford http://wexfordassociation-newyork.org

Cultural/Social

- Craic Fest http://thecraicfest.com
- First Irish Theater Festival www.1stirish.org
- Great Irish Fair of New York www.gifnyc.com
- Irish American Cultural Institute www.iaci-usa.org
- Irish Arts Center www.irishartscenter.org
- Irish Business Organization of New York www.ibo-ny.com
- Irish Cultural Society www.irish-society.org
- Irish Repertory Theatre www.irishrep.org
- Meetup: The Irish in New York www.meetup.com/NYIrish
- New York City St. Patrick's Day Parade http://nycstpatricksparade.org
- New York Irish Center www.newyorkirishcenter.org
- New York Police Department Pipes and Drums www.nypdpipesanddrums.com

Fraternal

- Ancient Order of Hibernians, New York City www.aohnyc1.org
- Ancient Order of Hibernians, Rockaway Park / Breezy Point www.aohrbny21.org
- Ancient Order of Hibernians, Yonkers http://aohblogger-mylesscullynews.blogspot.com
- AOH Home of the Brooklyn Irish http://brooklynirish.com
- New York Police Department Emerald Society www.nypdemeralds.com
- Staten Island AOH http://statenislandaoh.com

Genealogy

- Brooklyn Genealogy Information Page http://bklyn-genealogy-info.stevemorse.org
- Connors Genealogy New York City www.connorsgenealogy.com/nyc
- Cyndi's List Bronx Category Index www.cyndislist.com/us/ny/counties/bronx
- Cyndi's List Brooklyn Category Index www.cyndislist.com/us/ny/counties/kings-brooklyn
- Cyndi's List Manhattan Category Index www.cyndislist.com/us/ny/counties/new-york-city

- Cyndi's List Queens Category Index www.cyndislist.com/us/ny/counties/queens-long-island
- Cyndi's List Staten Island Category Index
  www.cyndislist.com/us/ny/counties/richmond-staten-island
- Dempsey Funeral Home Records (Staten Island, NY, and Bayonne, NJ) 1880–1948
  www.rootsweb.ancestry.com/~nyrichmo/cemeteries/Dempsey19021903.html#k
- Irish Immigrants of the Emigrant Industrial Savings Bank http://eisbirishnyc.com
- Irish Family History Forum www.ifhf.org
- Irish in New York City www.irishinnyc.freeservers.com
- Local Catholic Church and Family History & Genealogical Research Guide
  http://localcatholic.webs.com/newyork.htm
- Meetup: Irish British Genealogy Group
  www.meetup.com/The-Irish-British-Genealogy-Group
- NARA Famine Irish Passenger Record Data File, 1846–1951
  http://aad.archives.gov/aad/fielded-search.jsp?dt=180&tf=F
- New York Genealogy 101 www.nygenealogy101.com
- Rootsweb Irish New York Genealogy Mailing List
  http://lists.rootsweb.ancestry.com/index/other/Ethnic-Irish/IRISH-NEW-YORK-CITY.html
- Rootsweb Irish New York Genealogy –Assorted Records and Resources
  http://freepages.genealogy.rootsweb.ancestry.com/~nyirish/NYC%20index.html
- Rootsweb Staten Island www.rootsweb.ancestry.com/~nyrichmo

History
- American Irish Historical Society www.aihs.org
- Irish American Civil War–New York http://irishamericancivilwar.com/tag/new-york
- Irish Heritage Walking Tour www.nycwalk.com/iris.html
- Irish Speakers and the Empire City www.nyuirish.net/irishlanguagehistory
- New York Correction Historical Society http://correctionhistory.org
- New York Irish History Roundtable www.irishnyhistory.org
- New York Irish History Roundtable Blog http://nyirishhistory.wordpress.com
- The Irish in Five Points http://herb.ashp.cuny.edu/exhibits/show/five-points

Museum
- New York City Fire Museum www.nycfiremuseum.org
- New York City Police Museum www.nycpolicemuseum.org
- New York Transit Museum www.mta.info/mta/museum
- Tenement Museum www.tenement.org

Photographs
- Brooklyn Public Library–Historic Brooklyn Photographs
  www.bklynpubliclibrary.org/brooklyncollection/historic-brooklyn-photographs
- New York City Municipal Archives Online Gallery
  www.nyc.gov/html/records/html/gallery/home.shtml
- New York Public Library Digital Collections http://digitalcollections.nypl.org

Sport
- Armagh New York City Gaelic Athletic Association http://armaghgaany.com
- Gaelic Athletic Association of Greater New York www.ny-gaa.org
- NYPD Gaelic Football Club www.nypdgaelicfootball.org

Publications

Biographical

Burch, Wilhelmine T. "The Life and Methods of Charles F. Murphy." New York, NY: Columbia University, master's thesis. 1930.

Genen, Arthur. "John Kelly, New York's First Irish Boss." New York, NY: New York University, master's thesis. 1971.

McMahon, James B. "Henry Cruse Murphy–Brooklyn's First Party Boss." New York, NY: Columbia University, master's thesis. 1967.

Reid, B. L. *The Man from New York; John Quinn and his Friends*. New York, NY: Oxford University Press. 1968.

Catholic Church

Cunningham, Joe. *St. John's Home: From Brooklyn to Rockaway*. New York, NY: St. John's Home Press. 1993.

Dolan, Jay P. *The Immigrant Church: New York's Irish and German Catholics, 1815–1865*. South Bend, IN: University of Notre Dame Press. 1992.

Isacsson, Alfred. *Always Faithful: The New York Carmelites, the Irish People and Their Freedom Movement*. Middletown, NY: Vestigium. 2004.

Kenneally, James. *The History of American Catholic Women*. New York, NY: Crossroad Publishing. 1990.

McCauley, Bernadette. "Who Shall Take Care of Our Sick? Roman Catholic Sisterhoods and Their Hospitals, New York City, 1850–1930." New York, NY: Columbia University, PhD diss. 1992.

New York Mission of Our Lady of the Rosary. *Mission of Our Lady Of The Rosary For The Protection Of Irish Immigrant Girls*. New York, NY: Lauter and Lauterjung. 1900. [Reprinted by Nabu Press in 2012] Available online at: http://books.google.com/books?id=yUNDAAAAYAAJ

O'Brien, Michael Joseph. *In Old New York: The Irish Dead in Trinity and St. Paul's Churchyards*. New York, NY: American Irish Historical Society. 1928. [Also contains baptisms and marriages at other Churches; wills; letters of administration; etc.]

Shannon, Miriam C. "Early History of the Roman Catholic Church in the City of New York." New York, NY: Columbia University, master's thesis. 1929.

Shea, John Gilmary. *The Catholic Churches of New York City*. New York, NY: L.G. Goulding. 1878. Available online: http://archive.org/details/catholicchurches00shea

U.S. Catholic Historical Society. *Historical Records and Studies*. New York, NY: U. S. Catholic Historical Society. 1900.

Crime

Crystal, Pearl. "A History of Juvenile Delinquency in the City of New York, 1609–1900." New York, NY: Columbia University, master's thesis. 1938.

Gilfoyle, Timothy J. *A Pickpocket's Tale: The Underworld of Nineteenth-Century New York.* New York, NY: W. W. Norton. 2006.

Gordon, Michael A. *The Orange Riots : Irish Political Violence in New York City, 1870 and 1871.* Ithaca, NY: Cornell University Press. 1993.

Lombard, Anne S. "Fallen Angels: The Social Construction of Female Criminality, New York City, 1830–1875." New York, NY: Columbia University, PhD Diss. 1989.

O'Rourke, Hugh E. "Irish Immigrant Involvement in Collective Violence in New York from 1845 to 1875." New York, NY: City University of New York Graduate Center, master's thesis. 2001.

Employment / Industry
Bernard, Phyllis E. "The Movement to Regulate Employment Agencies for Domestic Servants in New York City 1904–1911." New York, NY: Columbia University, master's thesis. 1978.

Brooklyn Fire Department. *Our Firemen: The Official History of the Brooklyn Fire Department From the First Volunteer to the Latest Appointee.* Brooklyn, NY: unknown publisher. 1892.
Available online at: http://archive.org/details/cu31924082460407

Costello, Augustine E. *A History of the New York Fire Department, Volunteer and Paid.* New York, NY: self-published. 1885.

Costello, Augustine E. *Our Police Protectors: History of the New York Police From the Earliest Period to the Present Time.* New York, NY: self-published. 1885.
Available online at: http://books.google.com/books?id=JyYMAQAAMAAJ

Dallery, Marion. "Labor in New York City During the Civil War." New York, NY: Columbia University, master's thesis. 1957.

Fales, William E. S. *Brooklyn's Guardians: A Record of the Faithful and Heroic Men who Preserve the Peace in the City of Homes.* Brooklyn, NY: self-published. 1887.

Fisher, James Terence. *On the Irish Waterfront: The Crusader, the Movie, and the Soul of the Port of New York.* Ithaca, NY: Cornell University Press. 2009.

Gordon, Michael Allen. "Irish Immigrant Culture and the Labor Boycott in New York City, 1880–1886" in *Immigrants in Industrial America, 1850–1920.* Richard L. Ehrlich, ed. Charlottesville, VA: University Press of Virginia. 1977

Gutman, Herbert G. "Early Effects of the Depression of 1875 Upon the Working Class in New York City." New York, NY: Columbia University, master's thesis. 1950.

Houlihan, Timothy John. "The New York City Building Trades, 1890–1910 (Craft Union, Bricklayers, Carpenters)." Binghampton, NY: State University of New York, Binghampton, PhD Diss. 1994

Janiewski, D. E. M. "Sewing With a Double Thread: The Needlewomen of New York, 1825–1870." Washington, OR: University of Oregon, master's thesis. 1974.

Kapsalas, Maria A. "From the Gilded Age to Progressivism—Brooklyn's Horse Race for Wealth." New York, NY: City University of New York Graduate Center, master's thesis. 1990.

Kernan, Frank. *Reminiscences of the Old Fire Laddies and Volunteer Fire Departments of New York and Brooklyn.* New York, NY: M. Crane. 1885. Available online at: http://books.google.com/books?id=D2QEAAAAYAAJ

Laubach, F. C. "The Social Value of the New York Saloon." New York, NY: Columbia University, master's thesis. 1911.

Limpus, Lowell M. *History of the New York Fire Department.* New York, NY: E. P. Dutton. 1940.

Mendel, Ronald. "Workers in the Gilded Age, New York and Brooklyn." New York, NY: City University of New York Graduate Center, master's thesis. 1989.

McDonald, Brian. *My Father's Gun: One family, Three Badges, One Hundred Years in the NYPD.* New York, NY: Dutton. 1999.

Schwartz, Joel. "Morrisania Volunteer Firemen, 1848–1874: The Limits of Local Institutions in a Metropolitan Age." *New York History.* Vol. 55, No. 2. 1974. pp. 159–178.

Sullivan, Mary. *My Double Life: The Story of a New York City Policewoman.* New York, NY: Farrar and Rinehart. 1938.

Trout, Charles H. "The New York Longshoreman and His Union." New York, NY: Columbia University, master's thesis. 1961.

Ethnic Studies
Bayor, Ronald H. *Neighbors in Conflict: The Irish, Germans, Jews, and Italians of New York City, 1929–1941.* Baltimore, MD: Johns Hopkins. 1978.

Gerson, Jeffrey N. 'Building the Brooklyn Machine: Irish, Jewish and Black Political Succession in Central Brooklyn, 1919–1964." New York, NY: City University of New York Graduate Center, master's thesis. 1991.

Glazer, Nathan, and Daniel P. Moynihan. *Beyond the Melting Pot: The Negroes, Puerto Ricans, Jews, Italians, and Irish of New York City.* Cambridge, MA: MIT Press. 1970.

Tricarico, Donald. "Influence of the Irish on Italian Communal Adaptation in Greenwich Village." *Journal of Ethnic Studies.* Vol. 13. No. 4. 1986. pp. 127–137.

General
Alfred, William. "Ourselves Alone: Irish Exiles in Brooklyn." *Atlantic,* March 1971. pp. 53–58.

Bayor, Ronald H., and Timothy Meagher, eds. *The New York Irish.* Baltimore, MA: Johns Hopkins University Press. 1997.

Bourke, Angela. *Maeve Brennan: Homesick at "The New Yorker".* New York, NY: Counterpoint. 2004.
Casey, Marion R. *Ireland, New York and the Irish Image in American Popular Culture, 1890–1960.* New York, NY: New York University, PhD Diss. 1998.

Casey, Meaghan "From Irish Rags to American Riches?" *The Recorder: The Journal of the American Irish Historical Society,* Vol. 19–20, Summer. 2007. pp. 104–128.

Fitzgerald, Marie. "The St. Patrick's Day parade: The Conflict of Irish-American Identity in New York City, 1840–1900." Stony Brook, NY: State University of New York, Stony Brook, master's thesis. 1993.

Furey, Kieran. *Exiles : A Small Book About New York and the Irish in it.* Curraghroe, Co. Roscommon [Ireland]: Vampire Books. 1993.

Gordon, Michael Allen. 'Studies in Irish and Irish-American Thought and Behavior in Gilded Age New York City. Rochester, NY: Rochester University, PhD Diss. 1977.

Gunn, Thomas Butler. "The Irish Immigrant Boarding House (As It Was)." *The Physiology of New York Boarding Houses.* New York, NY: Mason Brothers. 1857.
Available online at:
http://books.google.com/books/about/The_Physiology_of_New_York_Boarding_hous.html?id=ItUaPDv tJvUC

Hadsell, Willard Leroy. "A Sociological Study of Certain Irish Organizations and Families in the City of New York." New York, NY: Columbia University, master's thesis. 1910.

Hogan, Neil. *The (Other) New York Irish.* Rock Hill, SC: Dept. of English, Winthrop University. 2004.

Ignatiev, Noel. *How the Irish Became White.* New York, NY: Routledge. 1995.

Jenkins, Leslie, and Bob Swacker. *Irish New York.* New York, NY: Universe. 2006.

Kelly, Mary C. *The Shamrock and the Lily : The New York Irish and the Creation of a Transatlantic Identity, 1845–1921.* New York, NY: Peter Lang. 2005.

Mann, A.P. "The Irish in New York in the Early 1860s." *Irish Historical Studies.* Vol. 7. 1950. pp. 87–108.

McGinnis. Grace V. "Irish Immigrants in New York City, 1840–1848." New York: Columbia University, Master's Thesis. 1940.

Museum of the City of New York. *Gaelic Gotham: A History of the Irish in New York, On View at the Museum of the City of New York, March 13–October 27, 1996.* New York, NY: The Museum. 1996.

Neale, Cynthia G. Norah. *The making of an Irish-American Woman in 19th Century New York.* Athens, OH: Lucky. 2011.

Reilly, A. J. *Irish Landmarks in New York.* Worcester, MA: Harrigan Press. 1939.

Ridge, John T. "Leitrim GAA in New York." in *Leitrim GAA story, 1886-1984.* Sean O'Suilleabhain, ed. Leitrim, Ireland: Leitrim County Board. 1984.

Rohs, Stephen. *Eccentric Nation: Irish Performance in Nineteenth-Century New York City.* Madison, NJ: Fairleigh Dickinson University Press. 2009.

Shea, Ann M., and Marion R Casey. *The Irish Experience in New York City: A Select Bibliography.* New York, NY: New York Irish History Roundtable. 1995.

Sheridan, Ann P. "The Irish Element in New York State Before 1798." New York, NY: Columbia University, master's thesis. 1935.

Silverman, Julius S. "Patterns of Working-Class Family and Community Life: The Irish in New York City, 1845–1865." New York, NY: Columbia University, master's thesis. 1973.

Ziegelman, Jane. *97 Orchard: an Edible History of Five Immigrant Families in One New York Tenement.* New York, NY: Smithsonian Books/HarperCollins. 2010.

Immigration
Dobson, David. *Ships from Ireland to Early America, 1623–1850.* Baltimore, MD: ed. for Clearfield Company by Genealogical Publishing. 1999.

Fitzpatrick, Franklin. "Irish Immigration into New York from 1865-1880." Washington, DC: Catholic University of America, master's thesis. 1948

Glazier, Ira A., and Michael Tepper. *The Famine Immigrants: Lists of Irish Immigrants Arriving at the Port of New York, 1846–1851.* Baltimore, MD: Genealogical Publishing. 1983.

Leach, Richard H. "The Impact of Immigration upon New York, 1840–1860." *New York History.* Vol. XXXI. 1950.

Smith, Clifford Neal. *Irish, British, and Some German Immigrants to New York, 14-21 January 1850.* McNeal, AZ: Westland. 1997.

Military
Bilby, Joseph G. *Remember Fontenoy!: The 69th New York and the Irish Brigade in the Civil War.* Hightstown, NJ: Longstreet. 1995.

Forde, Frank. "The Sixty-ninth Regiment of New York." *Irish Sword.* Vol. 1. No. 68. 1989. pp. 145–158.

Hogan, Martin J. *The Shamrock Battalion of the Rainbow: The story of the Fighting Sixty-ninth.* New York, NY: D. Appleton. 1919.

Kohl, Lawrence Fredrick. Ed. *The Irish Brigade and its Campaigns.* New York, NY: Fordham University Press. 1994.

O'Flaherty, Patrick. "The History of the Sixty-ninth Regiment of the New York State Militia, 1852–1961." New York, NY: Columbia University, PhD Diss. 1963. [Also privately printed in 1986.]

O'Flaherty, Patrick. "The Irish Brigade at the battle of Fredericksburg." *New York State and the Civil War.* Vol. 2. No 6. 1962. pp. 1–11.

O'Flaherty, Patrick. "The 69th Regiment at Bull Run." *Irish Sword.* Vol. 26. No. 7. 1965. pp. 2–4.

Toole, Arthur T. Roll of the 10th NY volunteer infantry, 1861-1865. *Irish Genealogist.* Vol. 9 No. 2. 1995. pp. 238–281.
Truslow, Marion A. "Peasants into Patriots: The New York Irish Brigade Recruits and Their Families in the Civil War era, 1850–1890." New York, NY: New York University, master's thesis. 1994.

Neighborhood
Curran, Patrick. "Growing up in the West Bronx." *Bronx County Historical Society Journal.* Vol. 24. No. 1. 1987. pp. 11–20.

Doyle, Joseph. "The Chelsea Irish and the Old Westside." *Ais Eiri*. Spring 1982. pp. 8–11. [*Ais Eiri* is the magazine of the Irish Arts Center]

Frank, Blanche, K. "Relocation in Two Contrasting Urban Renewal Sites in New York City: Seaside and Hammels." Brooklyn, NY: City University of New York, Brooklyn College, NY, master's thesis. 1965.

Giordano, Richard. "A History of a Neighborhood in the South Bronx: Morrisania in Three Periods: 1875, 1925, 1975." New York, NY: Columbia University, master's thesis. 1981.

Gonzalez, Evelyn Diaz. "City Neighborhoods: Formation, Growth and Change in the South Bronx, 1840–1940." New York, NY: Columbia University, PhD Diss. 1993.

Graham, Peter R. "Hell's Kitchen: The History of a New York City Neighborhood, 1855–1925." New York, NY: Columbia University, PhD Diss. 1977.

O'Hanlon, Timothy J. "Neighborhood Change in New York City: A Case study of Park Slope, 1850–1980." New York, NY: City University of New York Graduate Center, PhD Diss. 1982.

Ment, David and Mary S. Donovan. *The People of Brooklyn: A History of Two Neighborhoods*. Brooklyn, NY: Brooklyn Educational and Cultural Alliance. 1980.

McNamara, John. "Irish in the Bronx." *The Bronx Historian*. Vol. 5. No. 4. 1983.

Pernicone, Carol Groneman. "The 'Bloody Ould Sixth': A Social Analysis of a New York City Working Class Community in the Mid-Nineteenth Century." Rochester, NY: University of Rochester, PhD Diss. 1973.

Ridge John T. *The Flatbush Irish*. Brooklyn, NY: Division 35, Ancient Order of Hibernians. 1983.

Scherzer, Kenneth A. "The Unbounded Community: Neighborhood Life and Social Structure in New York City, 1830–1875." Durham, NC: Duke University Press. 1992.

Schick, Sandor E. "Neighborhood Change in the Bronx, 1905–1960." Cambridge, MA: Harvard University, PhD Diss. 1982.

Schoenebaum, Eleanora. "Emerging Neighborhoods: The Development of Brooklyn's Fringe Areas, 1850–1930." New York, NY: Columbia University, master's thesis. 1977.

Sullivan, Stephen J. "A Social History of the Brooklyn Irish, 1850–1900." New York, NY: Columbia University, dissertation notes–incomplete.

Symonds, Elinor L. "Population Shifting in Manhattan." New York, NY: Columbia University, master's thesis. 1924.

Tabachnik, Leonard. "Irish and German Immigrant Settlements in New York City, 1815–1828." New York, NY: Columbia University, master's thesis. 1960.

Weiser, Bruce L. "Hammels, Rockaway (1900–1976): A Case Study of Ethnic Change and Urban Renewal." New York, NY: City University of New York, Queens College, master's thesis. 1976.

Winsberg, Morton D. "The Suburbanization of the Irish in Boston, Chicago and New York." *Eire–Ireland*. Vol. 21. No. 3. 1986. pp. 90–104.

Newspapers
Joyce, William L., ed. *Editors and Ethnicity: A history of the Irish American Press, 1848–1883*. New York, NY: Arno. 1976.

Long, David F. "The New York News, 1855–1906: Spokesman for the Underprivileged." New York, NY: Columbia University, PhD Diss. 1950.

McGinley, Rita B. "New York Catholic Publishers and Their Publications, 1809–1952." New York, NY: Columbia University, master's thesis. 1941.

McShane, Kieran. "A Study of Two New York Irish–American Newspapers in the Early Nineteenth Century." New York, NY: Columbia University, master's thesis. 1980.

Pre–Famine
Doyle, Richard David. *The Pre-Revolutionary Irish in New York, 1643–1775*. St. Louis, MO: St. Louis University, PhD Diss. 1932.

O'Brien, Michael Joseph. "Irish Colonists in New York." *Proceedings of the New York State Historical Association*. Vol. 8. 1907. pp. 94–123.

O'Brien, Michael Joseph, New–York Historical Society, and Shamrock Literary Society of New York. *Irish Colonists in New York: A Lecture Delivered Before the New York State Historical Association at Lake George, New York, August 22nd, 1906*. New York, NY: Shamrock Literary Society of New York. 1906.

Van Denmark, Harry. "Irish and Dutch in Old New York." *America*. October 18, 1933. pp. 33–34.

Societies
Donohue, Joan, F. "The Irish Catholic Benevolent Union, 1869–1893." Washington, DC: Catholic University, PhD Diss. 1954.

Funchion, Michael F., ed. *Irish American Voluntary Associations*. Westport, CT: Greenwood. 1983.

Kelleher, Denis P. *Kerrymen 1881–1981*. New York, NY: Kerrymen's Patriotic and Benevolent Association of New York. 1981

Meehan, Thomas F. "New York's First Irish Emigrant Society." *U.S. Catholic Historical Society, Historical Records and Studies*. Vol. 6. Part II. 1912. pp. 202–211.

Mannion, Lawrence J. "The History of the Society of the Friendly Sons of St. Patrick in the City of New York, 1784–1835." New York, NY: Columbia University, PhD Diss. 1938.

Mannion, Lawrence J., and Richard C. Murphy. *The History of the Society of the Friendly Sons of St. Patrick in the City of New York, 1784–1835*. New York, NY: Society of the Friendly Sons of St. Patrick. 1962.

McLaughlin, James. *A History of the Donegal Association of New York, 1939–1981*. New York, NY: Donegal Association. 1983.

Purcell, Richard J. "The Irish Emigrant Society of New York." *Studies*. Vol. XXVII. No. 108. December 1938. pp. 585–587.

Ridge, John T. *The History of the Ancient Order of Hibernians and Ladies' Auxiliary in Brooklyn*. Brooklyn, NY: Ancient Order of Hibernians. 1973. Reprint 1985.

Ridge, John T. *Galway in New York, 1856–1910: Centennial Celebration of the Galway Men's Social and Benevolent Association*. New York, NY: Galwaymen's Social and Benevolent Association. 1981.

Society of the Friendly Sons of Saint Patrick in the City of New York. *Yearbook of the Society of the Friendly Sons of Saint Patrick in the City of New York, 1998*. New York, NY: Society of the Friendly Sons of Saint Patrick. 1998.

Society of the Friendly Sons of Saint Patrick in the City of New York. *The Society of the Friendly Sons of Saint Patrick in the City of New York, Past, Present, and Future: An Exhibition Organized by the American Irish Historical Society, May and June 1997*. New York, NY: The Society. 1997.

United Irish Counties Association of New York. *Irish Year Book*. New York, NY: United Irish Counties Association of New York. 1945.

Union
Comerford, James J. "Adjustment of Labor Unions to Civil Service Status: The TWU and the New York City Government." New York, NY: Columbia University, master's thesis. 1941.

Hurley, Jean. "The Irish Immigrant in the Early Labor Movement, 1820–1862." New York, NY: Columbia University, master's thesis. 1959.

Notes and Index

[1] In particular see Bayor, Ronald H., and Timothy Meagher, eds. *The New York Irish*. Baltimore, MD: Johns Hopkins University Press. 1997; Dolan, Jay P. *The Irish Americans: A History*. New York, NY: Bloomsbury Press. 2010.

[2] Moorhouse, B–Ann. "Researching the Irish–born of New York City." *The New York Genealogical and Biographical Record*. Vol. 112. No. 2. April 1981. pp. 65–71.

[3] Office of the City Clerk Marriage Bureau. *Marriage Records*. unknown year. www.cityclerk.nyc.gov/html/marriage/records.shtml: accessed 2 December 2012.

[4] New York City Department of Records and Information Services—Municipal Archives. *Births Before 1910*. 2009. www.nyc.gov/html/records/html/vitalrecords/birth.shtml: accessed 15 November 2012.

[5] Reilly, James. *St. Paul's Roman Catholic Church New York Baptism and Marriage Registers, 1857–1900*. Salt Lake City, UT: Redmond Press. 1996. p. i.

[6] Moorhouse, B–Ann. 1981. pp. 65–71.

[7] Reilly, James. 1996. p. i.

[8] Hodges, Graham. "Desirable Companions and Lovers: Irish and African Americans in the Sixth Ward 1830–1870" in Bayor, Ronald H., and Timothy Meagher, eds. *The New York Irish*. Baltimore, MD: Johns Hopkins University Press. 1997. p. 120–121.

[9] Moorhouse. 1981.

[10] Moorhouse. 1981.

[11] Davenport, John. *The Election and Naturalization Frauds in New York City, 1860–1870*. New York, NY: Self–published. 1894; Miller, Kerby A. Emigrants and Exiles: Ireland and the Irish Exodus to North America. New York, NY: Oxford University Press. 1988. p. 330.

[12] Ernst, Robert. *Immigrant Life in New York City*. Syracuse, NY: Syracuse University Press. 1949.

[13] Hodges. 1997. p. 114.

[14] Smyth, J. J. *The Impending Conflict Between Romanism and Protestantism in the United States*. New York, NY: E. Goodenough. 1871.

[15] New York City Department of Records and Information Services – Municipal Archives. *Almshouse Collection*. New York, NY. Microfilm Roll No. 4. Vol. 107. no page number. September 1848.

[16] New York City Department of Records and Information Services – Municipal Archives. *Almshouse Collection*. New York, NY. Microfilm Roll No.15. Vol. 105. no page number. September 1846.

[17] New York City Department of Records and Information Services – Municipal Archives. *Almshouse Collection*. New York, NY. Microfilm Roll No. 4. Vol. 110. no page number. February 1851.

[18] New York City Department of Records and Information Services – Municipal Archives. *Almshouse Collection*. New York, NY. Microfilm Roll No. 4. Vol. 107. no page number. January 1848.

[19] Hodges. 1997. p. 121.

[20] New York City Department of Records and Information Services – Municipal Archives, Almshouse Collection. New York, NY. Microfilm Roll No. 4, Volume 110, no page number, March 1857.

[21] New York State Library. *The Early History of Newspaper Publishing in New York State*. 2009. www.nysl.nysed.gov/nysnp/history.htm: accessed 29 June 2011

[22] Brooklyn Public Library. *The Brooklyn Daily Eagle Reporting on Immigration*. 2011. http://eagle.brooklynpubliclibrary.org/Default/Skins/BEagle/Client.asp?Skin=BEagle: accessed 6 July 2011

[23] Smyth, J. J. 1871.

[24] MacLysaght, Edward. *The Surnames of Ireland*. Dublin: Irish Academic Press. 1985. p. ix.

[25] Grenham, John. "The Origin of Irish Surnames." *Irish Ancestors*. 2011. www.irishtimes.com/ancestor/magazine/surname/index.htm: accessed 29 June 2011.

[26] Grenham, John. *Irish Roots*. 25 May 2011. www.irishtimes.com/ancestor/magazine/column/may25.htm: accessed 14 February 2012.

[27] For further reading on this topic, see: Bowen, Desmond. *Souperism: Myth or Reality: A Study in Souperism*. Cork: Mercier Press. 1970; Whelan, Irene. "Religious Rivalry and the Making of Irish–American Identity" in Lee, Joseph, and Marion R. Casey, eds. *Making the Irish American*. New York, NY: New York University Press. 2006. pp. 278–279

[28] MacLysaght, Edward. 1985. p. xi.

[29] Billings, John S. *Vital Statistics of New York and Brooklyn Covering a Period of Six Years Ending May 31, 1890*. Washington, DC: Government Printing Office. 1894. p. 19.

[30] National Archives of Ireland. "1901 Census of Ireland." database. 2009. www.census.nationalarchives.ie: accessed 12 December 2012. Search for "County/County of Origin–America."

[31] Riordan, Michael J., et al. *The Catholic Church in the United States of America: Undertaken to Celebrate the Golden Jubilee of His Holiness Pope Pius X, Volume III*. New York, NY: Catholic Editing Company. 1914. p. 308.

[32] Riordan, Michael J. 1914. p. 375.

[33] Riordan, Michael J. 1914. p. 565.

[34] Shelley, Thomas J. *Dunwoodie: The History of St. Joseph's Seminary, Yonkers, New York*. Westminster, MD: Christian Classics. 1993. p. 16.

[35] Shelley, Thomas J. 1993. p. 18.

[36] Shelley, Thomas J. 1993. p. 19.

[37] Shelley, Thomas J. 1993. p. 25.

[38] Eneclann. *President Barack Obama's Irish Ancestry*. 2011. www.eneclann.ie/exhibitions/barack–obamas–irish–ancestry/kearney–family–history/joseph–kearney–1794/: accessed 11 July 2011.

[39] Morse, Steve. *Obtaining AD/ED for the 1905/15/25 New York State Census in One Step–Frequently Asked Questions*. 2004. http://stevemorse.org/nyc/faq.htm: accessed 9 August 2013

[40] Diner, Hasia A. "The Most Irish City in the Union: The Era of the Great Migration, 1844–1877" in Bayor, Ronald H., and Timothy Meagher, eds. *The New York Irish*. Baltimore, MD: Johns Hopkins University Press. 1997. p. 93.

[41] Dolan, Jay P. *The Immigrant Church: New York's Irish and German Catholics, 1815–1865*. South Bend, IN: University of Notre Dame Press. 1992. p. 42.

[42] Dolan, Jay P. 1992. p.42.

[43] Dolan, Jay P. 1992. p.41.

[44] Dolan, Jay P. *The Irish Americans: A History*. New York, NY: Bloomsbury Press. 2010.

[45] Dolan, Jay P. 1992. p. 38–39.

[46] Kolko, Ed. *America's Most Irish Towns*. 2013. www.forbes.com/sites/trulia/2013/03/15/americas-most-irish-towns: accessed 4 May 2013.

[47] Anbinder, Tyler. "From Famine to Five Points: Lord Lansdowne's Irish Tenants Encounter North America's Most Notorious Slum." *American Historical Review*. Vol. 107. No. 2. April 2002. pp. 351–387. p. 368.

[48] Hodges, Graham. 1997.

[49] Rich, Kevin J. *Irish Immigrants of the Emigrant Industrial Savings Bank, Test Book Number 1 Volume II, Accounts 2501–7500*. New York, NY: Self-published. 2001. p. xii.

[50] Anbinder, Tyler. 2002. p. 368.

[51] Hodges, Graham. 1997.

[52] Rich, Kevin J. 2001. p. xii.

[53] Anbinder, Tyler. 2002. p. 368.

[54] Author Unknown. "Old County Divisions." *Hibernian Magazine*. Vol. 1. No. 6. 1896. pp. 142–143.

[55] Ridge, John T. "New York and County Kerry, 1851–1930." *New York Irish History*. Vol. 23. 2009. pp. 40–56. p. 47.

[56] Ridge, John T. 1995. "Irish County Societies in New York City, 1880–1914" in Bayor, Ronald H., and Timothy Meagher, eds. *The New York Irish*. Baltimore, MD: Johns Hopkins University Press. 1997. p. 276.

[57] Author Unknown. 1896. pp. 142–143.

[58] Rich, Kevin J. 2002. p. xii.

[59] Author Unknown. 1896. pp. 142–143.

[60] Wright, John D. *The Language of the Civil War*. Westport, CT: Oryx Press. 2001.

[61] Rich, Kevin J. 2002. p. xii.

[62] Author Unknown. 1896. pp.142–143.

[63] Rich, Kevin J. 2002. p. xii.

[64] Rich, Kevin J. 2002. p. xii.

[65] Author Unknown. 1896. pp. 142–143.

[66] Gilge Paul A. "The Development of an Irish American Community in New York City Before the Great Migration" in Bayor, Ronald H., and Timothy Meagher, eds. *The New York Irish*. Baltimore, MD: Johns Hopkins University Press. 1997. p. 74.

[67] Ridge, John T. 1997. p.296.

[68] Rich, Kevin J. 2002. p. xii.

[69] Homberger, Eric. *The Historic Atlas of New York City*. New York, NY: Henry Holt. 2005. p. 138.

[70] Homberger, Eric. 2005. pp. 136–137.

[71] Homberger, Eric. 2005. pp. 136–137.

[72] Casey, Marion R. "From the East Side to the Seaside: Irish Americans on the Move in New York City" in Bayor, Ronald H., and Timothy Meagher, eds. *The New York Irish*. Baltimore, MD: Johns Hopkins University Press. 1997. p. 401.

[73] Calculated by author with area of wards taken from www.demographia.com/db–nyc–ward1800.htm (accessed 6 July 2012). This website is maintained by Wendel Cox Consultancy, which publishes a range of measurements in relation to urban housing and population such as the Demographia International Housing Affordability Ratings. Example: The Fourth Ward Irish population in 1855 was 10,446 and the area was 0.13 square mile, giving a density of 80,353 Irish-born per square mile. Same for 1875 New York State census.

[74] Bayor, Ronald H., and Timothy Meagher, eds. *The New York Irish*. The Johns Hopkins University Press. 1997. pp. 552–553. Same for 1875 New York State census.

[75] Bayor, Ronald H., and Timothy Meagher. 1997. pp. 552–553. Same for 1875 New York State census.

[76] Silinonte, Joseph M. "Brooklyn's Cemetery of the Holy Cross in New York." *Irish History* Vol. 6. 1991. pp. 31–34. p. 31; U.S. Census Bureau. *1860 Fast Facts*. 2012. www.census.gov/history/www/through_the_decades/fast_facts/1860_fast_facts.html : accessed 20 April 2013.

[77] Burrows, Edwin G., and Mike Wallace. *Gotham: A History of New York City to 1898*. New York, NY: Oxford University Press. 1999.

[78] Benardo, Leonard, and Jennifer Weiss. *Brooklyn by Name*. New York, NY: New York University Press. 2006.

[79] Morrone, Francis. *An Architectural Guidebook to Brooklyn*. Provo, UT: Gibbs Smith. 2001. p. 117.

[80] Goldenburg, Stuart. *Only in New York: 400 Remarkable Answers to Intriguing, Provocative Questions About the City*. New York, NY: New York Times. 2004.

[81] Ridge, John T. 1997. p. 283.

[82] Ridge, John T. "When Williamsburg and Greenpoint Were Irish" in *New York Irish History*. Vol. 10. 1996. pp. 14–20. p. 20.

[83] Ridge, John T. 1996. p. 20.

[84] Casey, Marion R. 1997. p. 405.

[85] Rhatigan, Joe and Ginny Rhatigan. "Forum Tours Irish Flatbush" in *Newsletter of the Irish Family History Forum*. Vol. 22. No. 5. November 2012–January 2013.

[86] Bayor, Ronald H., and Timothy Meagher, eds. *The New York Irish*. Baltimore, MD: Johns Hopkins University Press. 1997. pp. 554–555. Same for 1875 New York State census.

[87] Bayor, Ronald H., and Timothy Meagher, eds. 1997. pp. 554–555. Same for 1875 New York State census.

[88] Casey, Marion R. 1997. p. 413.

[89] Casey, Marion R. 1997. p. 414.

[90] Casey, Marion R. 1997. p. 409.

[91] Diner, Hasia A. 1997. p. 93.

[92] Casey, Marion R. 1997 p. 413.

[93] Morris. Ira, K. *Morris' Memorial History of Staten Island, New York*. Volume One. New York, NY: Memorial Publishing. 1898. p. 414.

[94] Morris. Ira, K. 1898. p. 374.

[95] Salvato, Richard. *A User's Guide to the Emigrant Savings Bank Records*. New York, NY: New York Public Library Manuscripts and Archives Division. 1997. Available at legacy.www.nypl.org/research/chss/spe/rbk/faids/emigrant.pdf: accessed 17 December 2012

[96] Salvato, Richard. 1997.

[97] "New York Emigrant Savings Bank, 1850–1883" database. www.ancestry.com: accessed 7 December 2011. Entry for Daniel and Catherine Hanlon, account number 2571. Citing Emigrant Savings Bank. Emigrant Savings Bank Records. Call number *R–USLHG *ZI–815. Rolls 1–20. New York Public Library, New York, NY.

[98] For further reading about how this data was used, see: Anbinder, Tyler. "Moving beyond Rags to Riches: New York's Irish Famine Immigrants and Their Surprising Savings Accounts" in *Journal of American History*. Vol. 99. No. 3. December 2012. pp. 741–770.

[99] "Searching for Missing Friends: Irish Immigrant Advertisements Placed in The Boston Pilot 1831–1920", database. www.ancestry.com: accessed 30 August 2013. Entry for John Kelly, 18 April 1852; citing Harris, Ruth-Ann, and Jacobs, Donald M., Eds. *The Search for Missing Friends: Irish Immigrant Advertisements Placed in the Boston Pilot*, Volumes 1–8. Boston: New England Historical Genealogical Society. 1989–1993.

[100] Murphy DeGraiza, Laura and Diane Fitzpatrick Haberstroh. *Irish Relatives and Friends: From Information Wanted Ads in the Irish-American, 1850–1871*. Baltimore, MD: Genealogical Pub. 2001. p. 172.

[101] Moorhouse, B–Ann. "Notices of Irish-Born Persons in New York City Newspapers." *Irish Genealogist*. Vol. 5. No. 1. 1973. pp. 24–27.

[102] Jeremiah O'Donovan. *A Brief Account of the Author's Interview with His Countrymen*. Pittsburgh, PA: Self-published. 1864. p. 236.

[103] Anbinder, Tyler. 2002. p. 356.

[104] Archdioece of New York. *Search for a Parish*. 2011. www.archny.org/parish–search: accessed 27 June 2011

Diocese of Brooklyn. *About the Diocese*. 2011. http://old2.dioceseofbrooklyn.org/about/diocesan_stats.aspx: accessed 27 June 2011

[105] Moorhouse, B–Ann. 1981. p. 68.

[106] Miller, Kerby. 1985. p. 331.

[107] Dolan, Jay P. 1992. p. 12.

[108] Dolan, Jay P. 1992. p. 58.

[109] McDannell, Colleen. "Irish Catholics in New York City, 1870–1900" in Bayor, Ronald H., and Timothy Meagher, eds. *The New York Irish*. Baltimore, MD: Johns Hopkins University Press. 1997. p. 237.

[110] St. Patrick's Cathedral. *Journal of the Fair for New St. Patrick's Cathedral*. Volume 1. No. 1–31. New York, NY: Publisher unknown. 1878.

[111] Riordan, Michael J., et al. 1914.

[112] Works Progress Administration. *New York City Inventory of the Church Archives—Roman Catholic Church Archdiocese of New York Volume 2*. New York, NY: WPA. 1941.

[113] Diocese of Brooklyn. *Chronological List of Brooklyn Parishes, 1822–2008.* 2008. Diocese of Brooklyn old website http://dioceseofbrooklyn.org/wp–content/uploads/2012/10/chronological_list_brooklyn_parish_school_2012.pdf : accessed 1 August 2012.

[114] Diocese of Brooklyn. *Chronological List of Queens Parishes 1843–2009.* 2009. Diocese of Brooklyn old website http://dioceseofbrooklyn.org/wp–content/uploads/2012/10/Chronological–List–of–Queens–Parishes–and–Schools–4.pdf : accessed 1 August 2012.

[115] Diocese of Brooklyn. 2009.

[116] Corrigan, Michael Augustine Most Rev. "The Catholic Cemeteries of New York" in *United States Catholic Historical Society. Historical Records and Studies Volume I.* New York, NY: United States Catholic Historical Society. 1917. p. 374.

[117] Corrigan, Michael. 1917. p. 374.

[118] For nearly all cemeteries, opening dates (and where known, closing dates), location, and contact information have come from: Inskeep, Carolee. *The Graveyard Shift: A Family Historian's Guide to New York City Cemeteries.* Orem, UT: Ancestry. 2000. Other information from : Corrigan, Michael. 1917; French, Mary. *The New York City Cemetery Project Blog.* http://nycemetery.wordpress.com: accessed 1 November 2012.

Rural Cemetery Act (1847), 116

Printed in the USA
CPSIA information can be obtained
at www.ICGtesting.com
LVHW021341210924
791492LV00025B/157

9 780806 319889